DATE DUE

MY 20 99			
JE 2 '00			
OC 18 '00			
DE 28 '00			
AP 4 '01			
E '01			
MY 2 '02			
FE 7 '02			
JE 01 '02			
MY 23 07			

DEMCO 38-296

ELDER ABUSE AND MEDIATION

*For my family and friends
who gave me support and space
to work with and for other old people
whose wisdom and courage in coping with conflict
inspired this book.*

Contents

v

Part III: The social development of elder abuse and mediation services in Britain and Europe

Preface

A confluence of three socially significant episodes in the genesis of this book took place in the middle of the 1980s. Pillemer and Wolf's *Elder abuse: conflict in the family* (1986) was a major publication amongst those of other gerontologists which drew attention to the salience of unresolved conflict in contributing to the complex aetiology of elder abuse. British elder abuse theorists and practitioners also began to work on this critical contemporary subject, as recorded by McCreadie (1991).

At the same time I was involved with others in steering the British mediation movement into developing as the national voluntary organization now known as Mediation UK, and edited its quarterly magazine, *Mediation.* Through this and a co-operative, consultative and practical partnership which evolved with our American colleagues who pioneered alternative dispute resolution (ADR) thirty years earlier, I learned of the work of a retired barrister and staff member of the American Bar Association (ABA), Prue Kestner, who focused on mediation by and for older people.

In 1989 she and a younger colleague, working on the ABA's Commission on Legal Problems of the Elderly, wrote *Mediation: the coming of age* (Wood and Kestner, 1989) which included many examples of ADR being used successfully by older volunteer mediators in enabling peer group members to resolve their own later life conflicts, whilst safeguarding their rights to ongoing access to the law.

As I approached my 70s, retired as a social worker, counsellor and magistrate, but involved in the voluntary sector as a mediator and community activist, I became gradually aware of the increasing number of conflicts involving older persons which Mediation UK's member services had been asked to resolve. At the same time we were enriched by growing numbers of able (and disabled) elders who participated in 40-hour skills training programmes in a productive partnership with younger mediators, which provided effective experience of working with intergenerational conflicts.

I then began to evolve the idea that if mediation could empower older people to resolve their conflicts, this could contribute to the prevention of elder abuse in certain cases. I discussed the idea with gerontologists, colleagues working as professionals and volunteers in statutory and voluntary agencies involved in the care of old people, as well as with our older mediators, and many multicultural elders with whom I was in contact. They all encouraged me to develop the idea, whilst my academic friends warned me that this would require rigorous research. I followed their advice, although insisting that this would be participative action research which I hoped would be socially construed as a later life age group self-help initiative in contributing to understanding the potential of mediation for preventing elder abuse.

Although I was concerned to base the research on ongoing mediation work with and for older people, I found an academic anchor at the London School of Economics (LSE) as a postgraduate, where this book was conceived by multiple insemination, although an interim birth of Mediation UK's Elder Mediation Project (EMP) became instrumental to, and facilitated the present delivery.

There are three parts in the book's life course. The first is entitled *The social confluence of elder abuse and mediation*, and its initial chapter aims to be a critical inquiry into the theories leading to my interfacial placing of the two areas which are the subject of current academic and popular interest.

The second chapter considers a dominant theme of the book which refers to Simon Roberts' (1986) work on mediation as a minimal form of intervention. I suggest that this is of special social value in the sensitive complexities of elder abuse, where some law enforced adult protective services (APS) in America have been regarded as iatrogenic, although I discuss the countervailing critique of ADR.

The third chapter considers the praxis needed to test the emerging grounded theory that at early stages of relational conflict mediation can contribute to the prevention of elder abuse, and the chosen perspectives of participative and social action research from which to develop it.

The second part of the book is entitled *The social construction of elder abuse and mediation in America*, and its first chapter focuses on the context of American elder care, particularly its Long Term Care

Ombudsmen (LTCO) who use mediation as well as advocacy and other skills in their work.

The second chapter describes my active participant observer work in large and small Californian institutions and in community-based LTCO services.

The third chapter focuses on similarly organized research in mid-American heartland and southern States working with mediation services for senior citizens, using principally older trained volunteers.

The third part of the book is entitled *The social development of elder abuse and mediation services in Britain and Europe*, and its first chapter describes the development of the Elder Mediation Project and its acronym, EMP for EMPowerment.

The second chapter features an elder abuse project in Oslo in which mediation is used in typical and new ways.

The third chapter considers relevant current British social experience and policy issues in the context of potential European developments.

A brief conclusion reviews some of the new facts which the studies have revealed, and suggests that the ongoing research and collective work shows the potential of mediation for healing many of the painful later life conflicts from which older people suffer, and that they, and any multidisciplinary workers they consult, can be empowered to manage these in constructive ways to avoid abusive relationships. Thus this work, presently situated within the voluntary sector, can usefully contribute to evolving British social policy and planning for, and with, its ageing population.

The limitations of the book and its present studies are stressed throughout this provisional and modest attempt to draw attention to areas which need further extensive research before firm conclusions can be drawn. So this important area is wide open for others to explore the many issues and questions which have been raised, yet remain to be answered.

Acknowledgements

I am grateful to the many research funders who encouraged my work, especially the University of London Central Research Fund, the Centre for Policy on Ageing for its Marjory Warren Bursary, and the British Society of Gerontology for its Averil Osborn Award and grants to present papers at academic conferences.

I am also grateful to Mediation UK for helping to finance my workshops here and in international conferences, and its continuing administrative and practical support for its pioneer multicultural Elder Mediation Project which I started in 1990 with other older volunteer mediator members.

My thanks are also due to Dr Gail Wilson of the Department of Social Policy and Administration of the London School of Economics, University of London, and to Professor Simon Roberts in the Department of Law there, who supervised most of the academic research on which this book is based, and to the many other distinguished scholars from whom I learned so much.

Unfailing assistance has been given to me by the librarians at the British Library of Political and Economic Science, the University of London Library, the British Library, the Centre for Policy on Ageing Library, the National Institute of Social Work Library and many Public Libraries.

I have greatly appreciated all the support offered to me by my many colleagues who are professional, practitioner and voluntary workers in caring services for older people, and value the time, consultation and active co-operation which they have generously given me. In naming only three national voluntary agencies, Age Concern, its Action on Elder

Abuse, and its Advice, Information and Mediation Service for Retirement Housing, Help the Aged, and Counsel and Care, to whose staff I am indebted for advice and help, I wish also to acknowledge the important contributions to my work made by many other organizations of which I am a member.

During international conferences and research visits I have been given generous hospitality and full facilities for observing and participating in the work of my mentors, especially in the programmes arranged for me at the Justice Center of Atlanta by Edith Primm, the Olathe (Kansas) Dispute Resolution Services by Helen Wahl, the Californian (Concord) Long-Term Care Ombudsman Services by Lois McKnight, and the American Bar Association where Prue Kestner and Erica Wood pioneered senior mediation.

My deepest appreciation is offered to our volunteer co-workers in the multicultural Elder Mediation Project whose valuable varied life courses and trained mediation skills enable and empower members of our later life peer group to cope with their conflicts constructively so as to stop, avoid and prevent abusive situations. They, with many here unmentioned persons, groups and organizations all provide the inspiration and experiences which enliven the theory and praxis of this book.

However only I am responsible for the writing of this book, the ideas which it advances, the suggestions it makes, and any mistakes in facts, inferences or attributions, for which sincere apologies are offered.

Lastly I am grateful for the guidance of Jo Gooderham, from Avebury, Neville Young and Dorothy Stewart in publishing this book.

Yvonne Joan Craig.

Part I

THE SOCIAL CONFLUENCE OF ELDER ABUSE AND MEDIATION

1 Theories of interrelational conflict and relational justice in later life

Beatrice Webb was seventy when she produced her minority report on the reform of the Poor Law. Amongst its many recommendations she wanted a Society for the Prevention of Cruelty to the Elderly. Fifty years after her death in 1943, the 1993 European Year of Older People and Solidarity Between the Generations offered the opportunity for a similar critical inquiry to that which she pioneered in her early contribution to applied social research, and the understanding of the structural causes of elder poverty:

> The aim of the Webbs in doing all their research was severely practical ... The Webbs believed that it was possible to combine scientific research into social institutions with active participation in their operation (Bulmer, 1982:18).

This present critical inquiry into the contribution which mediation can make to the prevention of elder abuse acknowledges the example of Beatrice Webb by seeking to understand the context, typology and transformation of conflict which, unresolved, can lead to elder mistreatment in families, institutions and society (Gulliver, 1979, Phillipson and Biggs, 1992, Pillemer and Wolf, 1986).

Beatrice and her husband, Sidney Webb, are also examples of the vigorous and determined old people who make valuable contributions towards fulfilling their life course in ways which encourage intergenerational co-operation in understanding, confronting and coping with social conflicts. This book is based on such personal examples, and these, in later chapters, enliven the text whilst preserving their anonymity,

3

although being a more central feature of another publication, now in preparation, for practitioners in multidisciplinary services.

The book aims to contribute to relational justice in later life so that intergenerational solidarity, rather than conflict between individuals in different age groups, liberates energies for shared tasks in struggling against social oppression (Hobman, 1993). In this respect a major theme of this present book is to consider mediation as an emancipatory process in personal and social relations.

However it must be stressed that although structural social conflicts are a superordinate concern of this book, it only specifically addresses the interpersonal conflicts of later life, and the way these relate to elder abuse.

So the theoretical perspectives of this complex subject are introduced initially as an inquiry into the social confluence of the two central subjects of this book, elder abuse and mediation, the second being discussed first to point to the positive affirmations of this book. It should also be added that mediation is given a primary focus because its work and literature is less well known than that of elder abuse (Craig, 1994).

Definitions, boundaries and reasons for the research are given first, showing the significance of theory accumulation and innovation. Problems, limitations and restrictions are indicated, and the exploratory nature of the research is stressed.

Secondly other themes are discussed and autonomy, choice, and decision-making are shown to be critical factors in contributing to the empowerment and participation of elders as senior citizens seeking self-actualization (Maslow, 1970), self-protection (Korbin, 1991) and social justice (Jecker, 1991). It is these factors and values which are held to be central to mediation as a social process.

Thirdly the theme of communicative ethics and communicative action (Habermas, 1990; Moody, 1992) is developed as a theoretical and moral base in evaluating the idea that mediation has a potential for contributing to the prevention of elder abuse.

Mediation and elder abuse: a developing but unfinished paradigm

Theory formation may be seen as competitive or integrative. Rex and Mason favour theoretical dialogue which encourages constructive continuities in discourse, pointing out that for some 'a theory is little more than a set of working concepts or hypotheses'. This minimal alternative to the 'imperialist' construction of 'grand' or 'pyramid' theory

4

(Rex and Mason, 1989:1–2) fits the present modest aim of locating mediation in the domain of family conciliation in the hope of extending its shared knowledge base. It is also consistent with the view that in the social construction of knowledge there are 'many truths, many realities ... no monism or dualism ... but dialectical exchange' (Downes and Rock, 1979:61–4).

This theoretical perspective is especially appropriate as Mediation UK and National Family Mediation (NFM) in which elder and family mediation are respectively being developed, are associated national voluntary organizations with open channels of communication and co-operation. However as elder abuse in America has also been conceptualized as including crime as well as deviancy (Plotkin, 1988), reference must also be made to perspectives of mediation in the criminal justice system.

Reference to NFM is salient as its pioneer family mediation work has been instrumental to the Lord Chancellor's advocacy of this approach in the new divorce legislation now before Parliament. In this it is envisaged that all couples seeking divorce or formal separation will have the opportunity to consider using mediation instead of, or as well as, legal services, in order to reach an amicable, rather than adversarial, settlement. It is important to note that, through the insistence of the NFM, mediation is to be a voluntary option, so as to maintain the highest of the ethical principles on which the process is based.

Marian Roberts, the training co-ordinator of NFM, in her book, *Mediation in Family Disputes,* describes mediation as:

> a form of intervention in which a third party, the mediator, assists the parties to a dispute to negotiate over the issues which divide them ... The mediator has no power to impose a settlement on the parties, who retain authority for making their own decision (1988:5).

A 1992 annual report adds a salient sentence:

> The mediator is therefore responsible for the conduct of the process ... but is not responsible for the outcome (1992:5).

It is significant that the word 'outcome' is chosen in preference to the more commonly used 'agreement', 'resolution' or 'settlement' in commercial and industrial mediation, indicating that there may be general achievements of relationship improvement in the sensitive areas of marital separation and divorce, rather than any specific results (Ogus et al, 1989:3).

Although mediation fits comfortably within the definitional parameters of family mediation in civil justice, its concern with the prevention of elder abuse necessitates mentioning the use of mediation within the criminal justice system. In Wright's *Justice for Victims and Offenders,* he further qualifies mediation as 'negotiation between persons or groups in conflict, including victims and offenders ...' (1991:xi). This accentuates the offensive nature of serious interpersonal conflict, and gives recognition to the role of victims, for whom, therefore, mediation must also offer a protective process. This fundamental issue is highly contentious and Harshbarger (1989) and Heisler (1991), both lawyers, represent those within the American adult protective services (APS) who urge legal and police intervention in cases of suspected elder abuse. The critique of mediation situated in the next chapter will consider this more fully.

Blanton, an APS director, restores a personal dimension to the discussion by reminding us, in accordance with the principles of participatory research, that victims are subjects not objects, and may include caregivers as well as their dependants. His views are relevant to any construction of mediation as a form of social intervention, as it seeks impartially to promote the rights of all participants:

> Adult protective services are not primarily about 'legal interventions', as has frequently been argued; they are about human need (Blanton, 1989:33).

Marshall, a former director of Mediation UK, seconded from his position as principal research officer in the Home Office, is even more assertive about the role of mediation as 'an emancipatory process' representing 'a potent paradigm shift', saying it is 'capable of realizing a higher level of civilization' in the way people seek to fulfil their human needs and resolve their problems and conflicts (1990:2–3).

Here it should be observed that Mediation UK imposes no fixed operational definition of mediation on its individual and organizational membership as it is developing differentially in community, environment, family, housing, victim–offender and many other directions. However, codes of ethics, accountability and good practice stress that mediation is a voluntary and non-coercive process which can be combined with, or discontinued in preference to other forms of social, legal or law enforcement intervention.

Mediation services are developed as independent agencies with equal opportunities policies in the voluntary sector, primarily situated in socially deprived areas, aiming to provide free services to those in need. Mediators are generally volunteers, with expenses paid, often having special experience in the target area. They receive ongoing training to a good standard and their work is subject to supervision and review (Marshall, 1985). These critical attributes should be characteristic of any collaborative problem-solving process (Hudson, 1989) and intrinsically link praxis with mediation theory.

It should also be noted that the absence of dogmatic definition also marks the first American text on the subject of elder mediation, a term coined in this present book for describing British mediation with and for older people, whereas Wood and Kestner's *Mediation: The Coming of Age* (1989) refers to old people as seniors.

As a publication of the American Bar Association (ABA), which established its Commission on Legal Problems of the Elderly in 1978, and even earlier its advocacy and support of mediation in general, senior mediation has been advanced as the next obvious stage in widely developed popular services, although there are no specific references to its relevance for elder abuse work.

Here the construct of elder mediation has been fashioned in parallel with the currently accepted term elder abuse, and also for its simplicity, although recognizing that people in later life have ambivalent and changing views about how they wish to be named, preferences ranging from being identified as retired, or as senior citizens, to wishing to be known only as individuals. However 'the law of parsimony is a sensible guide to theory-building' (Pepinsky, 1991:25), so a definition of elder mediation should be as concise and simple as possible, although comprehensive in including the essential elements of mediation as noted above.

The following provisional definition is used here:

> *Elder mediation is a voluntary process in which elderly persons are enabled to make their own decisions in interpersonal conflicts with the help of trained independent workers, generally senior volunteers, who are concerned for the rights, interests and needs of all participants.*

However it should be noted that later life conflicts are often mediated by younger persons, sometimes in multidisciplinary caring agencies, or in community mediation services, and also in everyday encounters in families and among friends. Although an effort will be made to use the defined term of elder mediation in appropriately relevant ways, this book has a primary purpose of discussing the mediation process in general, especially in the theoretical context of this present chapter.

Elder abuse will not be subjected to a comparable definitional analysis, for it has been continuously and systematically investigated during the past fifteen years (McCreadie, 1991). The main problem for any critical inquiry is the degree of disagreement with which theorists have approached definitions of elder abuse and neglect. Hudson cities a three-year survey of the views of 63 experts on the subject who failed to agree on definitions and boundaries (1991:1–19). Stein makes a similar plea by urging definitional clarification as an urgent priority for 'a national agenda for elder abuse and neglect research' (1991:91–107).

In Britain two recent books followed McCreadie in pointing to various definitions, yet not formally constructing their own (Phillipson and Biggs, 1992; Pritchard, 1992). Eastman's early British work on elder abuse and neglect led him to describe it as 'systematic maltreatment, physical, emotional or financial, of any elderly person by a caregiver or relatives' (1984:23), but this does not include institutional or social abuse, nor self-neglect and suicide as destructive occurrences.

Johnson (1989), in her paper *Elder Mistreatment Identification Instruments,* charts the widest dimensions of elder abuse and neglect as variously noted by others. Her typology includes unintentional as well as intentional harm, and ranges from the physical, psychological (emotional, mental, spiritual and verbal), financial, material, sexual, medical, and sociological abuse and neglect of elders, as well as their own self-neglect or suicide.

She then reaches a heuristic conclusion which corresponds to the emphasis on the experiential perspective which distinguishes much feminist writing on domestic violence and victimology (Dobash and Dobash, 1980; Sanko, 1990; Walklate, 1989). It is also consistent with the principles of participatory research adopted here which stress that it is the feelings and thoughts of the subject(s) involved on which critical inquiry should be primarily focused. This view is clearly held by Johnson:

> The comprehensive term suggested here which might put us on more common ground is 'unnecessary suffering' ... The term 'unnecessary' is an important qualifier because sometimes suffering must take place to preserve one's quality of life. Suffering, rather than harm, has been selected because it implies a qualitative dimension (1989:28–9).

This concern is consistent with that of Blanton, the APS director mentioned above:

What is missing from existing literature and what is to be gained is a more fundamental vision of the problem of elder abuse, a vision that transcends the fragmentation, a vision that precedes labels and classifications (Blanton, 1989:29).

Whilst acknowledging the importance of the work of Felstiner, Abel and Sarat in 'naming, blaming and claiming' (1980–1:631–54) as essential stages in the recognition of conflict (to be discussed later), and whilst advocating the therapeutic and procedural utility of confronting abusive behaviour, it is also important to reinforce the humanistic values which Johnson (1989) and Blanton (1989) represent.

The dialogue about definitions and boundaries of elder abuse and neglect will continue, and it is here suggested that Beatrice Webb's early critical inquiry into the prevention of cruelty to the elderly and the structural causes of poverty, should be reconsidered in ongoing formulations, which should include a firmer focus on racial abuse, which has too often been apparent in this present research.

A provisional working concept for this present book which encompasses elder abuse and its interface with conflict could be construed as follows:

Elder abuse and neglect is the unnecessary suffering of elderly people, the prevention of which can be contributed to by appropriate social intervention in the interpersonal, institutional and structural conflicts which are among its complex causes.

Admittedly, the collapsing and cross-cutting of terms means that, for example, conflicts about alleged fraud can be located at the three levels cited, whilst interpersonal conflict can include unnecessary suffering caused by families, neighbours or criminal intruders. However, it can be argued that this reflects the real complexity and inadequacy of categorization, which is equally criticized in all other definitions.

Nevertheless it should be pointed out that the major multidisciplinary British initiative in the field of elder abuse, directed by Age Concern's Action on Elder Abuse (AEA) campaign, established in 1995 a provisional consensus among its individual and organizational members for the following definition:

Elder abuse is a single or repeated act or lack of appropriate action occurring within any relationship where there is an expectation of trust, which causes harm or distress to an older person (AEA, 1995).

Both definitions share the same concerns and principles, but the former is more useful for the purpose of this book as it directs attention towards devising appropriate social interventions to prevent elder abuse at different levels.

It is suggested that mediation is one of these, and although it is, like elder abuse, an unfinished paradigm, the foregoing introduction has created sufficient basic groundwork from which to go on now and explore the area, boundaries and reasons for exploratory research being begun.

Perspectives and parameters of mediation and elder abuse

Phillips and Pugh (1987:45) recommend the value of exploratory research in areas of social innovation. The present exploratory studies were primarily situated in three greatly different areas of America: the poor black south of Atlanta; the mid-range white heartland of Kansas; and the multicultural 'Costa Geriatrica' retirement coast of California, which has rich as well as low and middle income enclaves. Mediation services provided by and for elders, and also by Long Term Care Ombudsmen (LTCO), have been developed in these areas since 1989.

In comparison, elder mediation in Britain was only initiated as the multicultural Elder Mediation Project (EMP) of Mediation UK in 1991, and is dependant on funding for development. Its work is described in detail in a later chapter.

Increasing numbers of inquiries are being made by social workers, health care professionals and gerontologists about training in mediation for incorporation into their own elder care skills, as are referrals of individual cases for EMP to mediate.

In a one-year period, 50 elders, 25 of whom complained of unresolved conflicts, 25 of whom reported these included abusive relationships, were referred from various agencies, as well as seeking help themselves. EMP is still involved in working with and caring for some of these people, so a tabulated analysis of the cases is not presented here, although provisional findings will be discussed later and incorporated into the general exploratory research results.

Detailed reports of the American studies will be given in Part II of the book, although it continues now with charting some of the parameters and problems of research.

The limitations of research into social innovations are many and varied, ranging from the start-up idiosyncrasies of uneven and unrecorded

10

development, to the ethical and practical problematics of attracting approval for a critical inquiry into experimental events from the social actors involved who will be sensitive and uncertain, as well as possibly enthusiastic, about their individually different contributions.

Maguire writes perceptively and in great detail about this in *Doing Participatory Research* (1987), being influential in shaping these present studies which embrace the critical, exploratory and evaluative perspectives already noted.

However evaluation is mainly limited by the difficulty of obtaining reliable quantifiable data about the outcomes of elder mediation cases, as the voluntary processes involved precludes interrogative questioning by the mediators. Findings are based on what the old people say about their feelings, attitudes, needs and concerns, and these, in essence, are a product of their perceptions, subject to constant human change.

There are also the ethical problems involved in seeking to work with elderly persons using mediation services. Although an intrinsic theme in elder mediation is the valorization of elderly persons and their capacity for decision-making, nevertheless the onset of very old age may be accompanied by debilitating illnesses, including those of dementia such as Alzheimer's disease, in which decision-making capacity may be impaired or absent (Kapp, 1990).

While the use of mediation may still contribute to the preservation and enhancement of decision-making in conflicts of practical daily care, such as reaching agreement about dietary and toileting problems, it could be unreliable and counter-productive for old people with alcohol or senility problems. Work has to be mainly restricted to those people interested in, and able to participate in, the general objectives of mediation.

However the objective of making the research as participative as possible by older people is significantly reached because its aims and designs were initiated and continuously developed in consultation with the older members of many ageing agencies and national voluntary organizations, as well as those of Mediation UK, whose elder mediators were actively involved in EMP's work.

Also in 10 pilot interviews, some of which were tape-recorded, old people from mixed age, gender, socioeconomic and cultural backgrounds, talking about their life experiences of conflict and abuse, participated in the initial consensus about the value of researching the connections.

In addition, the design and development of the American studies was based entirely on the hosts' agreement with the research objectives, and their full participation in facilitating the work.

11

All participants knew that the research was only exploratory, that no claims for final answers to complex questions would result, and that the interests of the old people involved would be paramount to those of rigorous research methodology. This limitation in participative research is further discussed in a later chapter.

Another limitation in these studies is the well-known under-reporting of conflict which causes difficulties for APS workers and researchers who suggest that family loyalties, fear of institutions, and anxieties about future reprisals, are amongst the main causes (Pillemer and Wolf, 1986). Phillipson and Walker (1986) go further and say that elderly people may internalize, consciously or unconsciously, the political view that old age is a burden on the economy like childhood, and that, in their own second childhood, they should be neither seen nor heard.

Also victims of infantilization may develop resistance through maintaining silence with great dignity, or actively rejecting any perceived intervention. Old people have a generational tolerance of their personal conflicts, confusions and suffering which they prefer to keep in the private rather than public domain.

In addition the problem of chronic depression, which may be untreated or masked, may lead to withdrawal or disengagement behaviour which can inhibit active and passive co-operation with most social interventions (Knight, 1992). Wolf (1990) concludes that mandatory reporting of elder abuse in America may also have contributed to this silencing of the voices of elders in respect of their major experiences of mistreatment, through anxiety about facing interviews and investigations.

These difficulties partly explain why no major research inquiry and conclusions about senior mediation have yet appeared in America. However a more fundamental reason lies in professional uncertainty about its viability as a social innovation in a recessionary era, and the question as to how far major research is premature, speculative and, more importantly, fundable.

Review of the reports on American developing senior mediation services indicates that these are mainly descriptive narratives of work in progress, presented in brief papers. The ABA report already referred to (Wood and Kestner, 1989), and its *Family Dispute Resolution: Options for All Ages* (1990), which has a section on elderly people, are longer and more comprehensive, but not advanced as substantive texts analysing relevant theories. Nor, despite their general message that mediation enables seniors and associated workers to deal constructively with the conflicts of old age, does there yet appear to have been published any specific work hypothesizing that it can contribute to the prevention of elder abuse.

It is also useful to point out that, as will be shown in Part II of this book, there are general informal expressions by federal, state and organizational activists in the ageing network that such a hypothesis seems to be a common-sense notion which barely needs testing.

A closer review of the major gerontological texts on elder abuse show a similar consensus that unresolved conflicts are key factors in its aetiology, as shown in Pillemer and Wolf's seminal edited book, *Elder Abuse: Conflict in the Family* (1986), and also that of Wolf and Bergman's *Stress, Conflict and Abuse of the Elderly* (1989).

Conflicts feature strongly in other edited collections: Ammerman and Hersen's *Treatment of Family Violence* (1990), Block and Sinnott's *The Battered Elder Syndrome* (1979), Filinson and Ingham's *Elder Abuse: Practice and Policy* (1989), Kosberg's *Abuse and Mistreatment of the Elderly: Causes and Interventions* (1983), the Schlesingers' *Abuse of the Elderly* (1988), and Steinmetz' *Duty Bound: Elder Abuse and Family Care* (1988), to name but a few.

Authors with a predominantly social work orientation like Breckman and Adelman (1988), and British writers Pritchard (1992) and Phillipson and Biggs (1992), similarly identify unresolved conflicts as factors in the development of elder abuse.

Some of these texts mention mediation as a general process or skill which should, or should not be used, depending on each situation; many recommend its extension amongst various constructive problem-solving interventions which should be planned for the future.

Reading through the *Journal of Elder Abuse and Neglect* (1989–91) has yielded similar results, one important item being a brief review by Bergeron (1989) of Gwyther et al's *Older People and Their Families: Coping with Stress and Conflict*, an undated 55-page soft cover handbook whose curriculum includes a section on 'Prevention of Elder Abuse and Neglect: Coping with Family Conflict'. The review suggests that the perspective of Gwyther et al is that of this present research, and it is hoped to learn from this if a positive contact can be established.

So a case can be made for the value of the present research in extending knowledge of mediation as a useful process of social intervention in the prevention of elder abuse. It has already been suggested that this research can add to theory accumulation in its ongoing tasks of definition.

However there are more urgent and pragmatic reasons for researching this area. The demographic trends of ageing populations in industrialized nations, which will be detailed in Part II and Part III of this book, indicate that the increasing proportion of elderly people is already contributing to the socioeconomic conflicts of a recessionary era with a declining young wealth-creating population (Jeffreys, 1991; Minkler and Estes, 1991, Tinker, 1992). Nevertheless their books, and this one, like the most recent one of Walker (1996), do not subscribe to views of moral panic which are politically generated to polarize generations.

However the Family Policy Studies Report 1992 on home sales showed the suffering and embittered conflict which elders are increasingly facing if they need to sell the family's home to pay for residential or nursing home care that they had previously expected to be provided by the state.

The National Institute of Social Work (NISW) report on old people leaving hospital (Neill and Williams, 1993) indicates the rising inadequacy of provision for their future care, whether it is in the family, community or institutions.

Other reports feature statistics which suggest that maltreatment of the elderly, in families and in institutions, is now a problem of serious social concern, even though its increasing recording is an obvious factor. McCreadie (1991) suggests that Wolf and Pillemer's 1989 Boston study gives the most reliable estimate of the American incidence of elder abuse as 32 cases per thousand elders.

In Britain the 1992 Social Services Inspectorate report, *Confronting Elder Abuse,* accepts that 5 per cent of the elder population is at risk of abuse whilst Ogg and Bennett's (1992) report on their two-year Royal London NHS Trust Hospital study, found that 5 per cent of their 600 cases were verbally abused, 2 per cent physically abused, and 2 per cent subjected to financial exploitation. Analysis of 100 Berkshire Social Services Department cases showed that over 10 per cent of the elderly, and 15.3 per cent of those with mental health problems were maltreated at home (Jeffery, 1992). A British 1992 television survey, *Dispatches,* interviewing 2130 professional caregivers of the elderly in over 100 sites found that they also estimated that the rising figure of 5 per cent more accurately represented the incidence of elder abuse as they observed it.

Harman and Winn's report, *No Place Like Home* (1991), and the Royal College of Nursing's report, *A Scandal Waiting to Happen* (1992) drew special attention to institutional abuse.

Despite the statistical unreliability of figures about incidence and prevalence, and the fact that it may be observation and recording that is increasing, rather than its actual occurrence, it nevertheless remains true that there is increasing public and professional concern to find ways of preventing elder abuse.

This concern is also linked with emerging issues of bioethics, such as the use of physical and chemical restraints in both the family and institutional care of elderly persons, and the conflicts which arise with regard to Advanced Directives and guardianship, detailed discussion of which takes place in Part II. At this point it is mentioned to draw attention to the current search for appropriate forms of social intervention in complex and sensitive areas, and the hope that the present research into mediation will indicate its potential as a process for constructive decision-making for all involved, especially enabling old people to participate in it.

An even more urgent reason for considering the extent to which mediation can be used is that there has been a traditional British reluctance to follow the criminalization model of some American States by prematurely developing adult protective legislation and subsequent law enforcement procedures. Although there is certainly professional ambivalence on the subject, McCreadie at the influential Age Concern Institute of Gerontology, and her colleagues of the Action on Age Abuse forum, formed in 1992, are presently committed to establishing networks of support services for vulnerable people as their first priority. This has already been started in Lewisham, Camden and other local authorities and EMP has already begun to make its contribution to this approach.

Despite these reasons for the research, three main problems will recur. The first is that of language. The validity of critical theory and post-modernism in pointing to language and knowledge as power (Foucault, 1981) is accepted and is coupled with a concern to give voice to the 'muted groups' (Worrall, 1990:11) of elders and their carers.

Cain, in the context of the law, also notes the existence of 'repressed knowledge' and contrasts this with the 'self-closing knowledges' of professionals (1988:70). She shows how important it is for social innovations, or 'prefigurative institutions' as she calls them, to explore and expose these contradictions. However participative research into mediation, as a prefigurative institution, has necessarily to use the academic language in which theories are discussed, as well as trying to incorporate practitioner jargon and grassroots argot. This may lead to an uneven discourse.

Another difficulty lies in using condensed comments which illustrate points being made: if these comments are additionally discussed in detail and referenced, the text becomes overlong and unbalanced; without these comments significant connections may be lost.

A third problem lies in marking boundaries and relationships between central and satellite, or supportive concepts. Minor themes are as important as major ones, and some of these are now discussed.

Enablement and empowerment in elder mediation decision-making

The term enablement describes the function of the process of mediation. Its associated objective, empowerment, is in danger of losing its street credibility with many marginalized social groups. Also, for people over eighty, the memory of the powerful military gerontocracy which disposed of their brethren on the Somme battlefields, is uncomfortably connected with that of more recent aged political leaders of repressive regimes regularly represented on television screens.

It is here relevant to note that the major theorists of elder abuse stress the complexity of power relations in family violence. Wolf and Pillemer (1989) were amongst others who found that the abuser was often dependant on the elder who owned the home and financial resources: the abusive action resulted from the offender's pathological perceived powerlessness, often associated with alcoholism.

Steinmetz (1988) represents a general finding that elder abuse can be a continuation of spousal violence in which both elders can be involved, the weakest, mainly the woman, sustaining the greatest harm.

The intergenerational transmission theory of family violence (Gelles and Straus, 1988), in which asymmetrical power relations are perpetuated in altered domestic forms, is discounted by Wolf and Pillemer (1989), although it is acknowledged that there is insufficient longitudinal data for firm positioning at this point.

Thus issues of power in interpersonal relations are crucial in the aetiology of elder abuse, and this present research has uncovered some new examples of this in hitherto unexplored areas.

So, despite the caveat entered earlier, the social construction of empowerment theory is ongoing, often being conceptualized using advocacy principles as a base. Lloyd, himself an elder (as are a growing number of gerontologists), writes persuasively about this in *The Empowerment of Elderly People* (1991), and he and others see this as necessary for establishing the rights of older people, not only in family unequal power relations, but also in the social relations of capitalist society (Butler et al, 1988).

Evans, in *Liberation Theology: Empowerment Theory and Social Work Practice with the Oppressed* (1992), suggests that there are three major enabling processes of empowerment: the first is skill-building; the second is the enhancement of feelings of self-efficacy; and the third is consciousness-raising, which he relates to Freire's educational work on *conscientización* (1970):

> Taken together these processes have been described as developing a sense of critical consciousness (Evans, 1992:143).

It is this transformation which is the object of those who prefer the self-advocacy model because they say that advocacy is unfortunately disempowering in that it speaks for people rather than enabling them to strengthen their own voices. It is not relevant here to enter further into this important debate except to note that it is the enabling aspect of self-advocacy which relates to the processes of empowerment which Evans recommends, and to the self-determining process of mediation, in redressing unequal power relations.

Empowerment and enablement are terms with a circular relationship, but which also mean different things to different people in different situations. They are twin concepts of major importance which appear thematically throughout this book, and are in common gerontological usage.

Autonomy and independence are also closely related concepts. The first has regular academic and professional usage but has much less common currency with very old people who take pride in talking about their independence. Significantly, when their independence fails, they may have to be encouraged to realize that they can still be autonomous; that is, to be enabled to assert control over as many decisions and events in their lives as is possible, depending on the limits of their physical, mental and temperamental capacities, and the wish and will to use these.

The 1992 Social Care Association report stated that there is direct correlation between loss of autonomy and physical degeneration so that a social process such as mediation can make a direct contribution to maintaining and extending the sense of self-determination and well-being which is critical in health care (Lloyd, 1991; McDowell, 1989).

The literature on the human need for self-actualization (Maslow, 1976) supports these considerations which apply equally to elders and their carers. It has already been noted that some abusers have a sense of perceived powerlessness in their own pathological situations of dependency. They, and the great majority of responsible family and paid carers, can benefit from any services which contribute to feelings of self-realization.

17

In this respect Barusch's book, *Elder Care* (1991), usefully describes her own programmes for family carers' support groups, which provide practical and therapeutic assistance to encourage personal independence and caregiving interdependence with their elders. Constant reminders are needed that old people are increasingly being cared for by other old people so that unresolved conflicts can contribute to abuse of either, or both.

Autonomy and independence are also linked with the concepts of choice, consent and control. The Policy Studies Institute report, *Elderly People: Choice, Participation and Satisfaction* (1992) stresses the central role of choice in preserving autonomy, whether exercising preferences in food selection, or in the more problematic areas of choosing between community or institutional care. Even in the generally freer area of home care, Gaviland (1992) points out that housebound persons living alone may feel that their privacy, choice, consent and control is restricted by the way their visiting paid caregivers manage the domestic domain.

Consent is an attribute of voluntariness, the willingness to agree to suggested interventions and procedures, which, as has been stressed earlier, is the basis on which mediation services are offered. Formal consent to major legal, medical and social interventions is discussed in Part II where the views of Collopy (1992) and Kapp (1992a, b) are considered.

Control can be experienced as control by others, or as the ability to exercise direction and self-discipline in ordering one's personal life. It can be viewed as part of the social restraints of family, community or institutional daily living, and may be accepted or resisted according to the degree, style and purpose of the imposition. It may be perceived as a positive virtue in that it enhances feelings of self-efficacy (Evans, 1992).

The importance of locus of control issues in enabling old people to resist abuse is discussed with case illustrations later in this book, and it is relevant to note that in mediation participants are assured that it is they alone who control the outcome, and that the mediator only controls the process.

Nevertheless, despite the necessary and beneficial attributes of all these qualities, it is known that elders may withdraw from life, either as a deliberately structured disengagement (Moberg, 1990), or with diminishing interest in the events outside their shrinking world of daily routine (Severance, 1989).

In a study of institutionalized old people Wertle et al (1988) found that only 40 per cent wanted to have total information and consultation about the issues that involved them. In part this may be an unconsious or perceived attempt at self-protection of the personality, (id, and/or ego and super-ego) which seeks to avoid the uncertainties of confrontation, shocks and anxieties about future developments.

In this respect mediation is construed as a 'gentle process' (Acland, 1990), in contrast to often more painful psychotherapeutic or counselling interventions which demand patient and sometimes exhausting co-operation at a deeper level, and at greater length. On the other hand, mediation is likely to have more transitional than transformative effects, so there is the possibility that it could be dangerously superficial, when fundamental changes are needed.

However mediation is based on the consultation and co-operation which are necessary to all constructive human interaction. These feature in social exchange theory (Chadwick-Jones, 1976), where reciprocity is as important as it is in mediation, and which underpins much discussion about dysfunctional relationships in situations of elder abuse (Wolf and Pillemer, 1986).

All these concepts, and others which will emerge, relate to the importance of good communication so that needs, interests and rights of older people can be adequately expressed and represented in the search for social and relational justice (Burnside and Baker, 1993). These larger topics, in their relation to mediation and elder abuse, will be discussed later.

However it is suggested that the concepts so far considered have been shown to be intrinsic to mediation as well as to the gerontological consensus that these maximize quality of life in old age. These concepts, in fact, represent important human values, especially as they contribute to relational justice, and this chapter concludes by establishing an ethical base for these studies, adapted from the work of Moody (1992) on communicative ethics and communicative action, which he has derived from Habermas (1990).

Communicative ethics and communicative action

It has already been noted that there continues to be many disagreements about conceptualizing elder abuse, and this research follows Pillemer and Wolf (1986) in their pluralist approach to drawing on different theories for their explanatory power in understanding the varied aspects of a complex subject.

It also follows Phillips and Pugh (1987) in proceeding from a background theory, critical inquiry, to the focal theory, the subject of this section, concluding with the detailed theory of participatory research discussed in the third chapter. Both Habermas (1990) and Moody (1992) have developed their ideas from the foundation of critical theory, as has Maguire (1987) in her model of participatory research, so there is an internal conceptual consistency in this present approach.

This observes the fit between 'a civic model of communicative ethics' in which 'free and open communication does not suppress conflict or differences' (Moody, 1992:10), and the conflict resolution model (Burton, 1990) associated with mediation. Both are predicated on what Moody calls a 'procedural ethic' (1992:13). He goes on to argue that:

> The value of a communicative ethic is to find commonly agreed upon ways of negotiating our differences when we fail to agree on binding principles or rules (Moody, 1992:13).

This is essential for the complex bioethical work which Moody details in his book. He is concerned with decision-making in ageing conflicts, including those involving informed and negotiated consent in Advanced Directives and guardianship, autonomy and choice in nursing homes, the prevention of abuse and suicide, and a rational policy of social insurance to resolve issues of intergenerational equity. He takes a structural view of conflict, acknowledging competing social needs, but seeks to promote distributive justice through 'strategies for professional action and public choice' based on communicative ethics and communicative action (Moody, 1992:32).

This develops from the critical theory which exposes 'those forces which distort free communication, such as advertising, professional hegemony and the elite control of technologies' in the American nursing home industry (Moody, 1992:38). He goes on to say that:

> the 'ideal speech condition' is to promote the concrete conditions that promote such communication in all stages of life, including old age (Moody, 1992:39).

Here it is interposed that elder mediation provides one of these concrete conditions, and a lengthy quotation from Moody reinforces its rationale by arguing that:

> what we find in advanced industrial societies is a condition of systematically distorted communication, which serves to frustrate free and open deliberation ... everywhere we find an evasion of falsification of discourse ... we see domination by power or manipulation ... the nursing home industry does not empower

20

older people to make decisions about their lives ... Instead of freedom, we have the 'colonization of the life world' of old age ... The control of health care decisions by third party payers ... shows a bias toward elaborate medical technology or life prolongation, rather than social support for patient decision-making (1992:39).

Moody goes further in stressing that especially in old age should we older people be honoured as 'rights-bearing creatures', but that although bioethics should be based on 'a macro model of justice' in fact 'many of the most difficult problems of distributive justice arise at other levels of society, for example in reconciling competing claims among family members requiring 'a micro level analysis of justice' (1992:53). He further states:

Resolution of questions about distributive justice will depend on whether the family can achieve means of free and open communication about the problems they are facing ... abstract principles like autonomy and beneficence are secondary to the social process of communication itself (Moody, 1992:61, 64).

Moody is concerned throughout to establish constructive processes that will promote this:

The whole point of communicative ethics is to remind us insistently, in the tradition of Marx, to look more deeply at the practical and material conditions in which ethical ideals must be rooted if they are to flourish (Moody, 1992:182).

These ethical ideals are intrinsic to those of elder mediation, which needs to be grounded in such concepts of micro and macro levels of justice, if it is to contribute to the prevention of elder abuse, and develop integrity within the larger new social movement of mediation (Craig, 1991).

2 Rights-based mediation as a minimal form of social intervention

How far does Simon Roberts' model of mediation as a minimal form of alternative intervention (1983, 1986, 1988) meet the needs of elders and their carers in seeking to resolve their disputes?

This primary question is conceptually linked with a second one which asks how grievances and injuries are transformed into disputes through processes of 'naming, blaming and claiming' (Felstiner et al, 1987): are these experiences consistent or different to those of elders and their carers?

A third question relates to the interface of mediation with the law. To what extent do both succeed and/or fail in providing justice, protection from harm and the extension of human rights of those concerned? (Abel, 1982; Marshall, 1985; Hoggett, 1992; 1993a).

These questions are explored in the three sections of this chapter, and are central to a concluding analysis of the principal theme of this book that mediation, at early stages of conflict between elders and their carers, can contribute towards the prevention of perceived and actual elder abuse and neglect.

Throughout, the focus is on considering *processes* which have to accommodate colliding social and legal norms (Eisenberg, 1989), assure procedural justice (Hampshire, 1989), and reassure very vulnerable persons about the 'acknowledgement of one's selfhood' (Unger, 1975:216). These are the minimum criteria for any intervention in fragile family situations, or in institutional settings where unequal power relations prevail.

The strong ethical stance which has distinctively characterized all Roberts' work in promoting the autonomy and independence of the disputants provides safeguards for '(t)he very nature of mediation decision-making, in which the essence is an outcome constructed by the parties in accordance with their own meanings and objectives ...' (1988:148). His seminal contribution to the important contemporary discourse on family mediation has been to argue for it to move '(t)oward a minimal form of alternative intervention' (Roberts, 1986:25), so that sensitive and complex family dynamics are constructively respected, and coercive social manipulation avoided. It is this respect for their personhood and rights which elders and their carers especially need in the critical conflicts which currently confront them (Walters, 1992).

Elder mediation has yet to be established in the social policy of the United Kingdom but any decisions about the future direction that it might take will have to take account of the issues which will now be analysed.

Family mediation in elder caregiving decisions

The title of this section is taken from an influential article on American elder mediation which suggests that family conflict resolution is one of the five most frequent interventions by social workers in home health care agencies:

> Sources of family conflict around elder care decisions include feelings of guilt ... scarce resources for elder caregiving that demand commitment and substantial sacrifice from family members, limited experience with joint decision-making, and the rejuvenation of old conflictual family dynamics through the decision-making process (Parsons and Cox, 1989:122).

The social work concern is to prevent abuse developing, and to avoid the implementation of draconian powers under elder abuse legislation that, in many states, requires mandatory reporting, incontestable intervention and possible removal of the alleged victim from the family home. Senior mediation in America is thus conceptualized as a preventive process, and a constructive but minimal intervention.

This reference has been introduced to show the universality of Roberts' (1986) perceptions, the commonalities of family mediation and elder mediation, and to suggest that the attractions of minimalism, in the British context, were derived from comparable concerns to avoid 'the policing of families' (Donzelot, 1980), and to elude interventions which

23

'provide a cover for value-laden tampering with family life' (Roberts, 1983:139).

In an early article on mediation in family disputes Roberts (1983) gives a brief history of the 'ideologies' of conciliation suggesting that genuine party control of the process 'does seem incompatible with the call for a national conciliation service funded and organized by government' (1983:540).

> Such a development would almost certainly lead to an *increase* in state involvement in family disputes; at the least, a shift from one form of governmental intervention to another (Roberts, 1983:541).

Roberts then introduces four models of family mediation which, although they are ideal types, indicate some of the variations on which differently evolving British services are basing their practices.

The first is simple bilateral negotiation between the participants without the presence of a mediator.

The second, supported negotiation, relies on the activities of 'partisans' whose extended help 'may take innumerable forms' (Roberts, 1983:544).

> The intervention of partisans necessarily changes the shape of simple bilateral negotiations in several ways. First, the number or quality of partisans on one side or the other may alter the existing configurations of power ... Secondly ... some of the power over the decision-making process enjoyed by disputants ... is lost ... Thirdly, the universe of meaning within which negotiations proceed is extended and changed by the presence of partisans on either side; their interpretations, their understandings and their budgets of rules inform the process to a greater or lesser extent (Roberts, 1983:545).

This extract is necessarily long in order to make explicit some of the principles on which Roberts' views are based; their influential effect has contributed to the revision of mediation practice, and to an important book for practitioners by Davis entitled *Partisans and Mediators* (1988). In this he says that social workers are 'used to *exercising* authority' and that 'if one regards the ideal mediator as an *unobtrusive* figure, the "professional" expert is something of a contradiction in terms' (Davis 1988:10–11).

Returning to Roberts' typology, his third model is that of mediation:

> This limited role of the go-between, under which the third party constitutes no more than a conduit, a channel of communication, is of crucial importance (Roberts, 1983:546).

Although his preferences with regard to minimal intervention have already been clearly established, Roberts suggests that this must include two elements:

> first, the forum where they can get together; secondly, a normative framework, some ground rules, under which discussion can take place (1983:546).

Disregarding the fourth model of 'umpiring', in its varieties of arbitration and adjudication, which are not relevant to elder mediation, attention should be given to the way in which Roberts subsequently developed his views. He compares minimal intervention in mediation with that which is directive, and that which is therapeutic (Roberts, 1988).

He develops his early views of the tasks of the mediator by adding that 'a neutral presence supportive of the projects of negotiation' should be constituted within the family, leading to 'stimulating a 2-way flow of information' which enable the participants to develop their options (Roberts, 1988:144).

By contrast, the directive intervention has a mediator who actively influences the decision-making, interpreting those which are optimal, and persuading the participants to adopt the course of action which the mediator considers most suitable.

In therapeutic interventions, Roberts says that joint decision-making is postponed in favour of examining the relationships that have broken down within the family. For this purpose Roberts argues that mediators use 'openly or covertly, professional therapeutic techniques to reveal and correct pathological elements in the relationship' (1988:145).

Here it is useful to interpose Marian Roberts' detailed and profound study of family therapy in the context of conciliation which, significantly, she entitles *Systems or Selves? Some Ethical Issues in Family Mediation* (1990). In this she indicts family systems theory and practice for its determinist assumptions and social engineering management of family behaviour which she says coercively aims to correct its diagnosed dysfunctions. She also refers to the critiques which have raised 'grave ethical concerns within the field of family therapy itself' (1990:15).

Simon Roberts continues his own critique by saying that family systems theory is 'fraught with serious hazards, and is potentially extremely harmful' when practised in close association with attempts at joint decision-making' (1988:149). Neither he nor Marian Roberts deny that therapy, counselling, or social work advice and assistance may be helpful to participants in family crises or situations of chronic dysfunction, either before, after or in 'time out' taken in between mediation sessions, but they argue that the processes, and the agents of intervention, should be kept separate. Davis (1988), Davis and Roberts (1988) and Marian Roberts (1988) advance detailed cases for this division of role, which now appears to becoming a norm in good mediation practice.

However Simon Roberts allows that his model of minimal intervention has its own disadvantages in that it may not provide effective compensation in unequal power relationships between participants, and that they may reach an unfair settlement. He indicates that the model could be developed further to help people articulate issues and identify options that are available. He also strongly advises that access to the law, which should in any case always be freely available to protect weaker parties, may be the best option in such situations.

An interesting and important aspect of Roberts' minimal intervention model is its symbolic synthesizing role in what Cain and Kulcsar call 'the dialectic between theory and research' (1983:14). Auerbach, writing during the same period, also notes that 'recurrent dialectic between legality and its alternatives is one of our cultural constants' (1983:14). The vigorous antithesis mounted by the critical legal studies movement to the thesis that alternative dispute resolution (ADR) is a better mode for 'communitarian justice' (Auerbach, 1983:4), will be discussed later, but it is here relevant to observe that Roberts pioneered the scholarly middle ground between the erudite antagonism of Freeman (1984) towards the use of mediation in family conflict, and the benevolent paternalism of practitioners like Haynes (1981). Roberts' model may be justly regarded as meeting Freeman's critique, avoiding Haynes' active interventionism, and demonstrating an intrinsically valuable process for enabling participants to make their own decisions in resolving family conflicts.

A critique of Roberts' model is best incorporated into an evaluation of how far it meets the needs of elders and carers involved in conflict, and it is to this question that the present discourse now returns, having given a brief description of mediation in general as a form of minimal intervention.

There is a general professional view amongst social workers involved with elders and their carers that these social groups experience interpersonal and intergenerational conflicts which cannot constructively be dealt with by the law, in the majority of cases, and in which criminalization is too often counterproductive (Barusch, 1991; Breckman and Adelman, 1988; Eastman, 1984).

26

Parsons and Cox, in the article already referred to, agree that '(e)mpirical evidence for the efficacy of this approach (senior mediation) does not exist, except in what can be concluded from other family mediation' (1989:125). They quote mediation studies which support family views that:

> the mediation process had a more salutary effect on their ability to be reasonable and communicate with each other compared with adversarial clients using attorneys, perceived that the mediators had led them to more workable compromises, and believed that mediation intervention resulted in greater increases in cooperation (Parsons and Cox, 1989:126).

Furthermore these studies:

> found participants to be more satisfied with mediation than the adversarial process in nearly all outcome measures. Finally, they found no evidence for the often-voiced concern that women are disadvantaged in the mediation process because of lack of power in marital relationship (Parsons and Cox, 1989:126).

These findings have also been confirmed by Folberg and Taylor (1984) and Pearson and Thoeness (1984), and have important inferences for elder mediation in that much conflict is experienced between ageing spouses or partners, a fact now illustrated by international gerontologists in a recent cross-cultural review of findings from sixteen different countries (Kosberg, 1992). Also it is now well established that some elder abuse is a developmental form of prolonged domestic violence (Pillemer and Wolf, 1986; Steinmetz, 1988; Wolf and Bergman, 1989); this has a necessary interface with the law and will be discussed later, but is mentioned here to indicate that American senior mediation takes account of the 'lack of power in marital relationships' referred to above.

Prolonged family relationships naturally characterize the experiences of elders, notwithstanding the fact that living patterns are changing and that kinship and community networks widen forms of social interaction (Wenger, 1992; Willmott, 1988).

It is well known that elders suffer from feelings of guilt in proportion to their increasing disability and dependence upon their loved ones, or their families and friends, whose personal liberty and financial security may be amongst other social goods which have to be sacrificed, willingly or by default, as the ageing process develops (Block and Sinnott, 1979; Cumming and Henry, 1961; Filinson and Ingman, 1989).

27

These feelings of guilt tend to be residual, often unacknowledged, and difficult to modify or eradicate in ageing persons, who will also be mentally vulnerable to psychogeriatric illness and depression in particular, a condition closely associated with the sense of guilt. Depression is also often not recognized in personal, family or clinical terms, and, when untreated, can lead to chronic personality withdrawal states (Ryft and Essex, 1991), as well as to the condition of 'learned helplessness' (Seligman, 1975).

This factor contributes to the developing of *avoidance* as a conscious or unconscious trait and strategy in interrelationships, so that difficulties, problems and conflicts which are perceived to be overwhelming to the defensive and shrinking ego are ignored, suffered or sublimated.

Gulliver, a legal anthropologist, defines this *avoidance* in terms of its relation to dispute resolution:

> Third, there is avoidance: the more or less deliberate curtailing or limiting of further relations with the other persons, letting the matter rest, accepting the status quo (at least temporarily), seeking no specific decision on the dispute, and endeavouring to prevent the continuation or escalation of conflict because of the perceived difficulties that would result (Gulliver, 1979:2).

It is this avoidance which has been found to be critical in influencing elders not to respond actively and positively to American adult protective services, and to tolerate situations of abuse rather than involve those on whom they depend in the perceived perils of social intervention. Here it is hypothesized, therefore, that it is those services which can be perceived by elders as offering a minimal intervention in all that may remain to them of family life, which are most likely to prove acceptable. As it has been stressed throughout this book that mediation is a voluntary and non-coercive process, its appeal to elders in any free choice by them and their carers to accept its service, will largely depend on how far it restrains itself from any unwelcome examination of their deepest intimacies.

It is these which are often defended from the counselling and family therapy interventions which may well be necessary, but which are often resisted because professional outsiders or experts cannot be trusted with family secrets. Giddens has a significant comment on trust and 'the transformation of intimacy' in his book, *The Consequences of Modernity* (1990), when he suggests that this is an issue of particular contemporary importance:

Trust on a personal level becomes a project to be 'worked at' by the parties involved, and depends on the opening out of the individual to the other … which means a mutual process of self-disclosure (Giddens, 1990:121).

Roberts' model of minimal intervention has already been shown to encompass the sustaining elements of trust in relationships, and the encouragement of the mutual self-disclosure, which Giddens (1990) recommends if people are to maintain intimacy amidst the interventionist bureaucracies of modern, and post-modern society.

The consequent pressures reduce the already threatened and diminishing feelings of competence and self-worth which elders tend to experience unless they are especially physically, mentally and emotionally robust. Feelings of self-efficacy are emerging as key factors in protecting the elder's self from the effects of stressful situations, in strengthening the healthy, and in preventing disease.

Walker and Bates (1992) did an empirical study testing self-efficacy beliefs and elder health and found there was a positive correlation between the two variables.

Feelings of self-efficacy and the sense of well-being of elders has already been discussed earlier in this book, and has been shown to be related to the autonomy and independence which is enhanced as and when they are encouraged and enabled to participate in decision-making affecting their lives. This argument will not be rehearsed here except for pointing to the relevance of Cicerelli's *Family Caregiving: Autonomous and Paternalistic Decision-making* (1992) which stresses the importance of the subject, and Cox and Waller's paper for the American Health Association (1991) which advocates practical processes which improve communication between elders and their carers, a theme which will be returned to later.

Mediation is one of these practical processes, embedded in what Wehr calls 'bridging institutions' which use 'bridging persons', so described in his book, *Conflict Regulation* (1979). Smith suggests that these persons have essential functions of communication in being 'able to arouse (shared) meanings in others' (1973:15). He develops the theme of 'meta-communication' as a way of personal interrelatedness which can encourage the appearance of 'new facts and perceptions (which) can change attitudes' (Wehr, 1979:88, 77).

Here again there is a conceptual consistency with the work of Roberts (1986) in suggesting a mode of minimal intervention which, it could be extrapolated, creates the space and lack of coercive pressure, within which meta-communication can take place through the mediator's physical presence, restrained verbalism, modulated tone and attuned body language. It is sensitively and empathetically adapted to the needs of both parties, and, in particular, to those of very vulnerable elders and their carers.

It should be noted that American senior mediation training handbooks pay special attention to describing the age-related effects of sight, hearing and other sensory losses, and psychological traits which greatly affect the atmosphere of meta-communication in which the mediation takes place.

It is also relevant, from a cross-cultural perspective, to note that the Jewish Family Mediation Service and the Asian Family Mediation Service in the United Kingdom have been developed specifically to address the special needs of the social norms affecting their respective communities in ways that are consistent with Wehr's concept of meta-communication as developed in his book which is called *Transracial Communication* (1979).

It is similarly noteworthy that Christians, especially the Quakers and Mennonites who pioneered community and educational mediation in America and the United Kingdom, have had their philosophy of mediation influenced by Taylor's *The Go-Between God* (1972), in which Christ is portrayed as a model mediator. The Quaker emphasis on silence and waiting being positive qualities which enhance the value of active listening, as distinct from negative passivity, is especially pertinent to Roberts' model, even though he makes no comment upon it.

The role of go-between is one which is constantly discussed in all academic and practitioner literature on the subject of mediation, and is one amongst many others which this present narrow focus on the principle of minimal intervention permits no further elaboration. Nor is there space for a listing of the many other needs which elders and their carers have in respect of welcoming and co-operating with social interventions in their lives. Argyle, in his book *Cooperation* (1991), suggests that people in conflict situations have to be assertive, though not aggressive, in establishing their own and shared goals.

Here it might be hypothesized that the more assertive , dominating and intrusive the mediator is perceived to be, the less likely is it that the participants, especially elderly persons, unless they are particularly resistant, will feel encouraged to develop their own assertiveness and readiness to co-operate. Another way of expressing this is to suggest that the more active the work which the mediator is perceived to do, the greater may be the passive reliance of elders on this, and the lesser their inclination to take responsibility for personally contributing to it.

This may be an important factor for ageing persons, depending on how far their capacities are affected by dependence, and what kind of life-choices they wish, or feel constrained to make with regard to withdrawal or personal growth (Bitten, 1990). Nevertheless the model of mediation as minimal intervention affords elders the unpressurized space in which to prioritize their interests and constructively confront their conflicts, whatever outcome may result. It is a valuable, non-iatrogenic learning experience for all concerned.

However there are other mediators whose work has been developed to provide a more comprehensive intervention response to the conflicts which people experience, especially in the crises which can be typical in family mediation. It is similarly accepted that crises can also be characteristic of elder and carer conflict, as when the health of either party collapses temporarily or permanently, when decisions have to be made about the sudden necessity for hospital or residential care, and when an abusive situation appears to be imminent.

This suggests a critique of Roberts' (1986) model as being inadequate for the degree of intervention needed, although he has indicated that of course the necessary diagnostic and supportive services should be immediately at hand to help participants through any crises. He maintains that clear and cool decision-making is inherently problematic in the context of crisis, so that mediation is best reserved until essential needs for protection, treatment and care have been met.

However, Parkinson, one of the most respected practitioners in British family mediation, takes a different view:

> Conciliators can be catalysts for constructive planning during this crisis period ... The crisis theory of mental health ... suggests that if sufficient support is available, the crisis can be an opportunity for positive change ... (Parkinson, 1986:127).

Parkinson's extensive professional training in social work, counselling and family mediation equips her, as it does many multidisciplinary workers involved in the care of elders to offer intervention which is far from minimal. There are certainly indications in the work of Parsons and Cox (1989) that, as social workers, that they are aware of these issues. However, in their elder mediation service they insist that:

(t)he focus of mediation is on the process of problem-solving, not on the behavioral or personality issues of participants (Parsons and Cox, 1989:123).

Similarly the senior mediation projects in Atlanta and Kansas, described elsewhere in this book, based their approach on minimal intervention in practice, even though it was not conceptualized at such. Old people with more extensive needs were referred elsewhere.

Nevertheless in the emerging innovative uses of American senior mediation in guardianship and Advanced Directives disputes, it is as yet unclear as to how mediators will approach the extremely complex and sensitive issues involved. It appears that they will be acting in partnership with other professionals, so it may not be possible to keep the mediation process discrete.

However there is a case for arguing that mediation can play an especially valuable role in institutional ethics committees where the contributions of doctors, nurses, clergy, relatives and the patient will demand special skills from the mediator in ensuring that all voices are fairly heard and that the most appropriate outcome results. Roberts readily admits that there will be the situation in which his model should not apply which 'requires skills and brings hazards which require much more careful examination than has been attempted so far' (1986:39).

In returning to the principal question of this chapter as to how far Roberts' (1986) model of mediation as a form of minimal intervention meets the needs of elders and their carers, three conclusions emerge from the analysis.

Firstly its elements have already been incorporated, however unsystematically and unconsciously, in the American senior mediation services referred to. Secondly, in any evolving more complex use of elder mediation, the principles of minimal intervention might be regarded as a *standard* if not as a model. Thirdly, and more pragmatically, elder mediation, like mediation itself, is largely unknown to the older generation, who wisely seek to test new ideas and often approach innovative services hesitantly. There is probably more chance of them being willing to participate in mediation when it takes the form of minimal intervention. They will find it helpful if it is used at the earliest stages of relational conflict, when their own resources, and those of their carers, for dealing with it have begun to fail.

The transformation of disputes

An essential theme of this book is that elder mediation may be able to contribute to the prevention of elder abuse if it is used at an early *stage* in relational conflict. This follows Felstiner et al in their important seminal work which elucidates the way in which disputes develop (hereafter references will be made to Felstiner alone in the main text):

> the emergence and transformation of disputes – the way in which experiences become grievances, grievances become disputes, and disputes take various shapes, follow particular dispute processing paths, and lead to new forms of understanding (Felstiner et al, 1981:632).

However Felstiner insists that 'disputes are not things: they are social constructs' (1981:631), an admission that has earlier also been made with regard to the definition and interpretation of elder mediation.

He also insists that this means:

> studying a social process as it occurs. It means studying the conditions under which injuries are perceived or go unnoticed and how people respond to the experience of injustice and conflict (Felstiner et al, 1981:632).

This guidance has been an influential factor in planning the fieldwork for this book, in that it situates participant-observation research in American institutions where elders live, in which it is known that there are many conflicts and that some of these escalate into elder abuse. Similarly, the casework resulting from EMP mediation has generated basic empirical research data from studying social processes as they occur. The following extract supports this approach:

> One aim of transformation research, therefore, is to produce direct and reliable data about motives and interactions by studying them contemporaneously. Only in this way is it possible to catalogue the antecedents of a dispute before the issue is publicly joined ... the way in which grievances and injurious experiences are first perceived (Felstiner et al, 1981:651).

Felstiner develops his ideas:

> Things look very different, however, if we start with the *individual* who has suffered an injurious experience. That is what the transformation point of view makes us do. It encourages inquiry

into why so few such individuals get some redress. So the transformation perspective naturally prompts questions that have been largely ignored thus far: why are Americans so slow to perceive injury, so reluctant to make claims, and so fearful of disputing – especially of litigating? (Felstiner et al, 1981:652).

Felstiner, of course, is not referring specifically to elders, nor to institutional conflicts, but his words also apply to them.

To add to the comments that have already been made about the feelings of guilt and depression which result in many elders silently suffering from, rather than complaining about their perceptions of neglect or injury, it should also be remembered that patients in what Goffman has called 'total institutions' (1961) are often too afraid to indict those who care for them.

Felstiner has another possible explanation:

> One hypothesis tentatively advanced in some early research is that the cult of competence, the individualism celebrated by American culture, inhibits people from acknowledging – to themselves, to others, and particularly to authority – that they have been injured, that they have been bettered by an adversary (Felstiner et al, 1981:652).

As far as elders are concerned, it might contrariwise be conjectured that it is the cultural stereotype of *incompetence,* or the fear of it, which inhibits them from acknowledging their suffering.

Felstiner says that 'social scientists have rarely studied the capacity of people to tolerate substantial distress and injustice' but that it may 'represent a failure to perceive that one has been injured; such failures may be self-induced or externally manipulated' (1981:633). Decubital ulcers, or bed sores, which untreated have led to death and allegations of institutional abuse in American nursing homes, have generally resulted from staff failure to provide appropriate care, but, when elders live alone, may have developed through persistent lack of hygiene, or an unwillingness to change body-bed contact positions regularly.

This failure of some elders to care for themselves is named self-neglect, and has an ambiguous place in the categorization of elder abuse and neglect in as much as some theorists, and some American legislation, give it no definitionally distinct place in the index (McCreadie, 1991). So *naming* is a socially and politically important process.

Felstiner maintains that this *naming* is the first essential stage '(i)n order for disputes to emerge and remedial action to be taken' (1981:633). He then goes on to say that:

> (t)he next step is the transformation of a perceived injurious experience into a grievance ... We call the transformation from perceived injurious experience to grievance *blaming* (Felstiner et al, 1981:635).

An old person may blame her daughter for failing to provide nourishing and digestible food; the denial of this may lead to the development of conflict which, unaddressed, can lead to the risks of neglect, whether intentional or not.

> The third transformation occurs when someone with a grievance voices it to the person or entity believed to be responsible and asks for some remedy. We call this communication *claiming*. A claim is transformed into a dispute when it is rejected in whole or in part (Felstiner et al, 1981:635–6).

This process of *naming, blaming* and *claiming* neatly and clearly describes the transformation of conflicts which many elders and their carers experience in the difficult and demanding situations which interrelationship and dependency can create. It is an important process to understand for the purpose of this book, which conceptualizes that it is at the early *naming* stage, when the perceived injurious feelings or experiences are acknowledged, that elder mediation can play its most preventive role.

Here it is apposite to recall that the development of American senior mediation in family and community conflict has been primarily based on using elders as trained volunteer mediators, and that, because of their own ageing experiences, they are especially sensitive to the implications which *naming* may have in families. It may expose hitherto well-kept dark family secrets, as when the propensity of a grandson for petty theft from the pension money he collects, is brought into the light.

Felstiner also considers the initial event to be important:

> The early stages of naming, blaming and claiming are significant, not only because of the high attrition they reflect, but also because the range of behaviour they encompass is greater than that involved in the later stages of disputes, where institutional patterns restrict the options open to the disputants (Felstiner et al, 1981:636).

This view, although not derived from any specified knowledge of elder conflict, is nevertheless consistent with that of gerontology which has generally found elders to be reluctant, ambivalent and anxious about initiating and becoming involved in the transformation of family and institutional disputes, especially when they are members of ethnic minorities (Ammerman and Hersen, 1991; Kosberg, 1983; Norman, 1985). Once the *naming* has been made explicit, the old person may then become the subject of harassment, so that any future decision-making with regard to *blaming* creates further internal and external conflict.

As Felstiner suggests, if the *blaming* involves allegations about events which society construes as criminal, options of intervention may become restricted, initially at least, to involving the police and the law. This is perhaps the most critical stage in the transformation of disputes for old people who, even more than most of us, may be confused about the distinction between their interests, needs, and rights, and to what degree of social support and protection they are entitled.

In addition to this there are even more fundamental issues of family solidarity and loyalty, the values of which may be held to be of even more importance than personal comfort, security and safety.

It must also be recognized that the processes of *naming, blaming* and *claiming* may also be initiated by the carer. A daughter-in-law may feel her attempts at caregiving are being continually negated by the elderly parent's alcoholism and associated incontinence. Her own ageing, and increasing stresses of family life, may make her perceived injurious experiences appear impossible to bear any longer. She may decide to publicize her father-in-law's problems throughout the wider family and kinship network, where they have hitherto been recognized but unacknowledged. Blame will doubtless be attributed to her as well as to him, but it may lead to her *claim* to be free of the degrading smells and labours resulting from the addiction, and to have him admitted to an institution.

Here again, issues of family solidarity and loyalty arise, and conflicting norms and values can lead to bitter and tragic intergenerational disputes in which there can be several victims, some losers and no winners.

The main hope in such sad situations is that *identification*, as a pre-figurative form of *naming*, may take place sufficiently early in relational conflict between old people and their carers to enable appropriate diagnostic, support and treatment services to be provided, and then for mediation to be offered for voluntary acceptance by those involved who have to make critical decisions for the future.

Having said this, it is admitted that when issues of disputed values and norms are predominant, mediation, whether as a minimal or more comprehensive form of intervention, is seldom effective in establishing satisfactory outcomes. It may be possible to separate distinct and discrete items of a practical nature from the deeper and more fundamental cleavages in family life, and deal with these by mediation. It may also be possible that a specifically limited agreement may become the unexpected yet necessary catalyst for a beneficial change in the family situation, which may make the still remaining conflictual situation more tolerable.

For instance, the burden on the main carer of an increasingly senile but dearly loved grandmother may have become so unbearable that admission to a nursing home has to be considered despite the angry opposition of the grandchildren of the family. Family meetings may become increasingly characterized by personal attacks on its members for their failure to assume responsibility for the burden, and the grandmother, in her periods of cogency will become increasingly unhappy about the problems she is causing. She may decide to stop eating, or even to attempt suicide, in order to relieve her family of the burden of care, or the expense of a nursing home placement.

Yet, had the offer of mediation been made and accepted at the earliest stage when her increasingly disturbed behaviour had been named as Alzheimer's disease, it might have been more easily possible for family members to make an agenda of the various caregiving tasks involved, and to divide these appropriately by agreement amongst themselves. This would have reinforced their mutual sense of family solidarity and loyalty, giving them especial satisfaction in constructing their own agreement about an urgent problem. Their solution might only be temporary, but, more importantly, it would have established for them the experience of a creative process which could be used in whatever future decision-making had to be attempted.

So it can be seen that Felstiner's valuable analysis of the transformation of disputes fits helpfully with the concepts of elder mediation and its concerns to contribute to the prevention of elder neglect and abuse.

Also, on a more light-hearted level, his notions of *naming, blaming* and *claiming* fit equally well the maverick and malicious behaviour of some old people who defend the loss of their status, senses and sociability by deliberately developing difficult mannerisms in order to attract attention. For them, the *naming, blaming* and *claiming* involved in trying to get redress from their perceived and loudly articulated injurious experiences, may be their preliminary attempt at resistance to institutionalism, their first assertion of existential independence, and the last game that they may play at the ebb of life.

Felstiner, however, should be given the last word in order to provide continuity with the next part of this chapter which deals with the interface between mediation, the law and justice:

> Finally, attention to naming, blaming and claiming permits a more critical look at recent efforts to improve 'access to justice' ... Access to justice is supposed to reduce the unequal distribution of advantages in society; paradoxically it may amplify these inequalities (Felstiner et al, 1981:636–7).

Elder mediation: another form of social control?

Felstiner's concern that all citizens should have equal access to justice, where their claims for redress and protection can best be met through the law, has also been a founding principle on which senior mediation services are being built in America.

Although each is independent, one is situated in the Justice Center of Atlanta; another in the Olathe Legal Services of Kansas. The specially trained elder volunteer mediators, and their paid co-ordinators, have direct daily access to legal colleagues with whom they can consult about the best interests of disputants in their free choice as to the method of conflict resolution they prefer. The participants are informed that mediation is a voluntary, non-coercive process, in which only they make decisions, and that they are free to exit from it at any time to use legal and other available resources.

The general social history of mediation shows that it was initiated at the interface between formal and informal dispute resolution processes, although Harrington (1985) says these are 'in the shadow of the law'. For there developed a powerful critique of ADR in the 1980s, which Cain and Kulcsar (1983) described as 'second class justice' and about which Abel's *The Politics of Informal Justice* (1982) became one of the most influential academic texts.

These academic lawyers were mostly associated with Marxism and critical theory in the critical legal studies movement, and the legal philosopher, Unger (1987) wrote a profound study examining its considerable intellectual impact on the sociology of the law.

Although the decline of communism and consequent developments within formalism and informalism led to diminished vigour and rigour in the prosecution of the critique, which had been received more cautiously by British scholars, Roberts was one of those who introduced his *Toward a Minimal Form of Alternative Intervention* (1986) by giving the critique a very fair review. However he pointed out that, in the critique, 'few of the principal studies have been directed toward decision-making in the family and in the aftermath of family breakdown' (Roberts, 1986:26). Elder mediation, for the purpose of this book, has so far been situated conceptually within family mediation, and, in any case, developed in America *after* the first flush of enthusiasm for the critique had faded.

Nevertheless it is necessary here to evaluate its substance, because there is a continuing concern amongst lawyers and all other agents of social intervention, that in every area, with carefully qualified differences as in dealing with vulnerable elders, the most appropriate, constructive and protective services should be available and utilized.

It is proposed to refer briefly to the leading academics who have developed this critique, in order to show awareness of their place in evolving legal and social theory, and their perceived anxieties about the dangers of ADR. Even briefer comments will be made about any relevance their views have to the processing of disputes of older people, because these either did not specifically attract their attention, or were deliberately ignored by them.

Firstly it is necessary to refer to Auerbach's important historical review of the development of American ADR in his book, *Justice Without Law* (1983). He sympathetically describes the dissatisfaction of the early settlers with the injustices of the colonial legal system which had been imposed, and how they had pioneered their own various and alternative local dispute resolution services in efforts to promote 'communitarian justice' (Auerbach, 1983:4).

He then shows how these gradually became colonized by lawyers and co-opted by the state as providing cheaper and more cosmetically appealing ways of controlling its citizens. He exempts from his charge the genuinely independent community-initiated mediation projects, but shows that most ADR develops through state funding and court referrals: 'the new programs represent the justice system more than the community' (Auerbach, 1983:136). Thus the delegalized system has now become relegalized, and Auerbach is concerned that the new hybridism is dangerous, despite ADR having the propinquitous blessing of the courts whose formalism attracts him, because it alone can enforce people's rights. Unfortunately, as he sadly concludes, these are too often those of the rich and powerful, although the plight of the poor aged is not discussed.

Hofrichter represents the more extreme view of conspiracy theory in that he says that ADR has been established:

> as a disguised, quasi-bureaucratic police force that places itself between social classes so that it may stabilize as well as invade community life ... it is itself an agency of control (Hofrichter, 1988:109–10).

Hofrichter is interested in community conflict being used as part of the revolutionary struggle against class oppression, rather than in it being individualized by the resolution of interpersonal disputes. Nevertheless he gives a careful detailed study of neighborhood justice centres, showing their invasion by state interests, and saying that class action would be a more democratic way of dealing with local grievances. Yet he admits that 'given its contradictions and paradoxes, NDR (ADR) contains elements with a liberatory potential' (Hofrichter, 1988:153). He comments that this makes neighborhood dispute resolution a highly unstable subject to transform into political resistance, but it might be argued that, in his terms, this very instability should guarantee that it will never have the oppressive power he imagines. A dispute resolution service run by elder volunteer mediators for other elders would be unlikely to weaken any revolutionary struggle.

Hofrichter had been influenced by Harrington's earlier empirical research from 1978 to 1979 in a two-year pilot dispute resolution project in Kansas City. She drew attention to the 'ideology of informalism' (Harrington, 1985:14) by which the state extended its network of power. She said that 'the conservatism of this reform is evident in the social relations it constructs' (Harrington, 1985:34), which aims to preserve the legitimacy of the status quo. She also pointed to the high degree of tolerance for unresolved conflict in poor areas, and found that the dispute resolution services in Kansas provided no real redress for this. Harrington concluded that for most people 'alternatives offer a kind of shadow justice' (1985:169), although also, typically for the period, she makes no reference to the needs of old people. It was on account of these that the Kansas senior mediation service was set up in 1991.

In an article written about the same period, entitled *The Politics of Participation and Non-Participation in the Dispute Process* (1984), Harrington argued that for access to justice to involve effective participation in the formal system, people needed legal representation. Although there is no reason to attribute to her a concern for professional self-interest, her argument that lawyers are the gatekeepers to citizen participation in justice is one about which feminists have mounted their own critique.

Smart argues passionately about 'the power of the law as a discourse which disqualifies other forms of knowledge', attacking its 'phallogocentric' focus 'produced under conditions of patriarchy' (1989:86), and its 'juridogenic nature' in that 'the legal "cure" is frequently as bad as the original abuse' (1989:161). She concludes that in order to enable ordinary people, and women in particular, to participate in justice:

> it is important to sustain an emphasis on non-legal strategies and local struggles ... it is important to resist the temptation the law offers, namely the promise of a solution (Smart, 1989:165).

Smart indicates that she is partly thinking of single teenagers for whose problems of unwanted pregnancy the British abortion law appears to her to be counterproductive by disregarding their wishes and decisions. Smart also does not consider the special needs of old people.

It is relevant here to interpose the reminder that lawyers have not adequately safeguarded elder rights to participation in the struggle for justice. S.47 (1)(2) of the British 1948 National Assistance Act (1951 Amendments) allows the forced removal of certain persons, including elders, from their homes, following formal orders from magistrates' courts, where there has been an *ex parte* undefended hearing (Norman, 1987:133).

Cain, also a Marxist and a feminist, as she includes women in her list of marginalized and oppressed social groups, agrees, with Harrington, that informal justice reproduces hegemonic state power. Cain sees the tempting appeal of populist justice for the working or revolutionary classes, but agrees that it can be corrupted by a replacement authoritarianism, and instead proposes the ideal of 'collective justice' (1988:61).

> Clients are brought to a fuller understanding of their own class position and so of the political strategies necessary to counter the class oppression they experience (Cain, 1988:61).

She agrees that her ideal type has yet to evolve, and appreciates the contradiction of having to institutionalize and formalize it, if universality is required. Although Cain does not discuss the politicization of elders, which presumably would be included in her scenario, it might be speculated that their most dominant voices could well come from the more affluent groups, as in the Gray Panther movement in America,

41

possibly contributing to a gerontocracy which would fit uncomfortably with her ideals of democratic socialism.

Here it is interesting to note that although feminist lawyers tend to be critical of ADR, other feminists are enthusiastic mediators as they consider their work to be truly emancipatory.

Abel, in the first volume of his major work editing and reviewing contributions from these and other academics, admits that they see informal justice as instrumental to their political purposes, but argues that they show clearly that there is too often 'coercion disguised', 'covert manipulation' and 'characteristic modification' of people's interests in ADR (1982a:272).

In his second volume he allows that:

> informal justice has an important, if limited, role to play in revolutionary struggles. It can proclaim symbolically the autonomy and competence of a group of workers or peasants or a community of urban squatters, and it can confer on those who participate in the struggle a sense of collective empowerment (Abel, 1982b:12).

So he concludes that 'informalism remains problematic' as 'the struggle for informal justice never ends' (1982b:13).

Abel (1982), a liberal as well as a self-proclaimed libertarian scholar, leading the company of the other academics assembled here, does not include the aged amongst marginalized social groups who face discrimination, although he does broaden the parameters of informal justice by referring to its use as a diversion from the criminal justice system.

Matthews, a respected British scholar working in this area, in his *Privatising Criminal Justice* (1989), says that dispute resolution may offer 'an *extension* of justice rather than its dilution' (1989:18). and that it has sensitized people to demand better state facilities for victims and for deviants. Matthews had earlier edited a British critique, *Informal Justice* (1988) in which Marshall had presented a strong case for mediation and reparation providing restorative justice as a diversion from the penal system, arguing that 'community justice is participative justice' (1988:46). The coining of the term participative justice fits very well with the concept of relational justice which is thematic in this book.

It is also relevant to note that unpublished accounts from British mediators show that some older victims have benefited emotionally as well as practically from constructing their own mediation and reparation agreements with offenders. The evidence from the national voluntary organization, Victim Support, is that it is only since their introduction of the Victims' Charter in 1990 that lawyers and the courts have begun to consider the interests and needs of victims, elders in particular.

The foregoing references to some of the principal academics who shaped the critique of ADR has not done justice to the richness of their rhetoric nor to their scholarly achievements, especially as some, including Abel, suffered professional persecution from a few of the positivist legal theorists who rejected their views.

Other academics, like Henry, were more ambivalent, as he criticized Cain's (1988) advocacy of collective justice by saying that 'collective justice is no less subordinate to a range of inherent contradictions than the official criminal justice system' (1984:158), and later took a more pragmatically positive view about the value of ADR:

> short of revolution, change towards socialist legality is more likely to be fostered by mechanisms of community justice within institutions that do not challenge the basic premises of capitalism than through the development of more radical conflicting institutions (Henry, 1985:324).

This view is consistent with the experience of voluntary organizations who work for and with the aged, whose causes they advance through criticism which is co-operative rather than antagonistic in their social relations with the state.

Fitzpatrick makes an equivalent challenge to the theory of power relations, especially that of Foucault (1981) on whose seminal exposures of dominant power structures, many proponents of critical legal studies rely. He points to the shifting dialectics of power and counter-power, and how they are perceived to be located in state and alternative institutions, as well in those formed as a result of their critique. He suggests that the advocates of ADR are aware of the problematic and that 'the hidden terms of the engagement between such resistance and power are made explicit and subject to contestation rather than being contained passively' (Fitzpatrick, 1988:197).

Similarly British social activists, like Field (1989), who campaign for the elderly poor, publicly utilize any attributions to their apparent political weakness, by demonstrating their resistance to the establishment, and mobilizing alternative institutions into coalitions that have forms of popular counter-power.

Another aspect of the debate about the values of consensus and dissent in dispute resolution is that of those like Menkel-Meadow who point to the usefulness of settlement procedures by lawyers in preventing cases going to trial:

Adversarial assumptions affect not only the quality of solutions to negotiated problems, but also the process by which these solutions are reached. This is especially important because the type and quality of solutions may depend a great deal on the process used. The adversarial conception of negotiation produces a particular mind-set concerning possible solutions which then tend to produce a *competitive* process (Menkel-Meadow, 1984:775–6).

McThenia and Shaffer support this view in their article, *For Reconciliation*, in the *Yale Law Review:*

Settlement is a process of reconciliation in which the anger of broken relationships is to be confronted rather than avoided, and in which healing demands not a truce but a confrontation (McThenia and Shaffer, 1985:1664).

It should be mentioned here that it is well-known that 90 per cent of all cases, civil and criminal, that go to court, reach settlement before trial (Baldwin, 1985; Bottomley, 1979; Galanter, 1983; Mackie, 1991).

Bottomley (1979) goes so far as to say that legal rhetoric about the supposed supreme morality of the law should recognize that, in reality, there is a production ethic of routine justice which is as discretionary as that of any informal dispute resolution.

Trubek adds that 'critics say that there is no justice without law, but they do not believe in justice *through* law' (1983:834), adding that the mounting of the critique can be seen as a professionally defensive move by lawyers.

Turk (1975) goes further and says that legalism exacerbates and stigmatizes conflicts in an exploitive way, and that it regulates their symptoms, not their sources, so that any resolution is illusory.

As a conflict theorist, Duke (1976) maintains that the law operates from a base of superficial external values, whilst mediation proceeds by the discovery and affirmation of the internal values of the parties.

There is here a mixture of comments from family lawyers, criminologists and others who are concerned about the counterproductive effects of the formal legal system, and who deny the absolutism and determinism of the critique against ADR for its alleged propensity to extend the social control of the state.

Piven and Cloward insist that 'the very mechanisms that offer such a control at one historical moment generate the possibilities for political mobilization at another' (1982:143).

Having analysed, compared and contrasted views about the disadvantages and advantages of ADR, it is not now intended to rehearse the reasons given by those like Alper and Nichols (1981), Danzig and Lowy (1975), Deutsch (1973), Fisher and Ury (1981), Folberg and Taylor (1984), Folger and Jones (1994), Goldberg et al (1985) and Moore (1986) in America, and Mackie (1991), Marshall (1985) and Wright (1991) in Britain for the strong case they have advanced in support of ADR, and for its more democratically organized variant of community mediation in particular. This position has already been well established by the earlier discussion of the value of mediation.

Therefore in drawing this analysis of the critique of ADR to a close it only seems necessary to point out that it is from the experience of family and community mediation, rather than through any satisfaction with the law, that elder mediation has emerged as an innovative and, it could be argued, radical form of dispute resolution. The foregoing critique, while deserving respect for its championing of selected social groups, has substantially ignored those especially vulnerable persons who are impaired by age, disability and incapacity. They suffer from inequality and discrimination, and their silently borne and inarticulated interrelational conflicts need much closer social attention in this sphere.

Neither American informal nor formal justice institutions in the past have adequately succeeded in helping old people and their associates in interpersonal conflicts, and it is suggested that the above debate encourages a view that a good case has been made for the potential of elder mediation in contributing to the prevention of elder abuse.

It is to recent legal initiatives in Britain that the concluding section of this chapter now turns.

The protection of the rights of elders

Here it is not intended to catalogue the existing general legislation affecting elders which has been authoritatively described by Griffiths et al (1990; 1992), except to note that they chronicle in detail its many ambiguities, inadequacies and lack of safeguards for the protection of elder rights, and, for that matter, those of their carers.

In *Sharpening the Instrument: The Law and Older People* (1992) they point to the fact that 'the existing framework makes little or no provision for their special needs' (1992:7), and end by asking 'whether we should adopt a single codified system of law that applies exclusively to older people' (1992:42). They realize that this approach could be regarded as a form of reverse discrimination, and that it might isolate and stigmatize elders further:

> Law needs to be radically changed. But so do attitudes. Until society is prepared to abandon ageist attitudes and practices no amount of changes in the law will fully guarantee the rights of older people. In many respects the challenge for the law has much more to do with educating people and changing attitudes than it has with changing rules and procedures (Griffiths et al, 1992:44).

They therefore prefer the route to law reform, and commend the Law Commission for the path it has taken to this end. While this book has been in the process of writing the government has considered, and made a disappointing provisional response to the Consultation Papers now to be discussed, which will be considered on the basis of their original proposals.

In the Law Commission Consultation Paper No. 119, *Mentally Incapacitated Adults and Decision Making: An Overview* (1991), which pays particular attention to the needs of mentally frail elders and their carers, the following proposals are made:

> that people are enabled and encouraged to take for themselves those decisions which they are able to take;

> that where it is necessary in their own interests or for the protection of others that someone else should take decisions on their behalf, the intervention should be as limited as possible and concerned to achieve what the person would have wanted;

> that proper safeguards be provided against exploitation, neglect and physical, sexual or psychological abuse (Hoggett, 1991:n7, para 4.27).

It is interesting to note the consistency of the principles implicit in these proposals with Roberts' model of minimal intervention discussed earlier.

The consultation paper subsequently goes on to consider 'designated decision-making procedures', 'reformed emergency procedures', 'advocacy' and 'a new institution' which are among the options that should be made available (Hoggett, 1991:n7, para 6.1–6.61). It might be suggested that elder mediation services could well qualify for consideration as contributing to any new development.

A further Law Commission Consultation Paper, No. 128, on the same subject, reinforces the same principles, but focuses on the responsibilities

46

of carers. Three main provisos recur throughout the document, and its collected provisional proposals, emphasizing that these are equally important whether they refer to interventions by families, judicial and administrative bodies, health and welfare authorities, or those with enduring powers of attorney.

In exercising their responsibilities they must act in the best interest of incapacitated persons, taking into account:

1. the ascertainable past and present wishes and feelings of the incapacitated person;

2. the need to encourage and permit the incapacitated person to participate in any decision-making to the fullest extent of which he or she is capable; and

3. the general principle that the course least restrictive of the incapacitated person's freedom of decision and action is likely to be in his or her best interests (Hoggett, 1993a:103–4).

Once again the consistency of these proposals with Roberts' (1986) model of minimal intervention has to be noted. They also closely relate to the principles used in American senior mediation projects which are being developed to deal with the complex problems of guardianship and Advanced Directives, and which will be referred to in another chapter.

Another Law Commission Consultation Paper, No. 207, *Family Law Domestic Violence and Occupation of the Family Home*, (1992) makes innovative proposals which could affect elders. It is suggested that non-molestation and exclusion or occupation orders could be made in respect of other family members, including old people, who may be victims of, or threatened by family violence.

The objective of these proposals is:

to seek to avoid exacerbating hostilities between the adults involved, so far as this is compatible with providing proper and effective protection both for adults and for children (Hoggett, 1992:1).

There is a concern to avoid measures which:

would impede rather than assist communication, might well generate bitterness and animosity between the parties and hinder any attempt at conciliation or mediation (Hoggett, 1992:16).

Although Hoggett (1992) gives an informed and sympathetic review of the prevailing nostrums that family violence always merits police and legal intervention with the intention of considering criminalization, she nevertheless appears to concede that there is sometimes a place for conciliation and mediation at the earliest stages of family violence. It is fair to suggest that such a view may relate to her knowledge of the advantages (and disadvantages) of family mediation through her chairmanship of National Family Mediation (NFM).

There is no space now to discuss these contentious issues further, except to show an awareness of the important literature in the field. This shows the consensual views of establishment research criminologists like Edwards (1989) and Smith (1989), those of radical sociologists like Dobash and Dobash (1980) and Gelles and Straus (1988), and professional practitioners like Bourlet (1990) and Horley (1990), not to mention the feminist lobby, all arguing for increased police intervention in the area of domestic violence.

There is no conspicuous reference to the needs of old people who suffer from family violence, although it is known that they do not tend to be welcomed in women's refuges, which understandably wish to reserve their limited space and resources for mothers with small children.

However, as has been indicated in an earlier chapter, there is a connection between domestic violence and elder abuse, so the relevant Law Commission proposals could, if implemented by Parliament, provide practical redress for old people in making it legally possible to exclude from their homes any persons who can be shown to be abusing them, or threatening violence. The temporary or permanent nature of this would have to be contested with legal and other safeguards for all parties concerned. However, as the Law Commission proposals suggest, this does not preclude other constructive forms of intervention taking place in the interim period, whether by the health and social services, or by counselling, conciliation and mediation.

In America the Association of Family and Conciliation Courts (AFCC) has supported Girdner (1990), their foremost worker at the interface of family violence and mediation. She has considerable experience of using non-mandatory mediation as a screening instrument in family disputes, terminating it if abuse is active, but, subject to providing legally protective safeguards, continuing it if the parties wish and if no irremediable inequalities in power relations are present. The AFCC is currently piloting three very extensive research projects in different sites, which are being evaluated through the interest of the judiciary, and which may yield further information about an innovatory intervention.

At present, in America, senior mediation services only have consultative links with adult protective services, and, should any joint work be envisaged in the future, it is to be expected that even more extensive criteria than those described above would be developed to circumscribe the limits within which it would be safe and appropriate to offer mediation to alleged victims and their carers. In the terms of this book it is suggested that mediation has a *preventive* role in elder conflict, and that it is at the earliest stages, before abuse takes place, that it has its primary place.

Griffiths et al (1990) say that existing British law provides civil remedies through actions for tort based on proving some form of trespass on the person, and criminal proceedings for assault based on S. 45 of the 1861 Offences Against the Person Act. If police prosecute on behalf of an old person, then legal aid will be available, although the offence must be proved beyond reasonable doubt. If the prosecution is successful, compensation from the Criminal Injuries Compensation Board may be available.

Griffiths et al (1992) say that the civil torts of deceit, or of trespass to goods, can provide protection against financial abuse, and that criminal prosecution for theft and fraud is a possibility. A similar tort can arise in respect of false imprisonment or restraint, although this may be very difficult to prove if it can be shown that the restrictions were necessary for the person's safety, or for that of others. It is also possible to bring an action for negligence, or for breach of statutory duty with respect to public health, community and residential care, although this rarely happens. In as much as age discrimination in employment may be considered an abuse, the relevant British legislation only gives protection on grounds of race, sex or marital status.

Griffiths et al (1992) conclude that elders are poorly served by existing legislation:

> Doubts are sometimes expressed about the efficiency and heuristic value of using the law in the context of elderly abuse. Sceptics refer to difficulties relating to collecting satisfactory evidence, whilst others stress that many of the abusers are themselves elderly and the victims of community exploitation and neglect (Griffiths et al, 1992:130).

Greengross, director of Age Concern, in her book, *The Law and Vulnerable Old People*, (1986) asks a commonly voiced question:

> Should we not consider creating a framework granting limited powers of intervention to an appropriate body, following a complaint? Such a body would assess whether abuse was taking place, while not denying the right of the adult concerned to remain

in a household at risk if determined to do so. The right of a 'consenting' victim to self-determination must be safeguarded, and it is also recognized that there will always be some difficulty in protecting people from the consequences of active intervention in whatever form (Greengross, 1986:34).

Greengross sees intervention taking place in two stages. After an assessment of the elder has been made (a feature of the new 1990 National Health Service and Community Care Act) decisions would be made about that person's future care. If the authorities failed to respond appropriately to the needs of the elder and carer, they could apply to a court as an avenue of appeal:

> Therefore the purpose of an Intervention Order would be to provide a means of appealing against the action or failure to act by the local authority in carrying out its duty to consider the case of a vulnerable old person and their carers, who would be able to achieve a recognized status through an Intervention Order ... (Greengross, 1986:133).

In the second stage Greengross proposes an Emergency Intervention Order which could direct:

> 1. that specific help be brought to the old person where s/he resides, subject to the availability of such help;

> 2. that the old person be removed to a place of safety;

> 3. that named individuals be restrained from assaulting, molesting or otherwise interfering with the old person or be excluded from the old person's home (Greengross, 1986:136).

The idea of establishing an intervention order which could be used *against* local authorities is attractive, but the difficulties of implementing it can already be observed in current public debates at consultations over the new community care plans, which local authorities are required to produce. The phrase 'subject to the availability of such help' is being used by them to say that their statutory liability for meeting assessment needs depends on adequate resources, which they do not have. In fact few class actions have been successfully brought to require local authorities to provide facilities proscribed through legislation. As is shown in the chapter on American elder care provision and adult protective services, their early legislation was never funded for implementation, and few of the required resources for the social support of elders and their carers were forthcoming.

Following Greengross' (1986) important suggestions to their logical conclusion could lead to British adult protective service legislation comparable to that which, in America, has had negative consequences, particularly when the reporting of suspected abuse and neglect has been mandatory (Wolf, 1990), so it would have to be carefully drafted and publicly debated.

British multidisciplinary workers in the field are also ambivalent about the problems raised by the powers given through any emergency intervention order. The proposals of the Law Commission Consultation Papers referred to above, appear to be a more likely first step in the direction which Greengross advocates. Also, as was noted earlier, a great deal of public, professional and Parliamentary education will be necessary before any such proposals are adopted and implemented.

Cloke (1983), also writing for Age Concern, says that S.47 of the 1948 National Assistance Act should be amended to allow for the compulsory removal of any abuser, instead of any old person at risk being made to leave her or his home. In fact this section of the Act is generally operated in respect of elders who live alone, whose health and welfare is seriously endangered through self-neglect.

Greengross also has a fundamental concern for the *prevention* of elder abuse, and has championed and given leadership to Age Concern's Action on Elder Abuse:

> It is important to establish a mechanism, which is both preventive and protective, to avoid increasing the risks of abuse as more frail and vulnerable old people live into extreme old age in family or residential settings (Greengross, 1986:37).

In the contemporary British mixed economy of welfare and legal pluralism, it is likely that various organizational groups would suggest that more than one social mechanism should be constructed, if there develops a general will to address the sensitive and complex issues of elder abuse and neglect.

It is argued here that elder mediation could have a role to play, especially in the early critical stage of assessment, when both advocacy and mediation may be necessary to ensure that the voices of all parties are adequately heard, represented and enabled to contribute to the outcomes affecting their interests and needs. Mediation, with advocacy, could also contribute in other areas of dispute processing regarding the objectives, forms and safeguards proposed with regard to interventions.

Coser's comments on Simmel, the American founding father of conflict theory, include the observation that 'the need for safety valve institutions increases with the rigidity of the social structure' (1956:45), and any new British legislation, however desirable, will certainly increase the rigidity of the already extensively bureaucratized health and social services.

Dingwall and Eekelaar also make an apposite comment about a mixed economy approach to issues of social conflict in connection with family mediation:

> We are, in effect, advocating a 'mixed economy' in which lawyers and mediators are able to compete on equal terms offering a variety of means to ends defined by a set of statuary parameters. What is important is that clients retain a degree of choice which recognises the variety of their needs and circumstances (Dingwall and Eekelaar, 1985:180).

Whether or not a mixed economy approach has to depend on competition rather than co-operation is an ideological issue which can not be discussed here, but it is fair to say that the philosophical foundations of mediation give it a base in pluralism, whilst earlier chapters have noted that elder mediation is provisional rather than absolutist in its ongoing social construction.

In this connection it has to be observed that the philosophical foundations of elder rights has been here understated in the references so far given. However Greengross, in particular, has been a long term spokeswoman for elder rights, and for those of their carers, although Age Concern, which she directs, considers that most of its campaigning publications should pragmatically focus on the practical needs of those whom they represent.

Nevertheless she has been a prime mover in the construction of the International Federation on Aging (IFA) Declaration on the Rights and Responsibilities of Older Persons (1992). Age Concern publicized this for the 1993 European Year of Older People and Solidarity Between the Generations.

The emphasis on responsibilities as well as rights is a welcome contribution to the other rights literature which is emerging from different social groups. Freeden's important book, *Rights* (1991), says that in order for rights to function as a 'protective capsule' they must be *'essentially incontestable'*, and therefore culturally acceptable. They must 'meet rational and logical standards', be 'emotionally and culturally attractive' and 'translatable into codes of enforceable action' (Freeden, 1991:11).

The Declaration referred to above aims to attract this cultural acceptance, especially at a time of intergenerational conflict over decreasing social resources, by including responsibilities as well as rights.

For the purposes of this chapter, in which decision-making has been a critical issue, it is now intended to focus briefly on Principles 7–10 of the Declaration, which come under the heading of 'Participation'. Significantly, these have been designed to be consistent with the 1991 United Nations Principles for the Elderly (7–9), which also incorporates those describing responsibilities.

Participation

The IFA states that older persons have the right:

> 7. to remain integrated and participate actively in society, including the process of development and the formulation and implementation of policies which directly affect their well-being.

> 8. to share their knowledge, skills, values and life experience with younger generations.

> 9. to seek and develop opportunities for service to the community and to serve as volunteers in positions appropriate to their interests and capabilities.

> 10. to form movements or associations of the elderly.

The listed responsibilities of old people include their duties to try 'to make informed decisions about their health care ...' (IFA, 1992).

It can be seen that the substance of these principles are consistent with the advocacy of elder mediation as a process which increases the rights and responsibilities of old people in decision-making in the opportunities and conflicts which affect their lives.

However, although there are three principles relating to dignity which give elders the rights to be treated fairly, free from exploitation and abuse, and given the opportunity to die with dignity, there are no explicit suggestions that these should be extended to protect people from undesired social interventions. Roberts' (1986) standard of minimal intervention, and that of the Law Commission (Hoggett, 1993a) in its proposals for the least restrictive principles of care, could well provide a useful base for augmenting the IFA Declaration.

Meanwhile the ongoing debate about the interface of elder abuse, mediation and the law in the concern for human rights, especially those of older people, in the context of the issues raised in this book, will surely continue. An attempt has here been made to analyse some of the principles on which this debate has been founded, and to question the theories and facts involved, particularly in relation to evolving British legal and social policy.

It is concluded that Roberts' (1986) model of mediation as a form of minimal social intervention provides a valuable standard for safeguarding the needs and interests of old people, and that it is an important guide for developing elder mediation, here conceptualized as a primarily preventive service, which helps to enhance personal autonomy, independence and well-being. His model, and that of elder mediation, is compatible with, and complementary to the many other services which are needed to ensure adequate social provision for an ageing population.

Felstiner's (1981) theory of the transformation of disputes has also been shown to be consistent with the experience of elders and their carers, and that its processes of naming, blaming and claiming usefully point to the value of elder mediation as an early intervention in family conflict, and as a contribution to the prevention of elder abuse.

The critique of ADR mounted by Abel (1982) and others has been analysed with regard to its contributions about the dangers of social and quasi-legal interventions extending state control invisibly, coercively and unaccountably, and it has been seen that, in the British context, these have largely been avoided: mediation is voluntary and not mandatory.

Finally the evolving proposals for the safeguarding and advancement of elder rights and the struggle for participative and relational justice have been considered, and have been shown to be consistent with the aims of elder mediation.

Let Marshall, principal research officer at the British Home Office, which seconded him to be the first director of Mediation UK, have the last word:

> Justice may take a number of forms ... The movements away from the traditional legal system are movements towards not only alternative methods but also to alternative justice (Marshall, 1985:45–6).

3 Participatory action research into the unresolved conflicts of elder relations

In the first chapter elder mediation was conceptualized as a social innovation concerned with promoting elder decision-making in the issues that affect their lives. In the second chapter elder mediation in relation to the law was discussed, balancing the critique of ADR with a case made for considering that the processes of decision-making in both areas are complementary, not antagonistic, in relation to the interpersonal conflicts of later life.

In this chapter Maguire's text, *Doing Participatory Research* (1987) is examined as a methodological model which, like her work, is appropriate for an inquiry concerned with participative and relational justice:

> The inquiry should itself be educational and empowering for participants: outcomes should include action on attitudes and structures that inhibit self-worth, social justice or liberation (Maguire:viii).

Participation is then analysed as an extension of the discussion of decision-making begun in the first chapter, and is shown to be essential to social justice for all groups, especially for vulnerable elderly people. Then the question is raised as to whether elder mediation can be conceptualized, not only as a social innovation, but also as a part of any general new social movement concerned with intergenerational justice.

This discussion, although bordering on the speculative and social philosophical, is relevant to the way in which the research developed by linking Maguire's (1987) participatory and action elements with those of Lincoln and Gupa's (1985) naturalistic, and Reason's (1988) humanistic inquiries. These were also set in the context of Glaser and Strauss' (1967) grounded theory, and finally shaped by Robson's *Real World Research* (1993) and Hedrick et al's *Applied Research Design* (1987). The methodology was also greatly influenced by writers on sensitive topics including Harding (1987), Lee (1993) and Roberts, H. (1981).

This aspect of the research is then discussed in more detail, including a reference to using a video as an innovative research instrument, recalling in conclusion the caveats about its limitations considered earlier.

Uncovering generative themes: learning through dialogue

The above title is used by Maguire to head a chapter in her book, basing it on Freire (1970) and his 'concept of dialogue' and 'his problem-solving process' (1987:134, 137). This enables the participants in research to 'name their reality' (Maguire, 1987:134), a process similar to the exchange of accounts which takes place between participants in elder mediation.

Maguire argues that her critical inquiry into the conflicts of Navajo women 'enabled the women to analyse issues as they talked', beneficially to them, and productive of social information which could have been gained in no better way (1987:147). In elder mediation, which uses elders as mediators, a comparable analysis by the participants of the issues underlying their conflict is also encouraged.

Here it is pertinent to note that Maguire's work was with Navajo women who had been battered, so that her approach is particularly resonant with the subject of elder abuse. It also illuminates the debate about what contributions non-legal social interventions can usefully make in family violence involving vulnerable social groups like elders and minorities.

Having identified the area in which Maguire's work was located it is relevant to return to her initial explanation that it is premised on Habermas (1971), as was Moody's theory of communicative ethics and action (1992), which is entirely consistent with her approach. One of her objectives is to develop critical theory and praxis as a 'dynamic interplay between theory and practice' (Maguire, 1987:3).

Participatory research aims to develop critical consciousness to improve the lives of those involved in the research process, and to

56

transform fundamental societal structures and relationships (Maguire, 1987:5).

Following Habermas (1971) she develops her own version of critical knowledge which is consistent with the principles of this present research:

> Critical knowledge, a combination of self reflection and a historical analysis of inequitable systems, is produced by emancipatory or critical inquiry. Critical inquiry is structured to uncover the systems of social relationships and contradictions which underlie social tension and conflicts ... Critical inquiry is used to help people see themselves and social situations in a new way in order to inform further action for self-determined emancipation from oppressive social systems and relationships ... The dialectical relationship between inquiry and action, or theory and practice, is explicit (Maguire, 1987:14).

This approach which Maguire uses in her participatory research with Navajo women has been usefully adapted for this present approach to elder mediation services in Atlanta and Kansas, to be discussed in detail in Part II of this book. In this the critical inquiry will attempt to uncover the inequitable and oppressive social systems which contribute to the structural abuse of elderly persons, as well as helping them to see themselves and their social situations of conflict more clearly in self-reflective ways, through the emancipatory process of mediation.

Maguire goes on to describe the 'alternative paradigm' of her participatory research model (1987:22), which is given added emphasis here on account of the methodological principle which it upholds, and which is used in the present approach to elder mediation:

> *The purpose of research is shifted from constructing grand generalisations for control and predictability by detached outsiders to working closely with ordinary people, the insiders, in a particular context. The purpose is to enhance local people's understanding and ability to control their own reality (Maguire, 1987:22).*

This is particularly appropriate in studying a social innovation where people are in the early stages of experimenting with a potential service development. Maguire goes further in a section on professional research design and control 'versus local self-determination' (1987:24), when she suggests that premature research formulation is inconsistent with her model based on viewing social actors as research subjects not objects:

All participatory researchers stress a collaborative or participatory inquiry in which control over both the research process and production is more equally shared between researchers and participants ... Both the process and outcome should put more power and control in the hands of the oppressed. Research should give them a voice in articulating their perception of their problems and relevant solutions (Maguire, 1987:24).

It will be seen later that the critical inquiry made into the Atlanta and Kansas senior mediation services proceeded from a collaboratively designed interview schedule, continuous consultations about research questioning and shared conclusions about the future development of senior mediation in relation to its potential for contributing to the prevention of elder abuse. The research relationship with each service co-ordinator, both women, was firmly based on what Maguire calls 'the participatory research principle' (1987:37):

We both know some things; neither of us knows everything. Working together we will both know more, and we will both learn more about how to know (Maguire, 1987:37–8).

Maguire's concern is to 'help make people creative actors in solving their own problems' (1987:29), which is also the aim of elder mediation. She later makes two further important points:

Involving research subjects as partners in the entire research process also increases the potential to distribute the benefits of the research process more equitably ... by sharing directly in substantial policy and program decisions ... a deep and abiding belief in people's capacity to grow, change and create underlies this democratisation of research ... (although) participatory research is a tool not a panacea (Maguire, 1987:39).

So Maguire provides her own self-critique: she admits the limitations of what she names as feminist participatory research in another project described at the end of her book, because she and her female participants did not 'gain a structural analysis of capitalism, patriarchy or racism'. However she says they 'did gain experience and some skill in problem identification and solution building' (Maguire, 1987:188):

They gained appreciation of the value of collective problem-posing and solving. The group experience built their feeling of confidence that they could be active problem-solvers, decision-makers in their own lives, both individually and collectively, as well as contributing to group and agency problem-solving ... which strengthened their belief in their collective and individual abilities and resources (Maguire, 1987:188–9).

This linking conceptualization of decision-making and participation is now explored further with reference to other writers.

Participation, power and social justice

Croft and Beresford in an important article in *Critical Social Policy*, entitled *The Politics of Participation*, conclude it with a recommendation to 'enhance people's capacity to participate, by ensuring their involvement' through:

> *a participatory process of learning* based on shared learning which supports our self confidence, increases our assertiveness and encourages us to challenge the question
>
> *learning how to participate* both by gaining skills and having a say in our education and the services and policies connected with it
>
> *learning about participation*, finding out about the rights and responsibilities of a critical social policy (1992:41–2).

They view participation as an element in the human need theory of Doyal and Gough (1991).

> The objective and universal needs they identify are physical health and individual autonomy, because they are essential preconditions for *participating in social life* (Croft and Beresford, 1990:24).

It is here relevant to recall Blanton's earlier references to human need (1989:33), the fulfilment of which should be regarded as an essential precondition in the prevention of elder abuse. Burton, in *Conflict: Human Needs Theory* (1990), says that it is based on 'the premise that there are universal undivisible human needs which, when thwarted, result in deep-rooted conflict' (1990:270).

The notion that autonomy, independence, choice, consent and control are values necessary for free decision-making and social participation has already been explored. However Croft and Beresford develop this further:

The theory of 'normalisation' or 'social role valorisation' as it has also come to be called, with its emphasis on social integration and a valued life for people, offered a coherent value base and a participatory framework for services (Croft and Beresford, 1990:31).

Following this it is can be argued that the process of elder mediation has the effect of valorizing old people: firstly as they achieve the ownership of conflicts which participation in their management brings; secondly because the elder volunteers who act as mediators all report anecdotally that their work gives them an enhanced sense of self-worth, and that they are valued citizens in helping local community members. It should also be reiterated here that traditionally mediation has always been viewed as a natural and normal process in which everyone can informally participate.

Now Croft and Beresford bring power into the equation. They argue that as increasing numbers of people participate in influencing personal and social decisions and outcomes, the more the distribution of power will be changed, although perils resulting from this in a racist society, are insufficiently examined by them. They refer to Lukes' book, *Power: A Radical View* (1974):

> Hidden power is exercised, he says, when a conflict of interest has been excluded from public debate and decision-making ... the absence of overt conflict means only that they have been denied entry into the political process (Croft and Beresford, 1990:37).

The theory of power espoused by Foucault (1981) has already been discussed in the last chapter, where a case was made for considering mediation as a contribution to the counter-power of subordinating populations. A relevant quote suggests that in practice mediation has an empowering role for most people, including elders, in confronting the micro and macro conflicts of individual and social life:

> Mediation can open doors for older persons giving them a sense of empowerment in solving their own problems; and furthering the Older Americans Act objectives of enhancing the independence of the elderly (Hoffman and Wood, 1991:2:7).

Relevant American legislation and its implications for elder power and elder rights will be discussed in the next chapter in Part II but these attributes, like those of decision-making and participation and the other values listed, are essential components of human need, especially that of the human need for social justice.

It is not intended now to review general definitions of social justice, nor its versions of participative and relational justice which are especially appropriate for the themes of this book, but to draw attention to Tinker's point about 'bitter disputes over what has become known as inter-generational justice' (1992:242).

Moody refers to this as 'generational equity' dependant on 'intergenerational solidarity' (1992:208). He describes the bitter public disputes which arise between competing claims for insufficient structural resources, and the abusive conflicts that arise in families when inadequate personal resources lead to unnecessary suffering for old people and their carers.

He suggests that social justice has to be constructed:

> Justice across generations involves something more than a timeless logically supported set of claims about rights and obligations for old and young. It involves publicly visible practices or institutions that serve to teach successive generations how those rights and obligations can be up held in practice (Moody, 1992:230).

Jecker has edited a collection of papers on this subject in her *Aging and Ethics* (1991) in which she argues that 'distributive justice pertains to families as well as states' (1991:213). Callahan defends his argument for the 'age rationing' of health and social resources in his chapter, *Distributive Justice in an Aging Society* (1991:219–26). Farley, in her chapter, *Personal Commitments: Making, Keeping and Breaking* (1991:329–40), attacks Callahan's (1991) position in which she says that human society is held together by bonds and institutions of intergenerational solidarity and interpersonal commitments of mutual care which must not be abrogated:

> Promise keeping is one of the foundations of society. When it is commonly expected that promises will not be kept, people lose their moorings, society staggers into chaos, often at the beginning of violence (Farley, 1991:330).

The implications of this for the aetiology of elder abuse, in its structural and personal forms, is noted but not further explored here, in order not to interrupt Farley's argument. She continues to strike against Callahan's (1991) view that old people consume an inequitable amount of human resources and unfairly increase social costs, saying that most of these are borne by family carers:

To imply that most elders *drive* these costs is inaccurate and promotes scapegoating (Farley, 1991:330).

Although she acknowledges that there are critical intergenerational problems about distributive justice, she shares with Moody (1992) the view that social institutions must be created or used in which the general population can contribute to the policy and planning decision-making needed with respect to the allocation of human resources.

Under a section entitled *Promote Citizen Decision-making* she advocates the Oregon Model, which other social commentators have severely criticized, and which, from 1983 to 1989, based its elder policies on general directives from public consultative forums established through the state:

> The town meeting approach to decision making is now emerging as a consensus building tool in bioethics ... Decision makers must be affectable, meaning that they are obliged to be changed by the disempowered ... Our openness to be changed by the realities of disempowered people gives them the power to influence and assist us in resisting our tendency to homogenise, blurring the distinctions between people. Personal histories assist empowered people's abilities to hear and be affected by that which they cannot know – how individuals experience ageism, racism and sexism (Farley, 1991:331–2).

Although Farley (1991) is concerned with establishing public procedures for addressing the macro level of structural conflicts involving elders, her views can equally be applied at the micro level of the interpersonal conflicts which they experience. It is here that elder mediation services could contribute to more equitable decision-making, taking the views of all parties into consideration, through their participation in resolving conflicts.

Jensen, the next contributor to Jecker's book, in a chapter entitled *Resentment and the Rights of the Elderly* (1991, 341–52), says that resentment is a crucial factor in building conflict:

> Resentment is a response to deprivation of some value. More it is the awareness of the value of which one is deprived that is experienced by others ... resentment is, then, a sign of presumed injustice (Jensen, 1991:345).

He then relates this to distributive justice:

62

Resentment, then, is the alienation that results from dishonor. It is, as well, a form of injustice. Justice ... refers to the proper distribution of social goods, among which is honor and dishonor (Jensen, 1991:347).

He derives his understanding of justice as the 'distribution of honor' from Aristotelian Nicomachean ethics and from Rawls' (1971) theory of justice:

Thus, the honor of having achieved a life can be distributed equally uniformly. Just resentment arises, then, from uniform deprivation of honor to the elderly. If institutions of society can be so arranged as to mitigate resentment, whatever else they do, justice will be done to the elderly ... Due honor ... consists of creating and fostering social institutions that make life possible without resentment (Jensen, 1991:347–50).

Without repeating the references to the usefulness of elder mediation services just mentioned above, it can be seen that there is a case for considering that they can make an additional contribution to the other social interventions which the writers in Jecker's (1991) book deem essential in providing social justice for the elderly, and in preventing their unnecessary suffering.

It can be seen that there is a new social gerontology movement towards developing praxis from theory in respect to inter-generational justice, and it has been argued that elder mediation has the potential for contributing to this movement. However new social movement theory has its own progenitors, some of whose voices are relevant to this discourse.

Elder mediation: an emerging element in a new social movement?

In returning to Croft and Beresford (1992) it should be noted that they introduce and base their paper, *The Politics of Participation*, on the importance of new social movements. They begin by quoting from Oliver's *The Politics of Disablement* (1990):

These movements have been seen as constituting the social basis for new forms of transfigurative social change ... They are culturally innovative in that they are part of the underlying struggle for genuine participation, democracy, social equity and justice ... These new social movements are consciously engaged in critical evaluation of capitalist society and in the creation of alternative models of social organisation at local, national and international levels, as well as by trying to reconstruct the world ideologically and to create alternative forms of service provision (Oliver, 1990:113).

Croft and Beresford mount a useful critique of new social movements:

> They have resulted in an over-rapid retreat from class analysis and politics and the possibilities these offer of united action. Another concern has been that the focus on different ideologies may result in conflict and fragmentation rather than unity and concerted action (Croft and Beresford, 1990:22).

Nevertheless they agree with Oliver (1990) that new social movements have useful functions:

> They offer a critical evaluation of society as part of 'a conflict between a declining but still vigorous form of domination and newly emergent forms of opposition'.

> They are concerned with the quality of people's life as well as narrow materialist needs (Croft and Beresford, 1990:18).

They also highlight the concern of new social movements with participation and empowerment, saying that this, in turn, has led to the development of new *social work* movements (emphasis added), which have similar criteria in their location on the periphery of traditional social systems:

> (T)his conceives of their members in terms of services which their struggles are often concerned with challenging (Croft and Beresford, 1990:23).

Gilroy, concerned with the new social movements of black people, develops this idea of challenge:

> These new movements are part of a new phase of cultural conflict so far removed from the class struggles of the industrial era that the old vocabulary of class analysis must be dispensed with or modernised (Gilroy, 1987:225).

Nevertheless he also is critical of them, acknowledging that they are:

> systems of resistance to domination, defensive and dynamic, but unlikely to enter into more stable forms of politics until they develop more than grassroots consciousness (Gilroy, 1987:232).

However Castells, in the context of his concern for grassroots minority communities, believes that they are essential in providing opportunities for the participation and decision-making in society from which vulnerable people are otherwise excluded:

> Without social movements, no challenge will emerge from civil society able to shake the institutions of the state through which norms are enforced, values preached, and property preserved (Castells, 1983:294).

It is too early to develop opinions as to how far the Gray Panther movement of elders in America, the powerful mainstream American Association of Retired Persons (AARP) and the development of radical social gerontology might converge, but it would appear that the conflicting conservative, liberal and radical interests involved would inhibit the growth of any new social movement in the political terms discussed above.

Nevertheless, despite the caveats raised, an alternative view might more modestly make a minimalist claim that the voluntary association of social groups to further their own values, needs and interests constructively is an essential part of democracy. In America, the social groups of the ageing network come together in important coalitions concerned with elder care and elder rights, as will be discussed in the next chapter in Part II of this book. However it is not proposed now to distinguish between coalitions and new social movements, but merely to suggest that if ever elder mediation services develop in Britain in the future, they could make as useful a contribution to coalition-building of the British ageing network, as they can to the prevention of elder abuse.

Marshall expresses a strong personal view which links some of the ideas which have occurred thematically through Part I of this discourse:

> The ideas behind conflict resolution and especially the vigour of these ideas as a social movement themselves represent a potent paradigm shift away from the old adversarial competitive modes that have become more and more dominant in this century, to a way of living that is capable of realising a higher level of civilisation (Marshall, 1990:2–3).

Elder mediation is most appropriately situated in this social movement of ideas, for, as a social innovation, it may not yet emerge as a developing service firm enough to be integrated into any coalition of the ageing network, strong enough to resist co-optation by the state, or wise enough to be discerning about joining any other grassroots new social movements which may appear.

It is also necessary to know how far mediation is perceived by other social organizations and groups of people, especially by older persons, to be a useful process to add to those of advice-giving, advocacy and counselling, with which they may be more familiar. So one objective of the research was to find a form of methodology suitable for testing such social attitudes.

Using an elder abuse video as a research instrument

The difficulties of testing social attitudes before these could even be formed by long term, or even short term actual experience of mediation services working with elder abuse, appeared insurmountable for obvious reasons.

However the principles and practice of participative action research led to consultative presentations and workshops at conferences, seminars and study days with multidisciplinary community and residential care staff, and talks at old peoples' clubs.

These provided opportunities for showing these varied social groups a 24-minute training video, made by the Massachusetts Health Research Institute in 1984, called *Incident Report*, and then inviting them to complete a 20-question attitude survey of their reactions to it.

One of the reasons for choosing this video was that it dealt with a case of alleged institutional elder abuse, an area which is generally regarded as difficult to research, and which therefore usefully complemented the community-based studies.

In the video, a nurse (after 13 hours on duty) has her face scratched by an elderly nursing home resident refusing medication. The resident is restrained, and the next day her wrist is shown to be broken. The inspector arrives, interviews both parties, and the film replays the incident as seen from the perspective of each person. In the end, the home manager asks the inspector if elder abuse will be recorded, but discussion and decision-making about this is left to the viewers.

Seven groups, totalling 100 people, were invited to watch this video and contribute to the research survey. These included members of an old people's club, social workers, residential care staff, nurses from a teaching hospital, multidisciplinary professional and voluntary workers with older persons, holistic medicine conference participants, and mediators from a community mediation service.

The respondents to the questionnaire were asked if they thought abuse had occurred, and how it might have been prevented, providing choices of various interventions, including the use of mediating skills.

An analysis of the results showed that 53 per cent of the respondents thought that there had been elder abuse, with only 60 per cent thinking that it would have been possible to restrain the patient without force, the old people strongly represented in the majority views. Their own pride at not needing residential care appeared to influence them in thinking that good patients would not resist nursing care, and that bad ones should be controlled. They also felt, as did minorities in other groups, that the nurse had been abused, although this was not a key question of the research.

84 per cent of the respondents thought that the incident could have been prevented, and 85 per cent (the highest majority recorded) considered that the nurse should have sat and talked with the patient about the conflict before giving the medication.

An unexpectedly strong majority of 72 per cent considered that if mediating skills had been used, the conflict could have been resolved, and 65 per cent felt that these would have prevented the wrist breakage.

This brief report of a research project, which lasted a year, only summarizes the main findings relevant to this book, but indicates that these are supportive to its general argument. The research, whilst being fully participative, and showing a wide-based social interest in mediation, also served the useful purpose of raising the awareness of old people about elder abuse in a non-threatening way, as a video from America appeared to be safely distant from their experience.

However, there were more severe methodological difficulties in finding an equally non-threatening and ethically acceptable way of testing how far mediation could be useful in dealing with unresolved conflicts and abusive relations in 'real world' research.

The Elder Mediation Project (EMP) as a research instrument

The many general activities of EMP, described later, included accepting referrals from various sources of individual cases of old people distressed by unresolved conflicts. As the work of EMP became known and recommended among social agencies, referrals increased and in responding to them, it was found that many of the old people complained bitterly about the abuse from which they suffered.

EMP therefore found itself providing a free service, at the request of old people and their referring social agencies, in the context of situations in which unresolved conflicts might be associated with elder abuse, and which mediation might contribute to stopping or preventing.

It appeared providential that although EMP had its own intrinsic social value, its individual mediation service work could also be useful as a research instrument, if only for a limited period.

The intake of all referred cases could provide a random, representative and reliable sample which could be replicated for re-testing by other researchers. The intake could be divided into those cases where abuse was reported, and control cases where it was not a feature, so that comparisons could be made. The numbers were likely to be small, and therefore any findings could not be expected to be statistically significant, or reliable, although their validity and credibility should be acceptable.

Confidentiality was assured as this is anyway a feature of mediation services, where cases are always kept private, unless in exceptional instances, the participants jointly wish for publicity to attract public attention and action. The research data could be analysed in tabulated numerical form, and case illustrations recorded so as to provide anonymity. Any subsequent research colloquiums would similarly feature references in which anonymity was safeguarded.

Voluntariness was also assured, firstly because it was the old people who made requests for help, and secondly because the initial explanation given to them about mediation was that is a process which they can leave freely at any time. However, unfortunately there was no way of discussing with them the aims of the research, as this could have biassed their accounts, and the ways in which they either succeeded or failed in resolving their conflicts through mediation. In this respect, although they were fully participative in the mediation, giving informed consent to it, they were not able to discuss the research itself.

Through this useful opportunity, and despite its limitations, during a one-year period, a research sample grew of 50 old people seeking help with unresolved conflicts, 25 of whom said they were involved in abusive relationships, and 25 of whom did not.

Each group was divided into males and females of those between 50 and 75, and over 75 years, and there was data analysis of their marital, household and occupancy status, their income, employment and referral groups, their physical/mental health, disability and dependency status, their cultural, religious and social network backgrounds, and the types of conflict, response interventions, outcomes and personal affects involved.

Separate data analysis of the 25 older people reporting abuse showed its different types, whether physical, verbal, psychological/emotional, financial/material, racial and sexual, how many types said they experienced, and how many they admitted, or were perceived to give to others.

The qualitative work on which these quantitative results were based included home visits, face-to-face mediations lasting up to two hours, telephone mediations taking many hours, and shuttle mediation between the participants which took place over a much longer period.

Although there will be detailed discussion of some cases in a later chapter, only a brief report of provisional findings will be made now, because of the small numbers involved, and as continuing research promises to verify, validate and enlarge results more substantially. Such brevity may be regretted by readers of this book, but those with their own research agendas will understand that priority has to be given to increasing reliable data, and, probably, improving ways of processing it.

However one pointer to its relative representativeness and reliability is that many of the findings comparing abused and non-abused groups are consistent with those of general gerontological research. For instance abusive relations appear to be suffered by slightly more people over 75, most of whom are women living alone, the majority as Council tenants on low incomes and retired, although individuals in middle and high income groups also reported abuse, which is known to exist in all social groups, although less likely to be referred to social agencies.

It is also unremarkable that over half of the abused have frail mental health, although the majority had surprisingly good physical health, with little disability or dependency. The mental frailties, which included obsession and depression, doubtless contributed to the strength of perceptions that sufferers were feeling abused, and also, as the case illustrations will suggest, to their own problematic behaviour which itself was perceived as abusive.

The cultural background data showed that two-fifths of the abused came from ethnic minorities in comparison to one-fifth of the control group, but only a small number of both groups declared their religious affiliation as Christian or Jewish. It is here worth repeating that mediation is an elicitive rather than interrogative process, so that the facts from which the data was compiled came from the accounts given by the old people, rather than, in general, as answers to direct questions. This, of course, is another limitation of the data.

As the majority of referrals came from community mediation services who knew most about and wanted a specialist response from EMP, it is obvious that the sample was biassed here, although national voluntary ageing organizations referred one-fifth, a sheltered housing organization referred another fifth and almost a fifth were self-referred.

The chief type of conflict reflected the source of referral with three-fifths and two-fifths respectively of the abused and non-abused people suffering from neighbours. Only two people were involved in family abusive relationships, three in sheltered housing situations, and one in the residential sector.

The majority of all cases were responded to by some form of mediation, the rest receiving home visits only except for a small number who appeared sufficiently helped through their initial inquiry to cope with problems themselves. As a founding principle of EMP is that most old people, in many situations, have the ability to manage their own conflicts, and mainly need enablement and empowerment to resolve more difficult disputes, it was possible to help some people in this way through preliminary discussions, without further intervention.

The outcome of EMP interventions showed that three-fifths of both the abused and non-abused reached some form of agreed resolution of their situations, a fifth of each failing in this, and a fifth being referred on for further help.

However majorities in both group expressed positive effects from the intervention, and none reported negative ones.

The closer analysis of the abused group showed that almost all suffered psychological and emotional abuse, over four-fifths reporting verbal abuse also, whilst one third experienced physical abuse. There were also allegations of financial/material, racial and sexual abuse, just under one-fifth in each category. These findings are also consistent with other research on the subject.

There were three significantly different findings. The first was that so many relationships with neighbours were felt by old people to be abusive, and unbearably so, even though little serious physical violence was involved. This is an uncomfortable fact for those who are understandably concerned to restrict rather than expand categories of elder abuse. Nevertheless, as more old people choose to live alone, some of them socially isolated or with frail mental health, it is necessary to take into account their sensitivity and vulnerability to threatening neighbour relationships, as a new aspect of community care.

Other explanations may be that citizen education about abuse and other infringements of rights may now be raising old people's awareness of and resistance to social behaviour which earlier cohorts might have tolerated; and/or that they were exaggerating their feelings to attract attention, as in many cases no other agencies, including the police, had helped them; and/or that they were negatively projecting their general anxieties about money, health, broken families on to the nearest people who were felt to be causing them distress.

It was the high level of distress in these neighbour conflicts which was a surprising second factor, although this may be partly explained by the fact that these were long standing, and apparently resistant to other kinds of earlier social interventions. Very often the old people said they were desperate and that their retirement years were like 'hell' because of continual noise, bad smells, constant quarrels and the threatening social behaviour which resulted.

In case these observations should be considered biassed by heightened subjectivity, it should be noted that, often work was done by two visitors or co-mediators who checked out their mutual feelings periodically. Also, in an ongoing family case, a white older woman who had previously initiated sexual intercourse with a black teenager, but later complained of rape, showed far less levels of distress, even though the boy, a schizophrenic, was later charged with raping another woman, and is up for trial at the Central Criminal Court. So it is suggested that researcher response to, and analysis of distress, was sufficiently objective to provide reliable interpretations.

This case, besides indicating the variety that were referred, including an organizational one previously referred to the Charity Commissioners, also links with the third most significant but unwelcome finding in this study. This is that so many old people admitted to, or were perceived to be, behaving abusively themselves. Just under four-fifths appeared to have been verbally abusive, a fifth making discriminating racial and sexual slurs, while over three-fifths were said to have caused psychological and emotional distress. Only three of the 25 were reported as being physically aggressive, and these were relatively minor instances of pushing and seizing.

Some possible explanations already noted contribute to this finding, as does a popular view that some white old people have racist feelings and suspicions about the sexual activities of others. In addition, frail mental health and/or feelings of desperation can lead old people to assert what may be felt to be fading powers of virility and independence in unconscious, as well as intentional aggressive ways. Physical responses to unbearable situations tend to increase if people feel that their verbal communication is inadequate.

It is this important element in relationship conflict which mediation addresses, as its aim is to enable people to communicate constructively in a problem-solving way about their relationship and situational difficulties. Later case discussions will illustrate this central factor more fully, together with the other critical result of this mediation study, namely that the majority of people were positively affected, expressing a sense of self-achievement, self-determination and renewed autonomy. Their relief and self-confidence at having dealt with one problem, may enable and empower them to resist and prevent further abusive relations.

However, these two briefly reported research studies do not stand on their own in supporting the ideas of this book. They are triangulated with findings from the American research which Part II describes.

Part II

THE SOCIAL CONSTRUCTION OF ELDER ABUSE AND MEDIATION IN AMERICA

4 American elder care and elder rights

The American National Eldercare Institute on Elder Abuse and State Long Term Care Ombudsmen Services (NEIEASLTCOS), funded by the United States (US) Office on Aging (OoA), is a component of the coalition, the National Eldercare Campaign (NEC). Its central mission is:

> to assure that individual older people have their civil rights, autonomy and dignity protected, their claims to entitlements honored and their contracts and covenants for care and benefits fulfilled (NEIEASLTCOS, 1992b:1).

Significantly the focus is on individual elder care rights, whilst the challenge of class action to ensure structural redress of elder poverty, and the prevention of bureaucratic and institutional abuse through Medicaid and nursing home industry deficiencies is textually unaddressed. (*Washington Weekly* XVII, 1991:38).

Estes (1981) and Minkler and Estes (1991) have written major texts exposing these and other deficiencies in what they call 'the aging enterprise' of American federal and State provision for its older citizens, especially the economically marginalized and social minorities.

However the contemporary national forum for the American public agenda on elder care, elder rights and elder abuse has to be viewed in the context of the 1992 Presidential election, in which 42 seniors over 60 had votes, and when these issues received critical coverage in the press. Three headlines selected from many, reflect public fears and political anxieties about the collective challenges of elder care: 'One Fifth of the Elderly Live in Poverty' (*Atlanta Constitution*, 10 November 1992); 'In Spite of Federal Reforms, Elderly Opt for Hovels, Abuse, Suicide, the

Street' (*Wall Street Journal*, 3 December 1992). The President-elect responded by acknowledging that decision-making about elder care was of urgent social concern, assuring senior citizens that democracy means contributing to decision-making: 'Participation Means You're Going to be Part of It – Sharing the Decisions!' (*USA Today*, 13 November 1992).

A less populist affirmation of elder rights in decision-making about their interests was the subject of more detailed discussion at a Congressional meeting in 1988. *Mediation and Older Americans – Consider the Possibilities*, entitled the Forum presented by the Subcommittee on Housing and Consumer Interests of the Select Committee on Aging, and the Subcommittee on Courts, Civil Liberties and the Administration of Justice of the Committee on the Judiciary, House of Representatives (US Government Printing Office 1988). It is worth recording the full designation of the Forum to indicate the width of elder interests, and the extent of social issues, in which it was considered that mediation had an important role to play.

Its primary value and function was defined by the President of the National Institute of Dispute Resolution (NIDR) as 'to give people choices', but not, it was added, 'to replace courts or lawyers' with whom mediators were in a complementary alliance with regard to ensuring elder rights (US Government Printing Office, 1988:5). The conclusions of this Congressional Forum in respect of the worth of mediation as a salient social process for the advancement of elder care have been subsequently ratified by government public comment and by legal opinion. Dr Arthur Flemming, an elder care administrator, stated that 'mediation is going to play an increasingly important role in the life of the nation', suggesting that mediation is of general value to the whole population, as well as to 'the lives of older people' (*Senior Consumer ALERT*, 1992:7).

At the same time, Gottlich of the National Senior Citizens Law Center (NSCLC) emphasized that 'a dispute resolution proposal by the American Health Care Association (AHCA) is not consistent with the goals of dispute resolution, and will only harm the people we represent' (*NIDR Forum*, 1992:1). The legal remedies provided by the 1992 Amendments to the Nursing Home Reform Law/Omnibus Reconciliation Act (OBRA) 1987 were advocated instead.

These quotations are essential indicators of the tension within the conceptualization of the subjects in Part II of this book, and to understanding its purpose. This is to describe and interpret American elder care, elder rights and elder abuse in relation to the possibilities afforded by mediation processes in contributing to the constructive problem-solving involved, while not being traduced, or co-opted, so as to prevent social justice (Abel, 1982).

The rejected dispute resolution referred to above had been proposed by AHCA, the representative body of the American nursing home industry, as a means of avoiding or delaying the enforcement of penalties incurred following federal and State surveyor reports of institutional abuse to their elder residents. Clearly, whilst mediation can play a creative role in many nursing home conflicts, especially when used by Long Term Care Ombudsmen (LTCO) or senior volunteers, as will be discussed later, there would be a contradiction it its use to suppress complaints or public knowledge and action about elder abuse and neglect.

This tension between the positive and negative use of mediation, theorized earlier, is here distinguished as the difference between a social process 'guided by a new ethic of citizenship that incorporates elements of both individual autonomy and shared principles of justice' (Clark, 1991:638), and a social manipulation of conciliatory procedures to maintain and extend unequal power relations. In the first, the voice of the victim is strengthened; in the second, it is weakened.

The voice of an elderly person can be vulnerable: through poverty and homelessness it may be unheard (*Southern Exposure*, 1992); through suffering it may be uncharacteristic (Formby, 1992); through conflict with caregivers it may be unrecognized. Even though the collective voice of elders is politically heard in the lobbying of what is colloquially called the 'Silver Legislature', through the formal representations of the powerful American Association of Retired Persons (AARP), poverty lawyers point to the length of time taken to mount law reform campaigns, and then implement legislation.

Legislation in 1987 did not have its regulations completed until 1992, whilst their enforcement is still being debated. This is why the American Bar Association (ABA) in its publication, *Mediation – The Coming of Age* (1989), insists that the voices of elderly people involved in conflict can most speedily, audibly and powerfully contribute to its resolution when they are active parties in the process (Wood and Kestner, 1989).

The adversarial ambience of the law in non-violent domestic relations is professionally recognized as being generally counterproductive to amicable agreements (Roberts, 1988), and is relevant to American seniors who are the fastest growing sector of the divorcing population. Mediation in this sensitive, intimate area of microgerontology may be the preferred choice of old people, just as it can be the most effective remedial process in the macrogerontological task of establishing an ethical base concerning distributive justice in health care.

For it is in the domain of ethics that the argument for considering mediation as an important process in addressing major social conflicts has especially relevant advocacy. Moody, in *Ethics and Aging Society* (1992), suggests that the two most critical contemporary concerns are decision-making about patient autonomy, and decision-making about generational equity – justice between generations. He adds that the ethics which inform decision-making about elder rights, or entitlements, are 'part of a wider struggle for the rights of women, minorities, all oppressed groups' (Moody, 1992:3).

Moody, whose work has already been discussed, points out that 'from the outset, the doctrine of informed consent was based on the adversarial system of justice' (1992:9–10), but that what he calls 'negotiated consent' represents an alternative to the juridical model with its 'tyranny of principles' (1992:10). It is this negotiated consent which he considers to be a valuable option:

> I believe that, on both the small scale of clinical decision-making and the large scale of interest group politics ... this means both mediation of conflicts as well as political efforts on behalf of vulnerable groups where mediation cannot work (Moody, 1992:10).

Moody goes further and says:

> I favour a civic model of communicative ethics ... Free and open communication does not suppress conflicts or differences. But it achieves a compromise or negotiated settlement rather than a solution based on absolute rules and principles (Moody, 1992:10).

However Moody maintains that he is a pragmatist and historicist, and, having compared individual and collective struggles about inequitable practices, says:

> How we frame the problem – as 'conflict', as 'competition', as 'compromise' – will shape how we look for the terms of a resolution. As with negotiated consent at the level of clinical practice, the difficult problem is how to find a forum and a language in which 'fair negotiation' of intergenerational claims is possible, in which all parties with a stake in the outcome can have their voices heard ... (Moody, 1992:11).

Another factor necessary for the development of Moody's 'civic discourse' are 'institutions that promote communication and dialogue' (1992:12), and it is here, that in discussions at the Gerontological Society of America's (GSA) 1992 meeting, he attested to the value of formal and informal mediation services in contributing to 'procedural ethics' (1992:13) for intergenerational conflict.

It can be seen that the themes created by Moody, as one of America's leading gerontologists, are a source of additional legitimation for the argument that mediation can contribute constructively to the challenges of elder care, elder rights and elder abuse in the United States.

There now follows a more detailed discussion of these three major challenges, in which associated ones are incorporated. This will incidentally provide a useful contextual description of the demographic and other variables of America's ageing society in which the senior mediation services to be discussed in the subsequent chapter have evolved.

Elder care: 'The rich get richer'

The above headline of the American Economic Policy Institute's 1992 report referred to their statistics which showed that, between 1983 and 1989, the top half of the one per cent of the population's richest families received 55 per cent of the total increase in household wealth, while for the bottom 60 per cent of the population their income fell. Amongst these rich families are some of America's most powerful political and industrial gerontocracies. Many other elders have good incomes, enjoy good health and play important roles in public life.

Yet at the 1992 Joint Conference on Law and Aging, it was pointed out that, in addition to poor and nearly poor elders, there were 8.8 million living at home who were physically or mentally impaired, 2.5 million living alone and at least one million who were abused, neglected or exploited.

For old people do not represent a homogeneous social group, although they may share certain common needs, such as concerns to resolve family or community conflicts, and to make their own decisions about Advanced Directives or caregiving options. Such common interests represent one rationale for mediation evolving in universal, non-sectional services, although, as will be seen later, there is always a principal concern that positive action should be used to publicize their free availability to the poorest members of society.

Nevertheless, in America, as in Britain, it is not the poor who make most claim on the social benefits to which they are entitled, but the middle classes. A General Accounting Office (GAO) 1992 report entitled *Gaps between Poor and Non-Poor Elderly Americans* states that in 1990 only 30 per cent of the elderly poor had Medicaid; only 22 per cent received food stamps; and 50 per cent lived in households lacking any federal assistance.

The US Bureau of Census, (USBC), in its 1990 report, *Poverty in the United States*, stated that 3.6 million elderly Americans lived at poverty level, whilst an additional 2.1 million were near poor (USBC, 1990). Another report from the US Senate Special Committee on Aging (USSSCA), *Aging Americans: Trends and Projections, 1987–88*, pointed out that in 1986 there were 30 million people over 65, and that the poverty rate for those over 85 was 17.6 per cent, whilst that for those under 65 was 13.7 per cent. As it is estimated that by 2010 there will be 56 million Americans over 60, and that those over 50 will comprise one third of the entire population in 2020, it is projected that by then the nation will need three times as many social workers to deal with the social conflicts of the elderly in society (USSSCA, 1987–88).

Yet another recent relevant report, *Elderly Americans: Health, Housing and Nutrition Gaps between the Poor and Non-Poor* (GAO 1992b), points to a more serious source of social and political conflict, namely the gender, racial and age differential in poverty statistics. Amongst the 5.7 million, or 20 per cent of the American elderly who are poor, women are twice as likely to be represented, as are Hispanics; elderly black Americans are three times as likely to be poor; and those over 75 are twice as likely to be represented in comparison with those between 65 and 74 (GAO, 1992b).

An even more critical current report comes from the American Society on Aging which estimates that at least nine per cent of those over 60 were homeless, and that 140 used emergency shelters each night (*Aging Today*, 1991).

The social and political conflict generated by these facts, leads to a welcome reporting in the watchdog press, which adds a salient sensationalism at times of federal and State electoral change, an example of which was quoted at the beginning of this chapter. The conflict is fuelled partly by the fears *of* the ageing population, and partly by those *from* the ageing population. There is social and political anxiety about the rising costs of health care for an increasingly ageing population, to be borne by a decreasing young working population; there is individual anxiety and general awareness of the fact that the great majority of Americans hope to live long themselves, and rely on future supportive care.

These social and political fears led to the rhetoric of the Regan regime which correlated black Americans and elderly Americans as the joint chief charge on the tax burden. This resulted in the 1988 Medicare

Catastrophic Coverage Act, which was in itself catastrophic and repealed shortly after, because the electoral power lobby refused to meet the heavy surtax charges involved. So the bitter disputes about intergenerational equity have become more acute, and decision-making about public policy and planning with regard to social insurance and social benefits in elder health care has become more urgent. Additionally, justifiable concern about the increasing number of children coming within the poverty range has heightened the temperature of the ethical debate about intergenerational inequity and the competition for resources.

Here it should be noted that it is estimated that 36 million Americans have no health care insurance (AARP, 1992:2) and that only four per cent of the elderly population have coverage. Even this is restricted to the provision of long term care in skilled nursing facilities, and very limited assistance for home or intermediate care. In the Gerontology Institute (GI) 1990 research study, *Long Term Care Policy*, it is pointed out that although, in 1987, $36 billion was spent on nursing home care, only $9 billion was spent on the 80 per cent American elders who are cared for in their own homes. Put another way, only 20 cents of every dollar spent on long term care went towards home care. This gives rise to another social and political conflict in that there is increasing professional concern to develop community care of old people, either through assisted or congregate living projects, or by more supportive services to family caregivers. However, it is indicated that:

> some researchers worry that it will stimulate a 'woodwork effect'. Families who had been taking care of their relatives would ... 'come out of the woodwork' to claim federal dollars – and the costs to the federal and state governments would explode (GI, 1990:9).

As it is, Medicare benefits are exhausted when credit earned expires, and then patients have to be transferred to Medicaid. For instance Georgia, which is typical of the poor black south, is rated in the national State league as being 41st in its access to health care, and 37th in citizen coverage by health insurance (*Atlanta Constitution*, 10 November 1992).

It is not proposed to discuss in more detail the complex conflicts involved in Medicare and Medicaid controversies which are currently raging in America as the costs of health care, and long term elder care specifically, increase. Suffice to say that these occur often as a result of uneven and contested reimbursement to nursing homes by federal and State funds when patients' private resources are exhausted, and also over disputes arising about their free entitlement to supplementary services. Whilst Medicare and Medicaid do not provide general cover for

81

prescription drugs, dental and eye care, and various other needs there are continual individual conflicts about entitlement to specific items, and often collective complaints by nursing home residents about charged services which should be freely provided in Medicare and Medicaid licensed establishments.

Although the major social problems arising from the lack of a national health service and adequate insurance system have to be addressed by political measures, which is not within the remit of this discourse to consider further, it should be noted that AARP has not only played a lobbying role in challenging government, but has also played a constructive mediating role between the ageing network and successive administrations in trying to promote fundamental social change. For instance, following negotiations with all concerned, it published an important document, *Health Care America* with detailed proposals 'for a comprehensive health care system that provides health and long-term coverage for *all* individuals' (AARP, 1992:1).

Here it is important to note that the cornerstone of the plan is MEDICARD, a single health insurance access card, and that AARP is equitably promoting the interests of *all* age groups within the population, and not just those of its elderly members. It is consistent with AARP's organizational values and principles that it has been simultaneously promoting and financing the growth of American mediation in general, and senior mediation in particular, as will be seen later.

Another group of serious social conflicts are those between the nursing home industry, represented by the AHCA, and the Medicare and Medicaid licensing authority, the federal Health Care Financing Administration (HCFA), about the regarding the federal and State surveying of nursing homes, and the recording and penalizing of the deficiencies and abuses found. Not only have there been definitional disputes about what services proprietors and management should provide, and what should be categorized as neglect or mistreatment, but there has also been serious disagreement about the form and quality of the surveying process itself, about which allegations of corruption are made anecdotally by LTCOs who observe the system.

Although detailed discussion about the function and roles of LTCOs will take place in the next chapter, it is here relevant to note that they were formally instituted in the 1978 Amendments to the 1965 Older Americans Act to represent senior interests in residential care. In further 1988 Amendments to the same Act, each State Office on Aging was required to have an Office of the Ombudsman, with a duty to report malpractice and contribute to public policy-making. In fact, since 1971 when Nixon first called for an eight point plan to improve and monitor nursing home conditions, some States had initiated their own ombudsmen schemes, supervised then by the US States Public Health Service.

The majority of LTCOs are active members of the National Citizens Coalition of Nursing Home Reform (NCCNHR), which has led the campaign for nursing home reform, especially in lobbying for the 1992 Amendments to the Nursing Home Reform Law/Omnibus Reconciliation Act 1987, amongst the most critical of which were those relating to the institutional abuse of the surveying system.

Before considering this, it is worth noting that NCCNHR, founded in 1975 by 12 citizen advocacy groups, primarily funded by the federal Administration on Aging, is a research, development and information organization committed to increasing the participation, choice and decision- making of nursing home residents, most of whom are elders, and assuring their quality care. This has led to determined campaigning against physical and chemical restraints, and all forms of institutional abuse or coercive care. NCCNHR, with the support of LTCOs, have mounted a continuous critique against those owners and management members of the nursing home industry whose establishments show regular patterns of deficiencies on surveys, but used the ensuing conflict constructively to ensure a strengthening of the resident voice and LTCO role in the surveying process.

Prior to the 1992 Amendments many proprietors would intentionally exclude LTCOs from being present at the surveys, and thus be able to persuade poorly trained inspectors that the deficiencies found were uncharacteristic or solitary, not deserving citation. Surveyors were also given favours to prompt good reports and advance notice of when the inspections would take place. Through NCCNHR's research records, based on LTCO reports and its own special inquiries, it was able, not only to promote an adverse press campaign, but simultaneously and effectively to negotiate with the AHCA and the HCFA to ensure that the 1992 Amendments were passed.

In *The Impact of Adverse Nursing Home Survey Reports in Tort and Criminal Cases*, Harkins and Kelly point to the 'clearly emerging trend for persons suing nursing homes to use adverse survey reports to their own advantage in litigation' (1992:2). Nursing home proprietors have not only been afraid of this trend, but equal fear of contingency lawyers exploiting a profitable market brought them to the negotiating process with a considerably diminished power base.

83

The 1992 Amendments required the surveys to be unannounced, the LTCOs to be present, and the residents' views to be sought. So the Amendments have not only created opportunities for significant structural change within the administration of long term care, but have already begun to effect microsociological changes within institutional caregiving systems.

The long term educational objective of NCCNHR has always been to persuade the nursing home industry that quality care is ultimately the most cost-effective, and that encouraging resident participation, choice and decision-making, in addition to its intrinsic benefits for encouraging autonomy, independence and well-being, also reduces complaints and mistreatment. The social mediation role of NCCNHR between all the many federal, State, voluntary and commercial agencies involved in elder care, has been to ensure that the legitimate interests of all groups are listened to, considered and balanced against each other, with the LTCOs providing advocacy for residents when necessary, and encouraging the training and support of staff.

Here it should be recognized that many nursing homes provide excellent quality assurance for their residents. For instance some large chains of nursing homes have their own inspectorates whose aim is to monitor and manage nursing home conflicts constructively in the interests of residents and staff. Other good nursing homes advertise that their policies exclude any use of restraints, whilst many of those sponsored by charitable foundations are based on philosophies which encourage Family Councils and Residents' Councils to ensure quality care.

Nevertheless Bonnyman, in his article *Moral Malpractice*, points to the resident racial exclusiveness practised by some religious foundations, whilst simultaneously exploiting staff drawn from the minorities:

> There is another reason why until recently many church leaders have said so little on this subject. American religious organisations have a heavy investment, both financial and political, in the status quo. In some cases the religious orders or denominations own the facilities (Bonnyman, 1992:15).

Bonnyman goes on to point to a 1987 study in the *Journal of American Medical Association* (no references supplied) which estimated that '250,000 emergency patients are dumped from our hospitals each year in violation of the law' (1992:16). He then cites the cases of three denominational hospitals who contributed to this abuse and says:

only when the complicity of the American religious community ends and enough people condemn the moral bankruptcy of the current system will it be possible to achieve a just alternative (Bonnyman, 1992:17).

Bonnyman is a legal aid attorney who believes that lawyers are key workers amongst those professionals who should help all those involved find their 'moral voice' (1992:17). Significantly, it has not only been through the development of legal aid services in America that the moral voice of seniors has been heard more clearly but also, increasingly through the mediation services sponsored by them, as will be seen later in the Kansas study.

A closer look at American legal aid services appears more appropriately in the next section of this chapter, whilst recording at this juncture that they have been used in support of seniors in individual and collective actions against nursing home malpractice, when mediation could not establish the legal precedents or remedies needed. However mediation is a social process also concerned to encourage the moral voice of its participants, especially facilitating the emergence of the weaker voice in unequal power relations situations, so that elder rights are conceptualized as being a prime value in elder mediation (Craig, 1992:4–5).

Elder rights: perspectives, protection, participation

The above title was given to a conference held under the auspices of the Long Term Care Ombudsman Program and the Administration on Aging in 1992. Three principal objectives were to examine the context of the rising movement for elder rights, to consider the practical consequences of policies of protective restraints for nursing home residents or nursing home residents, and to explore the implications of the 1990 Patient Self Determination Act.

It is noteworthy that elder rights were similarly focused on in 1992, and earlier, by all major agencies in the American ageing network. For instance there were key features at the annual meeting of the Gerontological Society of America (GSA), especially in Estes' plenary address when she advocated an 'empowerment initiative' to increase elder rights in relation to the micro social construction of ageing, and the macro political economy of ageing (1992:15). She argued that 'universal entitlement offers the advantage of assured predictability in the supply of, and equity in access to, the community services for which it exists' and that 'the Americans with Disabilities Act of 1990 is a concrete expression in public policy of a transforming idea – empowerment' (1992:25–6).

Significantly, in conference discussion, practitioners involved in trying to obtain entitlements under that Act for their clients found that practical negotiation with the authorities concerned was often more speedily effective than the pursuit of the law.

The NCCNHR annual meeting also focused on elder rights in many sessions, whilst they were promoted as part of the National Elder Campaign of the US Administration on Aging at the 1992 5th Annual Joint Conference on Law and Aging. This important coalition comprises the American Bar Association's Commission on Legal Problems of the Elderly (ABACLPE), AARP's Legal Counsel for the Elderly (LCE), and the Center for Social Gerontology (CSG).

The fact that these legal agencies are also represented on the AARP Coalition on Mediation and Older Americans, which has a similar remit to promote elder rights, shows again how closely entwined are legal and mediation interests in advancing elder care. For instance the District of Columbia Department of Human Rights refers many of its individual complaints, including those of seniors, to mediation by the Center for Dispute Resolution in Washington, while retaining class actions or complaints against repeat offenders for enforcement.

This returns us to consideration of the role of legal aid services for older adults now referred to, as is the American custom, as legal services. Opportunities for the development of legal services for seniors were created by the 1965 Older Americans Act in order to provide free or means-tested legal assistance for poor or near poor people.

The services, funded by the National Legal Services Corporation and local State and charitable foundations, developed in a piecemeal fashion, depending on the political and economic power interests dominant in each State, and the idealism and quality of the professional law associations in each area. The ABACLPE has encouraged the universalization of this development to protect the rights of poor American old people, and also, pragmatically, to provide more areas of employment for its members who are retired paralegals.

The ABACLPE, in furtherance of these aims, has also urged the extension of professional legal education specializing in elder law through university and ABA courses. Similarly the ABACLPE has promoted university courses in alternative dispute resolution (ADR), in some of which modules of senior mediation training have been included.

Social workers also played a pioneer role in contributing to the protection of elder rights through the development of elder law, advocacy and other services. In an effort to merge the strengths of social work and law disciplines, the Institute on Law and Rights of Older Adults was formed as early as 1977 to serve five New York City counties, and has been a model for comparable developments elsewhere. The Institute has a 'holistic approach to elder law', in which mediation processes have their place as the attorney tends to form a close relationship with the client and frequently acts as confidante and social worker.

This complementary use of social work, counselling, mediation and legal skills in the protection of elder rights is especially appropriate in issues of guardianship which will now be briefly discussed, as mediation is also being developed in this sphere in America.

It is here that decision-making and choice by old people whose mental capacity may be questioned has to be most carefully safeguarded. In many cases of Alzheimer's disease and related conditions of senility, there may be states of 'variable capacity' (Formby, S, 1992) in which clarity of thought and understanding may change hourly, daily or periodically. It is well known, for instance, that decisional competence can be masked by chronic depression, if it is untreated.

Unscrupulous caregivers, whether in families or institutions, may have fiduciary and commercial interests in seeking premature legal orders of guardianship, whilst clinical opinion may be prejudiced in favour of providing the necessary medical support through anticipated increased ease of giving treatment.

Kapp, Professor of Community Health, and Director of the Office of Geriatric Medicine and Gerontology of Wright State University, is equally concerned. In conversation at the 1992 GSA meeting he argued that incapacity is not a legally authoritative definition but a working assumption made by clinicians, and that too many nursing home owners suffer from litigation phobia. He considered that guardianship should be a last resort, only to be applied for after careful mediation between all the interested parties.

He discusses this in more detail in *Alternatives to Guardianship for the Elderly* (1992) and says that:

> the purpose of this research program was to examine and delineate major actual and perceived legal, administrative and policy barriers to a more widespread development and of less intrusive alternative-to-guardianship services for older adults with varying degrees of mental or physical impairment (Kapp, 1992a:i).

His research found that:

> Eldercare service providers engage in a host of reactive techniques and defensive postures ... (which) ... contribute to and reflect habitual anxiety and usually are counterproductive to the development and implementation of alternative methods of service delivery to the elderly (Kapp, 1992a:123).

Kapp found that risks to elderly residents were minimal and that there were no reported judgements against service providers who used alternative decision-making processes in elder care, rather than persuading relatives to apply for guardianship orders. If there have been carefully mediated agreements, then, in legal terms, 'an array of available denial and affirmative defenses may be interposed in the rare event of a lawsuit (Kapp, 1992a:ii).

However, Kapp stresses the intrinsic value to old people of maintaining and enhancing their communication and decision-making skills as long as possible, and recommends the use of modern nursing management techniques to deal with variable problems of emotional, mental and physical stability more creatively.

In another article, *Health Care Decision-Making by the Elderly*, he affirms that:

> evidence is emerging that elderly people prefer informal practices of treatment and good communication for moral connectedness (Kapp, 1991:612).

He adds that this entails 'a continuous dialogue with others whose views are a dialectical part of one's own values' (Kapp, 1991:620).

It is for the purpose of encouraging dialogue in elder care that the CSG has started its own Guardianship Mediation Program. This seeks:

> to help parties in adult guardianship disputes to find a mutually satisfactory resolution that will, in appropriate cases, avoid the necessity for guardianship, while preserving family relationships, and allowing all parties, including the proposed ward, to have some control over the outcome. Such solutions created by the parties themselves, are more likely to work out than court-ordered solutions because parties are committed to them, having been part of the process that created them (Lisi and Burns, 1992:644).

Lisi and Burns go on to say that:

the area of adult guardianship is one in which the rights and autonomy of older or disabled persons are threatened more directly and significantly than in any other sphere. Currently in the United States, guardianships exist for more than 500,000 adults (1992:644).

The problems of unequal power relations among the parties, and the variable competency of the dependant, can be met, if necessary, by appointing a guardian ad litem. However the Guardianship Mediation Project will not use mediation when there is evidence of institutional or family abuse, and when the adult protective services agency (APS) has become involved.

However, Lisi and Burns conclude that:

> through mediation, the family may for the first time be able to focus on the needs of the proposed ward and the importance of having the caregivers and family working together to provide the necessary care for the person ... Mediation offers a way to explore the real abilities and needs of the proposed ward, find services that can provide those needs, and work out conflicts while preserving both the autonomy of the older or disabled person and improving family relationships (1992:645).

The mediation process is conceptualized as being part of personal care planning, a prime objective of good nursing care as endorsed by NCCNHR, either through initiating or reinforcing it, and can also be used in guaranteeing that the elder's voice is heard also in lesser issues of surrogate decision-making, which may be the last preferred remedy before guardianship is considered. The worth of mediation in these sensitive complex and variable predicaments of decision-making affecting elders is that it provides opportunities for the voices of all parties to be heard and considered, thus setting a model of good communication for future discussions of conflicts about elder care treatment.

The arguments for using mediation in appropriate cases of guardianship also apply to those involving Advanced Directives, the second issue of contemporary critical concern in America, preoccupying the public, its professional caregivers, its spiritual advisers, and those seeking hospital or nursing home care, whether they are elderly or not. Advanced Directives, or Living Wills, as they are called there, are different from Wills which deal with property bequests. They are documents which state a person's wishes with regard to resuscitation treatment or life-support measures should a terminal situation develop.

There is much public and professional conflict and anxiety about Advanced Directives because of competing interests between medical opinions, patients' feelings and relatives' views, in the variety of complex cases that arise. The protection of elder rights is especially important, as these are in danger of being regarded as more marginal and expendable than those of other age groups.

As a result of media pressure, the campaigning of the ageing network, and the government's concern that the euthanasia lobby should not hijack public concern, a Patient Self Determination Act (PSDA) was passed in 1990. This had the strong support of religious organizations such as the North West Interfaith movement, whose recent research report was entitled *The Patient Self Determination Act: Promoting Autonomy in Long Term Care* (1992):

> The Patient Self Determination Act provides a solid base in the fight for the recognition of the rights of all competent adults to control their bodies, and to make decisions about their medical treatment. It also provides the opportunity to plan for future care needs and incapacities by recognising the importances of Advanced Directives in extending autonomy in decision-making (Davitt, 1988:8).

The *Patient Self Determination Act State Law Guide*, compiled by the ABA, states that the Act requires all Medicare and Medicaid providers to:

> provide written information [to patients at the time of admission concerning] an individual's right under State law ... to make decisions concerning medical care, including the right to accept or refuse medical or surgical treatment and the right to formulate Advanced Directives;

> maintain written policies and procedures ... and provide written information;

> document in the individual's medical record whether or not the individual has executed an Advanced Directive;

> provide (individually or with others) for education of the staff and the community on issues concerning Advanced Directives (ABA, 1991:3).

The ABA then discusses in detail the conflicts that can arise and the abuses which may ensue, as pressure is put upon people, especially vulnerable seniors, to conform to a prescribed decision, that is not the patient's own. In situations of deteriorating physical, mental or emotional health, following traumas, or even at the crisis point of admission to a hospital or nursing home, the old person anxious to please, or placate, relatives and caregivers, may easily cease to make choices but acquiesce to the voices of others.

At the 1992 NCCNHR conference LTCOs documented their knowledge of nursing homes illegally refusing to admit patients until their Advanced Directives had been completed, coercion which the Act warns against. Here it should be noted that Davitt (1992), a LTCO, sees issues about Advanced Directives, like those about guardianship, best raised through the mediation approach of personal care planning, as discussed above. At times of initial assessment and regular review, Advanced Directives can be formulated and reformulated as often as is wished, to meet the demands of changing situations, and yet reflect the patient's continuing participation in decision-making.

The need old people have at times of considering Advanced Directives is for a flexible, gentle decision-making process, in which the voices of all who have a responsibility for contributing can be heard, questioned and balanced through the use of good mediation skills.

However, it is through the establishment of State Institutes of Biomedical Ethics, like the one in Kansas to be noted later, that the theoretical evaluation of these proposals must be researched. It is also through ethics committees, which are found increasingly in good hospitals and nursing homes, that the opportunity can be created for the fullest articulation of voices within what Collopy calls each 'moral community' (1992:9).

Nevertheless, even then, care must be taken to see that there is no inappropriate domination of clinical opinion, nor any chaplain's imperative, when a patient's quality of life is being considered. The process of mediation, with the help of a LTCO or staff member, generally a social worker, specially trained in communication and conflict resolution skills, may be the best guarantee that the patient's voice is encouraged, heard and respected, to ensure the fullest possible participation in the decisions to be made.

Clark, writing on *Ethical Dimensions of Quality of Life in Aging* says that:

> decision-making becomes a horizontal, interactive process involving negotiation, compromise and the recognition of reciprocities of common history and values (1991:634).

He adds that:

> crucial to this process are the key variables of decision-making, community development and empowerment and that medical decision-making must become guided by a new ethic of citizenship that incorporates elements of both individual autonomy and shared principles of justice (Clark, 1991:636, 638).

It is to considerations of justice, viewed in the context of restraints used to suppress and control old people, often in abusive ways, that this discourse turns next. Kapp, a lifelong campaigner against restraints writes in the *Journal of Legal Medicine* that:

> approximately 41 per cent of the American nursing home population, or about 500,000 people, are subject to physical restraints. According to the Nursing Home Community Coalition of New York State, up to 60 per cent of nursing home residents in that State are in physical restraints, and 93 per cent of those who are placed in restraints remain so for the remainder of their nursing home stay (1992b:2).

Following the determined campaign of NCCNHR, which lasted five years after 1987 laws first recommended the abolition of restraints when possible, the 1992 Amendments to the legislation finally contained specific regulations with regard to their use, and penalties for any abuse. NCCNHR documented these regulations, pointing out that restraints could only be imposed to ensure the physical safety of the resident or other residents, and only upon the written order of a physician that specifies the duration and circumstances under which restraints are to be used.

Despite the ambiguities contained within the regulations, and the threat that they present to nursing home managers who use bad methods, NCCNHR sees the 1992 Amendments as a radical watershed in elder care and the protection of elder rights. For overuse of drugs is a particular problem in American hospitals and nursing homes which have commercial ties with pharmaceutical companies, and which can overcharge patients for their medications. In this context it is worth noting that 'the Pharmaceutical Manufacturers' Association has 329 new medicines in testing for 45 diseases of aging' (*Newsweek*, 9 November 1992).

It is through being unjustly and inappropriately subjected to suppression or sedation by chemical restraints that the patient's voice is most commonly silenced, and autonomy threatened. NCCNHR's insistence on protecting patient autonomy through LTCO advocacy, and mediation with the nursing home providers, encourages the minimal use of restraints and is reinforced by Collopy in his paper for the American Association of Homes for the Aging. This is entitled *The Use of Restraints in Long Term Care: The Ethical Issue* and says that:

> to be at all effective, the principle of self-determination needs a context of open and ample communication. Patients can make responsible decisions and providers can respect or negotiate with those decisions only when there is an ongoing flow of information in both directions (Collopy, 1992:7).

Collopy, like Kapp (1992b), says that research shows that more physical and emotional harm results from using, rather than not using, restraints, and develops his ethics based on conceptualizing nursing homes as 'moral communities' (1992:9). He then goes on to say that:

> For an ethic that challenges paternalistic bonds on patient decision-making, bonds on patient *mobility* are even more untenable ... The public, physical nature of these restraints is a powerful *social* statement ... and ... can erode the basis of dignity – the individual's self-possession and self-esteem (Collopy, 1992:11–12).

It is here relevant to point to Moody's *Ethics in Aging* (1992) in which he suggests that dignity and esteem may be even more important to elders than the autonomy whose natural fading is more philosophically accepted.

Collopy concludes that:

> since providers and residents may disagree about the need for restraints, about alternative solutions to problem behavior, even about the very definition of 'problem behavior', there should be an established process for adjudicating disputes ... an established process of involving residents (and when appropriate their surrogates) in the discussion, of providing them with an opportunity to be heard in a fair and unbiased dialogue. The goal here would be not simply to provide some legal minimum of due process, but to establish consistent patterns of discussion and conflict resolution with the facility (1992:14).

The complementary roles of mediation and legal process are here indicated as being necessary to the resolution of conflicts. Significantly a recent Institute of Medicine (IoM) report, *Medicare: A Strategy for Quality Assurance*, is used by Collopy to support his views, and he quotes the IoM 'desired outcomes' as:

patient satisfaction and well-being, good health status and quality of life outcomes, and the process of patient-provider interaction and decision-making (IoM, 1991:4–5).

Kapp considers that ideological institutional change is involved in eradicating the prevalent misuse of restraints, and seeks to persuade providers that:

> resident and substitute decision-makers who share in the decision-making process are less apt to try to shift the blame on to someone else in the event of a maloccurrence (1992b:28).

He goes on to recommend documentation at patient care planning and review conferences, and says that it is essential that:

> the resident's chart should note the process of communication and negotiation, and the decision ultimately made ... and that a process should be designed for resolving disputes ... (Kapp, 1992b:30).

The *Long Term Care Management Newsletter* (1992) endorses these principles and refers to the HCFA proposed definition of abuse which includes *disregard of an individual* (emphasis added) to those which more commonly feature in the literature. The HCFA proposed definition of neglect is equally broad and includes the failure to provide *safe services* (emphasis added) to promote quality care. These are welcome indications that the authorities are beginning to upgrade their own values with regard to resident rights in elder care, especially in view of the evidence of other forms of elder abuse which will be considered next.

Elder abuse: ensuring an abuse-free environment

The above title comes from a Learning Program for Nursing Home Staff produced by the Coalition of Advocates for the Rights of the Infirm Elderly (CARIE), founded in 1977, and the Philadelphia Elder Abuse Task Force which it established in 1985.

Philadelphia has a tradition of conflict resolution through its historic Quaker development, and through its pioneer mediation services, so it might be expected that CARIE sees the prevention of elder abuse in terms of the constructive early handling of conflict, the theme of this book. It states that:

94

a 35 State survey of long term care professionals conducted by the Health and Human Services Office of Inspector General found that nursing home staff lack adequate training to handle conflict. As the staff with the most direct contact with residents, nurse aides have the greatest potential to defuse conflict and thereby reduce incidents of abuse and neglect (CARIE, 1990:2).

CARIE is one of the increasing number of elder abuse coalitions committed to training nursing aides in conflict resolution, as is NIDR in its major recent Californian nursing home programme where all staff were offered training in mediation, and which will be discussed in a subsequent chapter. Significantly California, a retirement State, has a bad record of institutional abuse, and NEIEASLTCOS, a federal agency of the OoA, indicts it strongly:

A 1985 study of 7 States that report institutional abuse found that of every 1000 elder residents, 1.6 – 8.5 had been abused. California, which receives approximately one-third of all complaints reported by State Ombudsman Programs nationwide, reported that of the nearly 30,000 complaints they received about nursing homes in 1988–89, over half were of abuse or neglect; 1336 alleged physical or sexual abuse, 804 alleged neglect; 39 alleged abandonment; 500 alleged fiduciary abuse; 357 alleged mental suffering; 3286 alleged violation of resident rights and 689 alleged thefts and losses (NEIEASLTCOS, 1992a:2).

In another document, *Elder Rights: A Call for Enhanced Leadership and Action*, from which excerpts are taken, NEIEASLTCOS states that:

approximately 2 million older people reside in an estimated 90,000 long term care facilities with growing reports of abuse, loss of autonomy and complaints concerning the quality of care. These growing and increasingly complex threats to, and violation of the rights of older persons call for the development of a comprehensive system of programs, services and protection at the community, State and national levels to assist older persons to … execute choice through informed decision-making … resolve questions and disputes … (which will) … establish consumer centered elder rights programs which facilitate change, promote autonomy and support decisionmaking with a minimum of administrative intrusion or confusion (1992b:1–4).

The emphasis is added to recall the earlier discussion of Roberts' view that mediation is most useful when used as 'a minimal form of intervention' (1986:25).

In the present context it is significant that NEIEASLTCOS is concerned that any innovative procedures of decision-making do not add to the burdensome bureaucratic interventions which have been an unintended negative consequence of many APS procedures. Hence there is an interest in the development of elder mediation services as a contribution to the prevention of elder abuse.

However NEIEASLTCOS also draws attention to the structural determinants of increasing instances of institutional abuse. Returning to the question of nursing aides, it recommends a registry with the names of staff who have been convicted of abuse. Unfortunately aides, who are mainly low-paid and untrained women who have to do more than one job to remain above poverty level, often being single parents, are often too tired to give residents quality care.

Also, some States, as in Kansas, subsidize providers for giving work to previously unemployed people: as the payment is for a limited period, owners find it profitable to encourage a rapid turnover of often dissatisfied staff, so that they receive further subsidies for new entrants. Ironically staff are dismissed for giving inadequate quality care, sometimes with the support of malicious residents whose generational racial abuse of black aides does not receive the attention it deserves in discussions about elder care, elder conflict and elder abuse.

NEIEASLTCOS also refers to the structural implications of Medicare and Medicaid legislation which is conducive to bureaucratic malpractice:

> Federal law says that each State Office of the Attorney General must have a Medicaid Fraud Control Unit to investigate and prosecute fraud and patient abuse and neglect in health care facilities which participate in Medicaid (1992c:3).

In passing it should be noted that police in every State are now constrained to investigate fraud, but that in only one third of America's major cities do they have guidelines for intervention in cases of elder abuse and neglect (Plotkin, 1988).

Medicaid fraud is committed by unscrupulous providers who overcharge residents for fees, and who submit false accounts relating to the reimbursement which they receive from federal and State agencies. This fiduciary fraud can be coupled with the dishonest editing of Residents' Councils and Family Council records to remove references to adverse comments on the nursing home care which would be inspected by surveyors, although, in addition, bribes might be offered to them.

The commercial abuse of elderly persons is also commented on by NEIEASLTCOS as coming from by non-lawyers who market defective services in advice about Wills or Living Trusts, or who promote investment scams which rob elders of their savings. AARP, through its Criminal Justice Service Program, has an ideological commitment to ensuring an abuse-free environment for its members. It warns them about financial and bureaucratic malpractice, through unfair evictions by landlords, discrimination in housing and employment, housing code violations, homeowner warranties, civil rights violations, utility fees disputes and landlord/tenant disagreements.

However AARP (1988) entitles its monograph on dispute resolution *Helping Seniors – Seniors Helping*, asserting that most elders actively contribute to their own, to their community's and to the national well-being. AARP supports the case for elder mediation by pointing to the creative roles elders play in dispute resolution and long term care programs as trained mediators using their long and valuable experiences of life to help other senior citizens.

Under another heading, *Older Volunteers – A Growing Asset*, AARP uses its considerable prestige and status in the ageing network to advance the idea of senior mediation as an important social trend for the future.

AARP is represented on the National Aging Resource Center on Elder Abuse (NARCEA) which was funded by the OoA in 1988 to provide information, written and video resources on elder abuse, and to encourage research on the subject. Whereas NEIEASLTCOS, through its LTCO connections, has a special focus on institutional elder abuse, NARCEA appears to concentrate on family abuse and neglect.

NARCEA estimates that nearly two million elders were victims of domestic abuse in 1988, and draws attention to the 1990 report of the Sub-Committee on Health and Long Term Care of the Select Committee on Aging of the US House of Representatives, entitled *Elder Abuse: A Decade of Shame and Inaction*, which says that about five per cent of the nation's elders are victims of abuse.

NARCEA indicates that the report concludes by saying that little has been done to prevent elder abuse and that existing knowledge in many of these areas is still very limited so that more varied research is needed.

NARCEA's research approach is consistent with that of the present study suggesting, as have other references in this section, that the model of co-operative problem-solving is appropriate for the complex and often contradictory conflicts which characterize issues of American

97

elder care, elder rights and elder abuse, and may help to ensure an abuse-free environment.

A brief review of this chapter recalls its initial purpose in describing the social context in which American concerns about elder care, elder rights and elder abuse have been evolving, and to generalize some of the major issues. No individual case illustrations have been included, as these will be given in the next chapter.

The issues raised have been chosen selectively for their focus on decision-making in elder care conflicts, and where mediation processes have possibilities in contributing to participation and choices for the elders involved. Mediation has been shown to have a base in current American research on ethics and ageing.

The theme of senior or elder mediation has also emerged in discussions about constructive ways of dealing with problems of guardianship, Advanced Directives and restraints.

In the social context of creating an abuse-free environment, mediation has been shown to have a role to play in contributing to the prevention of institutional and family abuse of elders.

No claim has been made that the developments described are anything more than social indicators of possible trends, but these provide the wider American social context in which to consider the evolving situation in Californian long term care which is the subject of the next chapter.

5 Californian long term care and institutional elder abuse

This chapter is divided into three sections. The first section analyses the structural, cultural and institutional conflicts affecting Californian long term care and the development of mediation for older people.

The second section evaluates mediation as used in a county LTCO service, a city public hospital for old people and a district nursing home.

The third section discusses issues relating to the protection of elder rights, the prevention of elder abuse and the role of mediation in long term care.

In these sections three principal questions are raised as to why mediation has developed as a new social intervention in California, what its impact has been there, and whether its work for promoting the interests of older people is being misused or underused.

Questions raised in previous chapters about mediation as a minimal form of intervention, the relevance of concepts of naming, blaming and claiming, and changing social definitions of elder abuse are recurrent themes. References are made to comparative developments in British Columbia, as American and Californian government agencies are currently considering Canadian financing of elder long term care.

The chapter has an introduction with statistics which provide a background to the structural approach to Californian conflicts in elder care. The research aims, limitations, sites and methods are also described.

The chapter concludes with a summary of the study findings, discussion of their implications for future social policy, and questions for further research about the viability and usefulness of mediation in the prevention of elder abuse in long term care.

The Californian context and a brief history of reform

California has a history of State initiatives to address the increasing number of social conflicts arising from its demographic situation as the now popularly called 'Costa Geriatrica' of America. Senior mediation is one of the most recent of these.

In 1929 California was the first State to introduce a mandatory system of pensions. In 1933 it led national radical political policy programs with its End Poverty in California (EPIC) campaign. When the federal plan of Medicare insurance was introduced in 1965, California simultaneously produced its own Medi-Cal system (Putnam, 1970).

Putnam, in his book, *Old Age Politics in America* (1970), shows how, during the period 1920–30, California had 20 per cent more old people than the whole of the USA, but developed innovative responses to rising social concern, as was the tradition of its earlier history. In 1867 the largest municipally-owned long term care hospital in America was opened in San Francisco for its aged poor and disabled.

This public hospital currently has a national reputation for pioneer work in elder care, as have other social agencies visited in this study. San Francisco police claim that they started the first elder abuse training for their officers, and were the first State to actively recruit homosexual and ethnic *majority* citizens, the City and County having an estimated white population of 40 per cent, with 132 languages being spoken.

California continued its general historic campaign against bad residential elder care and elder abuse by being one of the first States to develop a voluntary organization in 1985 specifically committed to this task, the California Advocates for Nursing Home Reform (CANHR). In 1988 its executive director became a key person in initiating senior mediation as a new social intervention to be developed for conflict management work in the nursing homes of four Californian counties.

Currently the San Francisco Superior Court Director of Probate Court Services is using mediation informally in some Conservatorship disputes. In addition the Californian Coalition on Elder Abuse has shown interest in mediation as a result of the research visit. The San Francisco Community Boards are also planning to develop a senior mediation service.

This brief history notes the varying estimates of California's population as about 1.5 million in 1900, rising to 29 million in 1993. Although there have been fluctuating proportions of elders, there have been residual similar problems. Putnam (1970) said that past initiatives, often politically challenged and defeated, had been inadequate in providing elder care,

100

while present concerns are illustrated by extracts from the following recent socioeconomic profile of 4.2 million Californians over 65 years:

60 per cent black elders living alone are below poverty
40 per cent elders live in poverty
21 per cent have one or more chronic disabilities
15 per cent cannot manage basic daily living activities
19 per cent depend on others for transport
8 per cent are homebound
80 per cent impaired elders have family carers
5 per cent live in institutions
10 per cent live alone
55 per cent nursing home residents have no family care
70 per cent of all Medi-Cal funds spent on nursing homes
(extracted from *An Aging Agenda 1993–95* (1993:5), Californian Association of Area Agencies on Aging).

These statistics provide a background for the subsequent analysis of the social conflict caused in struggling for the political and economic resources to reform elder care, and Putnam's concluding chapter, 'The Continuing Crusade 1940–69' (1970:126–42), can be identified as an early and clear warning about the structural abuse of old people.

While Putnam qualified his critique by the admission that rich elders also had been attracted to California, some of whom had played valuable roles in promoting elder rights, he queried how far the collective initiatives could lead to structural reform of elder care specifically, and poverty in general. Contemporary Californian critics of senior mediation, including members of CANHR, also question its capacity and competence as a social innovation to confront structural conflict. So does this present study.

Following Kuhn, an elder pioneer in nursing home reform, the subsequent structural analysis will include the political, economic and industrial issues of generational and social inequity:

I came to see all injustices, however small or seemingly unrelated, as linked (Kuhn, 1977:222).

The cultural analysis will focus on the racial, ethical and existential concerns of Californians in relation to the conflicts of old age.

The institutional analysis will look at conflicts between professional workers, the inadequacy of the law, and the problem of the medical hierarchy.

The Californian research project

The main aim of the study was to study patterns of conflict in the research sites, in the context of the Californian social conflict noted above. This involved contextualizing micro conflict within macro conflict, and analysing how the former was affected by the latter. For example, the State budget deficit dispute about whether funding should be given to schools or long term care directly affected staff shortages that led to residents' complaints.

Another principal aim of the study was to observe where senior mediation made a constructive contribution to resolving conflicts in long term care and preventing abuse, and to identify which these were. Disputes between residents leading to the risk of violence are recurring problems where staff and ombudsmen play a mediating role.

An associated aim was to see what forms mediation took, and whether the process was a formal, informal, minimal or any other kind of intervention. Another was to note how far disputes could be analysed in terms of a process of naming, blaming and claiming, and whether this can usefully contribute to understanding conflict management. For instance, budget cuts were named as being responsible for the way in which staff were blamed for inadequate care, and consequent claims by residents for better attention.

Another objective was to learn as much as possible in general about wider north American elder care, elder abuse and elder mediation to provide a background for the study. Additional invitations to speak about the research at meetings in Oregon, Washington and also in Victoria and Vancouver, British Columbia, led to unscheduled interviews with many other academics, practitioners and old people involved in mediation.

This included four retired Californian professors: one of 84 actively mediating as a university ombudsman in disputes about the staff abuse and neglect of students; one gerontologist over 70 was concerned about local conflict resolution, and another trained long term care recreation staff in mediation. Other elders included an American teacher and a counsellor who used mediation skills in their work, and a Canadian who had pioneered an elder abuse coalition. Canadian social workers involved with elder care and elder abuse also spoke about their use of mediation skills.

These meetings generated valuable data for comparative purposes in that it showed how active older people are contributing to the general use of senior mediation. Many others in this group were met socially during brief weekend camping and other engagements, and all supported the research concerns.

One limitation to the study was that a personal accident caused by the AMTRAK rail company, resulted in injury, hospitalization, and painful movement which restricted research activities. However this provided experiential learning of the way in which an old person was treated in an American emergency hospital unit, the risk of falls in old age, and how a complaint against AMTRAK went through the process of naming, blaming and claiming.

A further limitation was that almost all the residents in the research sites were people at various stages of senility. It was explained that, because of the recent emphasis on community care, and the rising cost of residential care, old people were not entering institutions until it became unsafe or impossible for them to live at home or in sheltered accommodation. Fluctuating mental capacity prevented formal interviewing and also restricted their participation in mediation.

The foremost limitation was that just before starting participant observation at one of two nursing homes, it became subject to closure through an alleged licensing violation, including a manslaughter charge. Although this featured in the research study and analysis, it meant that meetings with San Francisco professionals in elder care had to be substituted at short notice for the cancelled visit. So the second nursing home was the only one visited.

This nursing home was in Oakland, a poor district with a 29 per cent white population, and will be called Oakland throughout the study. It was a 38-bed skilled nursing facility, with a ratio of one member of staff to one resident. It was privately owned by a retired former director of hospital nursing services, actively co-managing Oakland since 1984 with her son and his wife, a registered nurse who was in charge of resident care. 50 per cent of the residents, and 50 per cent of the staff were from different ethnic communities. The nursing home was purpose-built as a one-floor circular cloister, with twin-bedded rooms opening into a central open patio, and externally on to a closed yard.

The public hospital and rehabilitation long term centre, had 1300 beds with 1600 staff. The residents were mainly between 60 and 90 years, suffering from chronic physical and mental disabilities, including Alzheimer's disease. However the hospital's rehabilitation policy meant that some old people were admitted temporarily for emergency or respite care. Others, more able, lived in an attached home-like unit. Selected community seniors visited the day centre where they also received all services. The hospital had a hospice, mostly for persons with AIDS. It also admitted some adults with chronic disabilities and diseases who were not accepted by nursing homes, or discharged from them.

The LTCO service studied was situated in an inland Californian county with a mixed income population. It was responsible for visiting 34 nursing homes, 230 residential care homes and up to 100 homes for developmentally disabled adults. There were two paid professional ombudsmen and a paid intake worker, who trained and supported (and were supported by) 28 volunteer ombudsmen, 15 of whom were active. The two professionals, one the director and a senior herself, and two older volunteers, had taken the Californian formal mediation training, and were enthusiastic about using it in appropriate cases. As the service was not completely State-funded but was supported by charities, none of the staff were pensioned, and consistently did unpaid overtime work plus their own office cleaning.

The research methods chosen included preliminary consultative letter-writing to various Californian authorities interested in elder mediation and/or elder abuse, followed by organising a visiting schedule in response to the research options offered. Hosts agreed to the study being based on participant-observation with the personal status of a volunteer, and findings to be reported so as to ensure anonymity and confidentiality. In accordance with the research principles set out in Part I, the research aims were approved by hosts as consistent with their own concerns, and findings were discussed with them, so that they might consider further action.

The residents and staff who contributed to the research had neither the capacity nor time to record formal interviews, as had been planned, but full notes were made of all the talks and events which fully filled the participant role that also included helping patients with feeding, toiletry and other activities of daily living.

The research observations were also based on what Andrews called the *verstehen* approach (1991:45), which consists of placing oneself as much as possible in the position of people from whom one is learning, and discovering their experiences and responses to life's conflicts. Her book, *Lifetimes of Commitment* (1991), introduces her own research difficulties in interviewing older public figures, although she solved them more successfully than was done in this present study.

Before considering the research sites, workers and residents in detail, it will be helpful to describe the specific social context in California that contributed to the environment of the studies when these were made.

The Californian climate of conflict and negotiation and its effect on long term care

The *San Francisco Chronicle, Contra Costa Times* and the national daily press, during the research period in June and July 1993, contained hot and cold comments on the structural crisis and conflicts within the current budgets.

The national Health Care Reform Task Force, headed by Hillary Rodham Clinton and a team of 400 advisers, aimed to reconcile universal access and cost containment in the American health system. Yet the federal deficit budget of $500 billion had to be reduced by a third. The Californian State Governor faced a $2.7 billion deficit, and that of the San Francisco Mayor was $184 millions.

The daily press reflected the icy contributions by medical and pharmaceutical hierarchies seeking to safeguard salaries and supplies, and the heated correspondence of old people and the poor who were afraid of projected cuts in services. The Clinton administration sought cuts of $8.4 billions in Medicaid, whilst Medi-Cal was to be reduced by $44 millions.

There was public pressure to follow Canada's 20-year national health insurance plan which covers everyone from birth to long term care, in which each Province negotiates its own payment system. However Clinton said that negotiations about American long term care insurance must wait until the end of the century. Californian State benefits to the old, blind and disabled were to be reduced by 2.7 per cent while inflation rose. San Francisco City Council proposed closing the day centre and rehabilitation units of their public hospital for old people.

The ensuing local conflict led to two City Hall public meetings during the research period, where angry elders, bused in with wheelchairs from the hospital, protested their rights, and said that any closure would be a form of collective elder abuse.

The hospital activity therapist who arranged the lobbying saw national, State and local political conflict as a direct cause of the conflicts within the hospital about the use of scarce resources:

> Closing our units would be a form of structural abuse. All the political emphasis on 'managed *competition*' in health and elder care leads to an *adversarial* atmosphere and residents suffer. I spend a lot of my time mediating between them in their troubles – and try to problem-solve when they are having difficulties with staff ... not to mention seeing if I can help to reconcile the staff

themselves when crises develop. We could do with some proper mediation in this vast hospital or some of us workers could benefit from mediation training. But there is no money for it. So we all get angry and don't know what to do with our anger. And we all get anxious and don't know what to do with our anxiety. We workers mustn't turn it on to the old people, and they, poor dears, haven't got any easy way of getting rid of their own anger and anxiety. It's not fair. The politicians are all rich – Californian Senators are millionaires! – and all of us in long term care work are poor ... except the doctors and the nursing home owners!

In order to cool the atmosphere the Mayor said that he would try to negotiate some more acceptable solution to the unresolved situation. An analysis of this suggested that the extreme disparity between wealth and poverty in California has to be reduced by structural reform of the tax system. However there was no indication that negotiation between the rich and the poor was likely to take place, whilst California's economy was under threat.

In June 1993 California's unemployment rate rose to 9.1 per cent, the national rate then being 7 per cent (US Dept. of Labour; California Economic Development Dept.) This unemployment was set to increase by the 25,000 workers due to be made redundant through five military bases being closed in San Francisco, plus others in seven more bases in California. There would be consequent further manufacturing jobs lost in the technical and service supply industries. Environmentalist pressures were also causing a severe contraction in logging employment.

The conflict between employers, employees, the State and federal governments about this crisis led to conflicts between banks and their customers who had little credit. This was the situation of the owner of the nursing home threatened with closure, mentioned above. The director of the ombudsman services, trained in mediation, and asked by the owner to mediate in his case, pointed to the problem:

> Bill and his wife bought the nursing home with insufficient capital. They had to arrange a mortgage loan with the previous owner. Because Bill has been a good and compassionate owner, allowing residents to stay on when their Medi-Care is exhausted, and giving them the same services on Medi-Cal, he makes little profit. He enjoys developing creative activities for his residents and he took the NIDR mediation course and was very enthusiastic about this. He is keen on encouraging resident independence and participation in everything, and CANHR think highly of his work. But he is not

a good business man. His roof is in bad shape. He knew this, but said that it never rained in California. Unfortunately for him, we have just had the worst downpour of the century! The rain poured through the roof of a resident's room – and she got pneumonia and died. The Licensing Authority (quite apart from their consideration of bringing in the police and a charge of manslaughter) have threatened to close the nursing home within ten days if he does not get the roof repaired. That has caused another conflict for him – the roofers say the *whole* roof must be done (and so does the Licensing Authority) and that will cost thousands of dollars, which he does not have! Worst of all – the banks have turned cold on him and won't lend money to him. Now I have just heard that the previous owner for economic reasons has decided to foreclose on the mortgage and take Bill to court if he doesn't settle outstanding amounts within a set time.

The ombudsman knew that Bill ran a happy nursing home, and that the residents could have heated arguments with the Licensing Authorities if they were evicted with him, so she was considering whether she could mediate informally with all the parties involved. It should be noted that Bill asked the ombudsman to mediate rather than turning to one of the professional associations of the nursing home industry for advice, financial assistance and support.

The American Health Care Association (AHCA) is a trade group of 11,000 for-profit long term care facilities with more than one million residents. There are also other associations. Some members belong to powerful chain groups with heavy financial investments to protect, but with less interest in providing protection for poorer members. In any business based on competition, co-operation tends to be a secondary concern.

However one association requested that all its members should be trained in mediation, and approached the University of California academic involved in the National Institute of Dispute Resolution (NIDR) State senior mediation project. As an elder and radical activist working on the Berkely campus, she responded to a research question as to whether a trade association might misuse mediation in dealing with member and customer complaints, saying she was aware of the danger:

> But the incentive in teaching mediation to such an important group is that it gives us the opportunity to put over the powerful values and message of mediation – values of justice and democracy, and the message that conflict must be fairly confronted, and that the

parties involved should have equal rights in presenting their cases, and reach their own decisions about any agreements. It is also very important that owners realise that if they use mediation properly and ethically at early stages of conflict, then complaints won't escalate, and abuse is less likely. Also, if owners are trained in mediation, they might eventually have their staff trained, and they would certainly be more sympathetic to ombudsmen offering to mediate. This could change nursing home culture. We found in evaluating the NIDR project that, even though nursing homes could seldom set up formal mediations, informal conciliatory approaches to problems created a much more open, responsible and responsive atmosphere between residents and staff.

However there is another aspect to industrial conflict in long term care in California. The Service Employees International Union (AFL-CIO) has 13,000 members in San Francisco who won a new contract at the time of the hospital closure crisis. They were hotly criticized for raising hospital costs necessitating closures. So they issued leaflets at an information booth in the hospital public corridor, protesting that some departments had one supervisor to four workers, and that 65 per cent of the City's new appointments had been in high-pay jobs, whilst too many low-paid workers were classed as temporary. When questioned about the value of mediation in such industrial conflicts, a union member coolly replied that he preferred it to arbitration or strikes.

The more complex question about temporary workers is best addressed by turning from structural to cultural conflicts. However this analysis of structural conflicts has shown clearly that they contribute to perceived and actual elder abuse, as in the case of hospital closures and the resident who died from pneumonia under a leaking roof.

The tolerant and permissive culture of San Francisco with regard to its sexual minorities and predominant non-Caucasian ethnic communities is also reflected in California's white heartland. In all the research areas these cultural groups were proportionately represented amongst residents and staff, although not amongst owners of nursing homes.

There was conflict about this. In the public hospital, there appeared to be more upward mobility for African Americans, two senior administrative appointments having been given to them. In only one out of over ten nursing homes visited was a black manager seen, and he was leaving when new Asian American owners arrived. The ombudsman co-ordinator gave her view:

African Americans don't like the increasing number of Asians coming into the market. These generally have better business skills. They also employ a lot of Filipinos at very low wages. These people are often small and tend to push around our large American white residents when caring for them. There are lots of complaints about this, and allegations of abuse. When is 'firm handling' abuse? Also there is a language problem with many Asians. At the moment there is a conflict going on with the Licensing Authority as to whether it is an abuse of residents' rights for staff to speak to one another in their own language which residents can't understand, and suspect this includes verbal abuse of them. The Asians deny this. The owners won't pay for them to have training. I try to mediate and cool things down in nursing homes when things get heated.

The primary cause of the cultural conflict in California is the racial problem of immigrants, 20 per cent of whom are illegal. The State's population growth rate of 2.2 per cent each year, compares with the national rate of 0.8 per cent, and is equal to that of many developing countries, the Egyptian percentage being 2.9. The Californian population is estimated to double to 63 million by 2040, the Hispanic birthrate being the highest at 3.9 births per mother, with the great majority of illegal entrants coming from Mexico. There is national conflict over negotiating trade with Mexico to improve their economic situation and thus the immigrant inflow to California, but the State fears that its manufacturing companies will emigrate to sources of cheap labour, causing more local unemployment.

This affects the nursing home industry which also relies on cheap Hispanic labour, adding to the interracial conflicts which ombudsmen try to mediate.

Another aspect of cultural conflict lies in public and professional attitudes to medical ethics debates about Advanced Directives and elder mental incapacity. This has already been discussed in detail in Part I, but a reference to the Californian context came from the medical director of a hospital visited:

We have a medical ethics committee here and I am very interested in the new proposals for using mediation in this area of elder care. But there would have to be legislation in California to permit this, and anyway there would be no funding available to develop a demonstration project. I cannot even find the funds to develop my own interests in using volunteers as surrogates in decision-making

109

for mentally incapacitated elders – that would require legislation too. These are all heated issues.

Frosty relations between professional groups were observed in the study. At one Elder Abuse Coalition meeting the adult protective service (APS) worker complained at the lack of support from doctors, police, social workers and others:

> I have to *respond* to all referrals of elder abuse but, under Californian law, I have no *power* to be effective. I cannot remove people against their will. I cannot force victims or offenders to change their lifestyles if they're on drink or drugs. I cannot pressurise old people to go into hospital or nursing homes. Others have the power, but don't use it – geriatric services and the Public Guardian. I asked them to come to this meeting so we could debate the matter coolly, but no-one has come.

A research presentation on mediation at that meeting attracted comments from the police, social and medical social workers that they all used mediation informally in senior conflict situations. But they had different institutional responses when violence and crimes were alleged or caused, and there was institutional conflict about responsibilities for these. How could this be mediated?

The role of the law was also being hotly debated as an effective institution, even in dealing with class actions against nursing homes accused of elder abuse. In one case there was doubt about a criminal prosecution succeeding, so that State civil action was taken. The case was taken up by the district attorney in 1976, filed in 1978 and was not concluded successfully until 1984, after costly delays caused by constitutional and legal appeals by the defence. During this period, the nursing home's substandard care continued to the detriment of residents.

The medical profession was also subject to heated criticism for its institutional response to elder care, especially through its management by drug prescriptions. One hospital resident complained angrily:

> I suffered terribly from rheumatic arthritis. When the doctor visited me at home *all he did* was to prescribe expensive brand drugs. In the end I had no money left, so I had to be admitted to this public hospital. They gave me physio and activity therapy, and a special diet and reduced all the drugs, and I now feel better than I have for years. That doctor was *abusing* me, medically and financially!

110

A national research study on medical bills shows that doctors overcharged patients by $45.7 millions between August and December 1992 (*AARP Bulletin*, June 1993, 34/6:1–14). However medical and pharmaceutical institutions have powerful financial defenders in the current conflict affecting elder rights. A new federal bill, S514, being hotly debated, would give elders and others the right to be reimbursed from detected overcharges.

It is significant that these two institutions have made relatively little contribution to social concern and action about elder abuse. It has also been shown in this section that structural, cultural and institutional conflict have contributed to the general factors which can lead to elder abuse, although it must be said that many nursing home staff and professional workers have developed constructive ways of preventing this. Mediation is one of these.

In concluding this section, it is suggested that mediation has begun to address the problem in a climate of uncertainty, which, like that of San Francisco, can be very cold, foggy, windy or hot, all on the same day. In the next section mediation is examined in the context of the visits to the research sites.

Long term mediation in California

In this section the original NIDR senior mediation project from 1988 to 1991 will be briefly described. Its impact on a county ombudsman service, an Oakland nursing home and a San Francisco public hospital will then be analysed. In conclusion its relation to community services concerned with elder rights will be discussed.

The project was located in two areas, Georgia and four San Francisco Bay counties. The reasons for the initiative are explored in the chapter on the Justice Center of Atlanta, and will not be repeated here.

In California CANHR was the principal organization involved, together with the area's ombudsmen. Constraints on funds and time resulted in ten nursing homes participating, representing a variety of types. So it was hoped that the demonstration project would have State-wide influence.

In size the nursing homes had between 26 and 400 beds. Four were non-union. Six were partly or entirely unionized. Two were non-profit. Seven were commercial, three belonging to large chains. One was owned and managed by a county.

In 1989 40 people attended an initial three-day training in communication and mediation skills. They included members of nursing home staff, administrators, ombudsmen and volunteer ombudsmen. Certification was provided. In 1990 a further cycle of training began, designed to train trainers, with five one-day modules on intercultural issues, conflict resolution, negotiation, mediation and multi-party mediation. Only 25 people attended. This resulted in future training being developed at only seven sites, in four ombudsmen services and three nursing homes.

In 1992 an evaluation was published by NIDR based on the ongoing research which had been built into the project. This clearly showed the successes and failures of the project, but was convinced of the benefits of mediation in nursing home conflicts (Hanawi and Goodman, 1992).

A main problem was the constant changeover of staff, a recurring difficulty in nursing homes. Administrators were not invested in sending staff for mediation training, although those that moved on took their skills to other nursing homes where they might or might not be welcomed.

This linked with another problem: the willingness of nursing home management to become involved in a project which they had not designed. The evaluation recommended that when a further initiative took place, the nursing homes should be invited from its inception to 'own their project' and plan the training, using exercises and role-plays based on the actual situational conflicts they experienced in their work.

However the greatest problem was that formally conducted mediation sessions were generally experienced as being inappropriate to the resolution of the actual conflicts that arose amidst the activities of daily living in nursing homes. Mediation was needed most when interpersonal crises threatened, when problem-solving was urgent, and when the decision-making rights of elders – and of staff – had to be considered immediately.

The evaluation found that the training:

> failed to create the broad understandings and mediative consciousness that are needed to change a conflict culture ... essentially a re-acculturation from a confrontive to a mediative approach to conflict (Hanawi and Goodman, 1992:19, 21).

Although their report included many references to individual cases which had benefited from mediation, Hanawi and Goodman found that these were because:

participants in the project, trained at the start in a particular and formal model of mediation, gradually developed an array of mediative interventions to use in various situations (1992:30).

Hanawi, in conversation, was critical of the NIDR project, but amplified her belief in elder mediation by saying that nursing homes institutionalize a closed conflict culture. Any approach which encourages elders to participate in opening decision-making processes adds to their quality of life. Mediation also provides a setting for acknowledging feelings, for increasing mutual understanding, for apologies and reconciliation. It gives people the chance of non-destructive, non-injurious peaceful change and development. It helps people to communicate and learn about values. Above all it helps people to respect relationships and avoid harming them. A mediative consciousness and a mediative approach is essential if nursing home culture is to be reformed.

As Hanawi co-directs with Goodman an ADR program at the University of California, she was interested to hear of Roberts' (1986) work at LSE on mediation as a form of minimal intervention. She felt that this was consistent with the evaluation findings that the principles of mediation are best served in the nursing home context by facilitating communication and negotiation between the parties as simply and directly as possible, and avoiding processes of maximum intervention.

Hanawi was familiar with the work of Felstiner et al (1980) on naming, blaming and claiming in the transformation of disputes, and considered it a useful concept in analysing nursing home conflicts, especially where abuse was alleged. It was important to identify grievances openly, to assess responsibility for them (through mediation where possible), and see that any rightful claims for apology or reparation were made.

These views have been dealt with in depth because they reflect the consensus of opinions expressed by the workers at the research sites, and colleagues associated with them.

The work of the county ombudsman service

The service chosen for the study was one where its director had taken the NIDR training, and now continuously trained her own volunteer ombudsmen in mediation. This was at their request, and in addition to their ombudsman training, which initially took 40 hours over six weeks, plus periodic supplementary trainings and annual re-certification.

During the week spent 'shadowing' them in their work, visits were made to six nursing homes, a meeting of a local Elder Abuse Coalition, an Alzheimer's Support Group evening, a seniors' life history group evening, and a supper visit to the home of an elderly ombudsman volunteer.

In addition, office work included reading the documentation on one month's complaints, 400 in number, the general average, observing the ombudsmen dealing with incoming telephone calls, relatives and colleagues, plus their report writing, and discussing their activities with them.

The ombudsman director gave an overview of this:

> We all have too much work to do. We suffer from burn-out. My other professional ombudsman here has a broken marriage as a result. I haven't had a holiday for two years. I come in on Sunday (unpaid) to clear the decks for the coming week, and cope with all the heavy paperwork for the State ombudsman and the Licensing Authority. But I love the work. I love standing up for old people when they have been wrongly treated. I enjoy doing on-the-spot mediating between quarrelsome residents. And it's a challenge when I report elder abuse and become involved in the outcome. Having many roles is part of the fun of the work. But I am over 60 and get very tired ... at least I'm able to locate the best nursing home for *myself*, which I shall need soon!

A visit was made to this home which was the only one in the county which had no deficiencies or violations recorded against it, and in which its owner-manager and nursing director, both elders, had never received any complaints during their long professional careers. The home was a skilled nursing facility with 42 beds, and most of its culturally mixed residents were poor and received Medi-Cal. It had an anti-segregation policy for its Alzheimer's and senile residents, and provided as many activities as possible for everyone. The residents looked happy and were on first name terms with the owner and his staff who were constantly in and out of the community rooms. Yet the material conditions of the nursing home were not good. There was no wall-to-wall carpeting, and some rooms had three beds in them.

In contrast, another skilled nursing facility visited, which had just been purpose-built as a national and State model of good standards, had 120 beds with family suites, single and a few double rooms which were expensively gilt-decorated. Chandeliers, a white grand piano and marble-topped dining tables graced the common rooms, which included a library and visitors' room. The home was commercially owned, and administered by a business manager who had just installed a vast computer system in her office. There were no Medi-Cal residents, and although there were full activity programs scheduled, and many choices on meal menus, the mainly white residents appeared socially reserved or withdrawn, depending on whether this was interpreted as due to their personal status, or to luxurious institutionalization. This nursing home had not participated in the mediation project, and the business manager said their residents had no complaints.

A visit to another home with 99 beds and a mixed population led to a typical ombudsman intervention:

> A relative had complained to the ombudsman about an injury to her husband, who was found with a gashed, stitched and bandaged face. The ombudsman firstly sympathized with the man, and listened to his story of another resident's attack. She asked him if she might photo the injury, and she was given his permission to name the alleged culprit, in reporting the incident to her State office and the Licensing Authority. She then spoke to the administrator, blaming him for not having called her immediately, but learned that the victim had provoked the attack by aggressive insults. The offender had been made angry, but now regretted his actions. The ombudsman then tried to make peace between the two residents, but the victim claimed that the offender was partly senile, and often acted violently. The nursing director agreed. The ombudsman blamed her for not having set up a policy to avert such violence, but was told that their efforts had failed, and that they were not allowed to sedate the man. After much discussion it was decided that the ombudsman should mediate with the offender and his relatives and reach an agreement about transferring him to a home with a closed Alzheimer's unit. This could prevent further abuse, and also the need for criminalization, if the victim and police agreed, as was expected, that charges should not be made.

At the local Elder Abuse Coalition, where a brief research presentation was made, the police member said that he felt uniformed officers should play a visible protective role in the naming, blaming and claiming process, especially when fraud was alleged:

> Fraud is one of the most common nursing home forms of elder abuse, as it is in families, and San Francisco City and County Police have a special unit investigating this. When fraud is suspected,

the police should be called at once, and the incident exposed, investigated and claims for reimbursement made. In order to hear all sides of the question, the police generally have to use mediating skills, but when firm evidence of crimes are found, the police have to consider prosecuting offenders. If they are mentally incapacitated or emotionally disordered, there are problems for us all.

The ombudsman spoke about the way in which she tried to *prevent* financial abuse:

> When residents or staff complain to me about relatives not paying fees out of the benefits they administer, I then write to the relatives saying that I know about the situation, and that they are being blamed for it. I offer any problem-solving that may be needed, but firmly *inform* them of their legal and criminal liability to meet the claims. My letters often produce immediate cheques in settlement! Early confrontation is a good remedy!

The visit to the Alzheimer's support group meeting took place in a nursing home with 200 beds and a closed unit. The staff member responsible for its social services, and an elderly member of the Alzheimer's Society, was on that occasion welcoming a new relative. He movingly described his past and present conflicts with his wife and family:

> We were childhood sweethearts and have had a wonderfully long and happy marriage. But then she started to wander and became violent when I tried to discuss the dangers. Life has gradually become hell and I am exhausted. There is constant conflict outside me, and constant conflict inside me as I feel so guilty about putting her away. I still love her so much. My children are bitterly divided too. They can't provide effective help, but my daughter won't speak to me since I've made plans to admit her here.

The man was encouraged to speak as long as he wanted about the family suffering, and then other relatives assured him that they had had similar experiences, but had been gradually relieved as their loved ones seemed to stabilize in a residential community setting adapted to their needs. The elder ombudsman volunteer, who regularly attended the group as part of her work at the home, said that mediation between family members might help the children express their pain openly and reach helpful agreements about visiting their mother. She added that it would be difficult to include the resident because of her fluctuating mental capacity, but that as a trained mediator herself, she thought that a mediative approach might heal the family conflict.

It could be observed here that in severe illnesses, processes of naming, blaming and claiming are inappropriate, and that conciliatory rather than confrontational approaches to relatives, residents *and* staff are best. It was noted during the study that staff appear to be trained increasingly not to label their residents as having Alzheimer's or any other disease. However, this causes conflict with some relatives for whom such medical labels provide a hope of cure, and an acceptable diagnostic status to stop local gossip. If mediation is possible in restricted instances, it would certainly have to be a minimal form of intervention.

The visit to an 84 year-old life historian resulted in an unexpected and hilarious potluck supper with other octogenarians and an evening swimming party. People spoke about their own healthy, happy and active lives with loving families where there had always been mutual help. Their descriptions reflected the findings of Wenger in her study *Help in Old Age* (1992). Interest in the research study was keen, people recognising experiences of naming, blaming and claiming in their own lives when dealing with conflict. They felt that they had often unconsciously or consciously mediated in family and neighbourhood life, but that it had been *very* informal and *very* minimal! But they knew their rights and would always call their lawyers or the police if these were breached!

A more serious supper visit to the home of an elder ombudsman volunteer aged 82, now a widow, produced her experiences of mediation:

> I had a father who I dearly loved, as did my mother, his fourth wife after the three previous ones (all sisters) had died of TB. Though we were very poor, we never *felt* poor. My parents taught me courage and to stand up for justice. I remember a serious conflict with a Minister's wife, but I stood up for the truth quietly, and eventually became the Sunday School Supervisor in my teens. Then I became a teacher ... and my mediation work started and lasted for 34 years! I was always dealing with disputes between students, their parents and other staff! (My husband was a teacher, as is my daughter.) I became interested in this approach and started counselling, especially crisis counselling ... mediation wasn't talked about in those early days ... After I retired I became an ombudsman volunteer, and later jumped at the chance of doing *proper* mediation training! But there is never the *time* to arrange anything formally. You just have to respond spontaneously and appropriately to conflicts

when they occur ... I personally don't find any conflict between my roles of advocacy, investigation, mediation and the rest ... I seem to move into whichever mode is needed naturally, and generally unconsciously. I found the training very helpful in that it sharpened my old skills for the new context, but I think that if we were required to set up *formal* mediation sessions it would be very inhibiting for everyone in nursing homes. I do a lot of shuttle diplomacy amongst relatives, especially if their loved ones are senile. But I also make a lot of complaints!

A analysis of the 400 complaints records was impossible because the information was incomplete. Ombudsmen said they often could not find the time to write up whether complaints were substantiated and how conflicts were resolved. They drew attention to types of sex abuse that they had not seen discussed in the literature, for which mediation and counselling appeared to be the most sensitive processes of prevention, whilst criminalization was the least appropriate.

In these cases husbands used daily visits to their wives for forced intercourse with them; in one instance the resident had intragastrinal tubing in place. Husbands, also often mentally confused, argued that they wanted to give comfort and love to their wives, and that they knew touching was encouraged. Wives were fearful of losing visits and affection, but hated regular interference when they were bedridden. The unoriginal comment was made that as some men aged, their sexual capacity increased in proportion to the decrease of their mental capacity.

Amongst the professional visitors to the ombudsman office was a retired accountant ready to set up a representative payee scheme there which would be especially valuable for the residents of the numerous adult care homes. Ombudsmen seldom had time to visit these unless a grave complaint about abuse was received.

Another visitor was the director of the local community Conflict Resolution Panels, who had senior mediators and trainers, and who had heard about this research study. As a result of discussions, including reference to the principles of participatory research on which the study has been based, it was suggested that future co-operation between the two agencies would be beneficial. A community senior mediator volunteer might play a useful role in nursing home conflicts, when the ombudsman's main task was to act as advocate.

A concluding analysis suggests that mediative interventions were constantly made, but not formally. Participant-observation noted that the telephone hot-line for crisis reporting was always in use, and that there was a constant flow of people in and out of a very small office. All the ombudsmen were friendly, and gave undivided attention to each person's questions, including those of the researcher. Their overwork was sustained by their humour. Their noticeboard, filled with photos, had a large printed card with popular mispronunciations of their name: OMBUDSMAN – ONBOSOM OR AMBUSHMAN? The study suggests that nursing home residents and abusers symbolically experience ombudsmen in both roles.

The Oakland nursing home

Mrs S, the elderly owner of this 38-bed skilled nursing facility, gave a brief account of its history and her present aims:

> In 1983 the previous owners brought me in as director of nursing services to do a clean-up job. I found 30 residents had decubitus ulcers! The owners wanted out, I liked the place, and the residents liked me. The daughter of one of them offered to lend me $40,000 to buy the place. I did. In 1984 I moved into management with my son, John, and his wife, a registered nurse. I have 32 staff to just under 38 residents. I run this place as *their* home. They are free to go wherever they like inside. No-one is labelled. There is no segregation unit. I don't use restraints or over-medication. People with Alzheimer's and other conditions share all activities and meals with the others. Most of the residents are on Medi-Cal, and I never move them when their Medi-care has run out. I aim to keep an open door, a keen eye and close ear for anyone with a problem, resident, relative or staff. I invite everyone to talk it out freely and I stamp immediately on any abuse that I find. Staff are immediately sacked, even for a minor theft. I encourage the independence of residents wherever possible, but most of them are confused, and many of them are senile ... ideas about decision-making and mediation are *nonsense!*

Mrs S, a practical and pragmatic person of great experience in elder care, and with firm values about freedom and good standards, thought that her residents' potential for participation was strictly limited. She said that most of them had become passive and dependant before arrival at the home, and that although she employed a full-time activity therapist, their conditions were not reversible.

At the time of the visit a Californian State Bill was passed giving doctors the power to make treatment decisions for incapacitated patients

119

who had no surrogates. Mrs S supported that Bill (as did the public hospital medical director), although CANHR had mounted a public campaign against it, and a later judicial decision threatened to negate it. Mrs S said that she could never persuade relatives to make decisions for her senile residents, and that they were too poor to go through the expensive process of applying for Conservatorship or Enduring Powers of Attorney.

She was also critical of ombudsmen. She had a good record of no violations (a later research check verified this), so when two young ombudsmen inspected her home two years ago and objected to her policy of allowing smoking in an outside patio, she told them they would not be welcomed again, and no visits have been made since.

Yet her son had been recommended by CANHR as a manager who had done the NIDR mediation training. He gave his views:

> We are not able to carry on all the formal aspects of mediation in this place. But we practice all its values as far as possible. We're very keen on as much freedom for people as possible. And we insist on each person being treated with respect. We encourage them to dress smartly and groom themselves well. Our staff and nurses don't wear uniform so that residents feel this is a homely community. We all use first names. We try to approach everything in a problem-solving way. And we have a great activity therapist, K, who is a born mediator even though she had no training in it.

K fulfilled his description. She was a young academic with vocational training, devoted to the residents, each of whom she knew intimately. Although she was a Mormon she gave no special attention to Mormon or any other residents. She gave much free time, and on Independence Day, during the research visit, came in to help the residents make ice-cream. They said they loved her.

The residents brought all their non-physical care problems to her. It was typical of her responses to situations to ask all those involved in them if they would give her permission to intervene. She always checked with the nursing director if she might act.

In one incident of a recurring pattern a resident complained that her glasses had been stolen and she named the culprit with silent mouthing. The alleged thief was an old prostitute with criminal convictions, although this was never referred to in the home, who was now quite senile. K listened to the complainant, comforted her distress, and promised immediate action. In a conciliatory way she reminded her that people were forgetful, as she was herself, and that perhaps someone had found

120

her glasses and put them elsewhere for safe keeping. Perhaps no-one was to blame. A search was made and the glasses were reclaimed, although their location was not disclosed.

K had what she called a conciliatory approach to all the issues involved in her work. She began each day (as did this researcher) by talking with every resident individually, asking them how they were and whether they had any problems, and responding to any invitations for handshakes or kisses. An analysis of her work is best evidenced in a transcript of extracts from her Daily Newspaper session, the dotted lines indicating spaces for residents' participation:

> Good morning everybody! ... What do you think of the weather today? ... *The Oakland Tribune* says that the President is going to cut senior pensions: what do you think about that? ... Do you think the government ought to give more money to the schools as our State governor says? ... B, are you having trouble with your wheelchair? ... Would you like me to fix it for you? ... The paper says there is more violence today: has anyone an opinion on this? ... *My* opinion? Well, I think that there are different kinds of violence. Some people start trouble. Then others try to defend themselves. I believe in peacemaking. M, instead of standing there, would you like to join us in our discussions? ... Here is an news item about too much sex on TV: do you agree? ... That is an interesting view, B ... Thank you for that statement of values, R ... You always stand up for the under-dog, don't you, J! ... *My* view? Well, everyone has different labels for sex. Films can be seen as funny, loving, naughty or evil, depending on your perspective. If you want to go to the rest room, J, I'll get the nurse for you ...

This account shows how K made every stage of her work an opportunity for giving attention to residents' needs for individual validation. She encouraged their decision-making and participation in issues affecting their lives, as far as their physical and mental capacities allowed. Her approach, similarly adopted by most of the nursing staff, was a creative influence pervading the home.

One resident, with repetitive speech, would continually say 'This place is only as good as I am'. Another would incessantly repeat: 'It could happen to anyone ... it can't be bad'. An elder with Alzheimer's disease had views on the causes of conflict:

You can't put what's in your heart into someone else's heart … God gives everyone a different heart and puts different things in each person's heart.

S was a retired teacher, and was still able to enjoy reading. Her philosophy was that each stage of life has its own meaning, and that it is often painful discovering what that is, especially at the end of life. She suffered from sharing a room with her sister, also a teacher, but who shouted and wandered freely during the night, as no restraints were used.

No residents wished to leave the home and none complained of neglect or abuse. The relatives met were all appreciative. Although only a 'mediative consciousness' prevailed, an opportunity came during the study for a research study 'mediative intervention' (Hanawi and Goodman, 1992) to be made.

A resident had died. The strapped blue plastic body box was quickly wheeled out through the residents crowded in the lobby where they enjoyed gathering to watch the outside world and talking to the nurses at their station. The residents were visibly distressed.

A research inquiry was then personally made to Mrs S asking for her view of the situation. She was ready to name the problem but said that no-one was to blame as there were two conflicting issues. The first was that she would never interfere with residents' rights to go where they wanted in public spaces. The second was that if she moved them all away, this would negatively reinforce their fears of death, and upset relatives. Having affirmed Mrs S's sensitivity to these points, information was given about hospice practice in the UK whereby a simple but beautiful cloth is draped over the body box before removal, and that where possible it is escorted by a senior member of staff to show respect. This has a symbolic value of reassurance to watching residents that their death will be accorded a similar dignified status passage. Other options were raised, but Mrs S liked the first one, and agreed to accept a gift (in appreciation of the research visit) to choose her own cloth. A subsequent suggestion was made that she might invite her Residents' Council to consider whether they might wish, collectively or individually, to participate, or not, in observing their friends' final departing in some way.

The importance of mediating *issues* was raised more consistently during the hospital visit.

Mediation considered in a large public hospital

The old hospital had been imaginatively renovated to cope with increasing numbers of old people and dependant adults with mental and physical disabilities. The long corridors and large wards were brightly painted and curtained, decked with original paintings, live plants and flowers, filled with comfortable settees, chairs with cushions and tables with magazines and books. The conflict between hygiene and homeliness had been solved by allowing untidiness despite constant cleaning.

Yet some of the deficiencies named by the Licensing Authority in its previous survey related to chipped paint, cigarette ends behind radiators, and cans with moisture on them in the dry foods storage room. The survey had spaces for the hospital to identify who was to blame for deficiencies or contest them, and further ones for them to state what corrections would be made. The survey had to be available for public inspection in the hospital. So this process might be interpreted as a valuable variation on the theme of Felstiner et al (1980) with regard to the satisfactory transformation of institutional complaints.

Other conflicts were less easy to solve. The recent survey had blamed the hospital for allowing a resident to walk around in the corridors, where he fell to his death down the stairs. The medical director, who strove hard to remove the asylum image of the hospital by focusing on its rehabilitation work, now included in its title, explained the issues:

> I want to humanise the hospital. I want to promote people's autonomy, independence and freedom. I want residents to use the hospital as their home and enjoy walking around it. We have a policy of avoiding physical and chemical restraints. This means that we must have some locked wards otherwise fatal accidents happen. There is a conflict in this vast place between safety and liberty for our mentally incapacitated residents. It is a terrible responsibility making decisions about these issues. We try to do this through regular assessment by multidisciplinary teams, and to bring in relatives to discussions. I can see that mediation could here be a relevant skill and process.

It was the medical social workers who said they would find training in mediation useful, and it was they more than doctors and nurses who came to the research lecture on Elder Mediation, Elder Rights and Elder Abuse, and later discussed their casework problems and professional conflicts. The following points were made:

It is our job to find relatives and encourage them to play a role in decision-making about their residents when necessary. But we can spend months trying to trace them, writing letters and making appointments only to find that they don't want the responsibility, and can't afford to arrange for Enduring Powers of Attorney. Or we get them together for what might be called a mediation, and we can't get them to reach any agreement. If they do, there is often a change of mind. The issue becomes unresolvable, so the doctors make the decisions. This hospital is run on the medical hierarchy model. The Social Services Department was one of the last to be developed, and we are not accorded equal status with the medical and nursing teams. We are short of staff and there are constant conflicts about increasing our resources. Our views are often regarded as the least important in resident assessments. Even in situations where residents want counselling, the nurses are encouraged to do this ... we can see that the nurses benefit by enlarging their experience and that they are immediately available day and night when help is needed, but they are not trained as we are in formal counselling.

Here the medical social workers showed the professional concern for set standards and processes that some professional mediators feel about senior mediation developing as a 'mediative intervention' (Hanawi and Goodman, 1992), without formal rules. In conversation, Hanawi commented that they had been in dispute with NIDR which had not wanted to publish their critical evaluation of the demonstration project.

The hospital ombudsman, an older mediator, held conciliatory views as should be expected:

I was a business man, and after I retired I took training as an arbitrator in which I got a lot of experience. I also took the NIDR mediation training which was very extensive. So I know the value of formal set-ups and processes. But life in hospital just doesn't lend itself to them. Although I come in two whole days a week to visit residents and check if they have any complaints, I find they want them dealt with on the spot. Of course I report anything that can be named as abuse or neglect, although generally this has already been raised with the ward manager. With minor complaints I start a kind of shuttle diplomacy around all the people involved and try to get people listening and talking to each other. Often an explanation and apology is all that is needed ... an apology from hospital staff heals the blaming mood more than anything.

The ombudsman had lifelong experience of helping people to negotiate together, so the concept of mediation as a form of minimal intervention seems consistent with the way in which he adapted his training to meet the realities of hospital life.

V, a senior resident, was the grand-daughter of a plantation slave, and for 17 years had been paralysed from the armpits down:

> We were a large happy family and my parents brought us up always to sit down and talk things out when there was trouble. But I married a man who started to gamble and drink, and there was no talking with him! He just went off! And when my sister had a row with her boyfriend and I tried to help them settle it, he shot me! So I became paralysed. But I am a Southern Baptist and I know that although I had to suffer, there was no point in making a misery of it for others. So I got the family together to sit down and talk about it. My mother – who I had looked after earlier – was also becoming bedridden, and I could see that my sister couldn't look after us both. Then I got diabetes and had to come into hospital, and later we all agreed it would be best if I stayed here. I like the place. It's got purpose. It goes in for problem-solving.

V went on to say that she had become a volunteer and helped to organize committees and outside visits because she was good at getting people together. She was interested in talking about mediation, and said that peacemaking was her 'way of life', and that of the hospital too.

However the previous survey had listed deficiencies about the way in which the hospital had failed to listen to grievances, or indicate in medical records schedules for the progressive removal of necessary restraints. It was stated that in 17 out of 17 care plans studied, it was seen that multidisciplinary assessments were not systematically done. The hospital's written responses had been to blame lack of funding for adequate staff and resources for their 1300 residents, but, as required by regulations, included plans for correction.

There had not been a full correction of the failure to have survey results publicly displayed. A research inquiry found the entrance lobby copy on an interior office high shelf, and the second one on the fifth floor in an alcove outside the nursing director's office.

The 1993 survey was being conducted during the week of the research visit. Notices were displayed throughout the hospital inviting anyone, residents, staff, relatives or public to consult privately with the surveyors, and, on one day, an open meeting was arranged for general discussion. The medical director would not grant a research request for attendance at this meeting as an *observer*, although a later inquiry of the State licensing authority confirmed that this would have been in order, and welcomed by them.

An analysis of this situation, consistent with that of the nursing home, was that surveyors are putting increasing pressure on institutions to conform to higher standards at a time of financial depression, causing them continuous paperwork and staff adjustments, and concern that researchers report issues fairly. A State survey statistician later asserted that California had the most rigorously detailed survey system in America, and, consequently, the highest number of recorded deficiencies and violations, feeding the myth that it had the worst elder care and elder abuse.

No deliberate or accidental abuse or neglect of individual residents was observed in the research visits, and this might be expected from institutions which were open to receive them. Where standards needed raising, depleted energies and scarce funds fostered frustrated inaction.

This especially affected the possibility of an improved initiative in extending the use of mediation in such an institution, although all those consulted welcomed the idea, if it cost nothing and was appropriate to needs. It was consistent with the principles of participatory research to ask whether they might consider inviting in the services of community mediation services who had trained older volunteers. The response was favourable and networking contacts were given. Personal research meetings with these contacts were arranged so as to give them notice of possible inquiries.

Community meetings with multidisciplinary workers

The most relevant meeting was at the centre of the Community Boards which had, since 1976, established 83 community mediation sites in the city, and, in 1992, had developed 871 cases from 1379 intakes. It had 300 volunteers, one-third of them 'colored', and the director, herself an old person, had recently developed a senior mediation program:

> I welcome the possibility of co-operation with residential institutions … co-operation is another name for the Community Boards! We also often use 'conciliation' instead of 'mediation' which has been captured by some groups in an over-formalised and over-professionalized way. So I am sensitive to nursing homes not being able to cope with formal mediation set-ups. We are used to responding

quickly to emergencies on the streets of San Francisco! Also I agree that if our elder volunteers were welcomed, it would be a creative way of the community permeating institutional culture.

At other meetings issues already raised were further discussed. It was observed at the Probate Court that informal mediation played a hidden but constructive role in monitoring surrogate decision-making for incapacitated elders, and that research information was given about the hospital's needs to find ways of dealing with similar problems.

At CANHR the 1990 Americans With Disabilities Act (ADA) was discussed as it increased public focus on other impaired adults, and complaints were being currently filed at the rate of 2500 per month, taking two and a half years to clear. Through public pressure four mediation programs in major American cities had been started experimentally to bring speedier justice to people who were too disadvantaged to wait for the longer legal process. The future of these was uncertain because of funding problems, but they highlight issues about social remedies for complaints by adults with developmental disabilities.

CANHR's concern was that 41 national Fraud Control Units were to be cut, and that there would only be State, and no more federal surveys in California. Instead there was to be increased stress on giving people information about their rights, and encouraging them to make their own decisions about exercising them. Analysis suggests that this rhetoric subscribes superficially to current concepts about promoting personal autonomy and independence, and also affects critical attitudes to mediation.

Here it is important to stress that mediation services should not *displace* other ones, but only complement them, although unfortunately governments may seek manipulative changes using voluntary rather than statutory agencies to save costs, thus unfairly giving mediation a bad name.

As groups of vulnerable adults and their needs for dispute resolution expand, could mediation be misused? In California mediation has attracted radical activists who support improved access to the law and the promotion of rights. It is said that mediation is about *how* not *whether* to achieve these.

It has been shown that only a minimal form of mediation developed in long term care, although mediative approaches to conflicts proved valuable. There is also no evidence that the older mediators did other than support CANHR in its campaign for more effective regulations and implementation, although the bureaucratic paperwork was experienced as being oppressive. Mediation appeared to supplement regulation and the law usefully, although the practice of each needs improvement. Mediators were certainly keen to prevent elder abuse.

When reviewing changing concepts of elder abuse in California, it is worth noting that the early classic texts of Townsend (1957, 1964) on the experiences of old people, included descriptions of how they suffered, but never formally named this as 'elder abuse'.

In California, as in British Columbia, there are signs that the definitional borders are not rigid. In both areas police have developed elder abuse services from out of their experience of domestic violence, and elder abuse projects respond to inquiries from middle-aged women too. Whatever the age, police find it difficult to act on uncorroborated statements by people suffering from mental or substance-related incapacity.

In British Columbia the Seniors Advisory Council has suggested that naming elder abuse services like this may be socially construed as infantalizing elders in an ageist way. As British Columbia then had no elder abuse legislation, but only an increasing number of elder abuse services, this leaves a space in which mediation could make a contribution.

All the professional elder care and elder abuse workers contacted there during an earlier informal research visit indicated that they used mediation skills informally, but would value training, and perhaps special services. The Justice Institute had just been invited by a nursing home to train its *residents* in mediation, but wanted to establish whether this was a genuine decision by the Residents' Council, or a managerial ploy for reducing institutional complaints. Suggestions were offered as to how this query might be resolved constructively.

In California mandatory requirements to report, and powers to intervene in elder abuse are uncertainly applied, depending on local workers and their resources. In discussions with Elder Coalition workers they also said that they used mediating skills in situations of family and institutional conflict, and that this did not prevent them from taking any other measures to prevent or stop criminal acts, *when* these were legally and materially available. Here again, low funding meant that there were inadequate community support, respite and residential care resources to deal effectively with difficult problems.

In *A Shared Concern*, the Newsletter of the British Columbia Coalition on the Prevention of Elder Abuse and Neglect, a contributor suggests that interventions should 'avoid rescuing, be non-judgemental, help generate options', as the holistic approach means that 'abuse and other imbalances cannot be healed by attempting to heal isolated individuals apart from their family and community' (Spicer, 1993:8).

Rescuing may sometimes be essential, but the point being made is that in family conflict the rights of *all* parties have to be considered, and that they all have *responsibilities* as well as rights, although differing mental, physical and temperamental capacities modify these. The situation, and those involved in it, have to be assessed in developmental terms.

In this sense mediation is a developmental model, and not a rescue one. However it should not be used as an alternative to rescue action, when this is necessary.

Dukes, in Canada, goes on to argue that:

> in transformative practice the focus is upon the creation of sustainable relationships ... a sustainable democracy – a society not dependant upon dominance and coercion – cannot exist without a capacity for engaging different viewpoints, confronting difficult issues, and resolving difficult problems (1993:7).

Although Dukes is writing about public disputes, he is aware of violent and unequal power relations in general social conflict, and his views have special relevance to the stress in this chapter on the structural, cultural and institutional connections with elder abuse, and the effects on the development of elder mediation.

It has been public Californian consciousness of its social conflicts, and its history of devising reform innovations in elder care, which created the climate for the emergence of elder mediation. There has been a transformation of elder mediation as a model, as has been shown, but its impact has been beneficial, and not harmful to date.

In conclusion, the American and Californian social conflicts about financing elder care suggest that there are no present prospects for publicly funding further developments in senior mediation.

Yet there is continuous political, economic and industrial *negotiation*, public and between groups, to prevent hospital closures, and to improve elder care. The powerful Health Insurance Association of America spent $4 million on advertising in one month to publicize their plans for a new co-operative approach to structural problems.

The original NIDR mediation program has been shown to be over formalized for the needs of residential institutions. Any new initiative should be based on their planning and participation in its design and programming. However, there is evidence that the use of mediation skills is widespread and valued by many workers who would like further on-site training specific to their situations.

Future social policies with regard to American health and elder care and its financing are continuously debated in both Houses of Congress. The decisions taken in respect of ongoing social conflicts will determine the extent of planned reforms, especially in health insurance.

It is the consideration of the needs of increasing numbers of senior citizens in long term care which is causing most political and economic uncertainty. For these people are electors, with 'grey power' in America:

> where it has depended on mass pensioner movements (the American Association of Retired Persons had 30 million members in 1990), allied with the trade unions and a political system which gives a great deal of power to lobbyists (Wilson, 1993:3).

From consultations with American and Californian social policy planners, professionals and volunteer mediators concerned with elder care and the prevention of elder abuse, it seems that senior mediation is regarded as a valuable form of intervention. However it has no priority for public funding in the present American and Californian situation, although the government is financing pilot mediation schemes to work in the context of the Commission set up to enforce the 1990 ADA.

This is outside the scope of the present research but is obviously a highly relevant one to its continuance, as older people represent the largest group in the disability population.

Further American empirical research is needed for more detailed study of residential institutions where elder mediation is being used, whether minimally, or linked with therapeutic or formal interventions. This could test how far mediation resolved conflicts in the long as well as short term, which kind of cases responded best to the process, and whether the older residents involved experienced any immediate or lasting benefits in communicating skills, decision-making and general empowerment in participation.

It may be more difficult to set up studies which can provide computable data about conflicts which lead to elder abuse, and the ways in which senior mediation can contribute to its prevention in American residential care. However there is an expressed need for such research to be done.

The effects of mediation on institutional culture also need studying, with attention being paid to the needs and rights of management and staff in their difficult responsibilities.

In addition careful evaluative work should be done on the misuse of mediation as a covert social control mechanism, and it is recommended that all research should be contextualized in its structural, cultural and institutional setting, as has been attempted in this present chapter.

6 Atlanta and Kansas community mediation and elder abuse

This chapter describes mediation in its interface with elder abuse in two greatly contrasted community settings. The social context of the development of the mediation services is briefly described, and aspects of their management are noted. Cases are discussed, together with the principles involved with these, and a conclusion evaluates the significance of the problems and achievements recorded.

The Justice Center of Atlanta senior mediation programmes

In 1978 an activist lawyer in the Carter administration initiated the Neighborhood Justice Center of Atlanta which he wanted to serve the needs of its poorest and predominantly black population living in the slum area where Martin Luther King had his ministry. Shortly after, a young Atlanta woman attorney from Georgia University became the centre's director. In the following 14 years she transformed it into one of the acknowledged world centres of excellence in mediation, where hundreds of American and international scholars have studied.

By 1993, 3000 people from 20 States and 20 countries had been trained in mediation, 15,000 conflicts had been addressed, and over 250 Atlanta citizens had each received over 40 hours' training in mediation. In addition, hundreds of workshops and special programmes had been devised in special areas involving the Peace Corps, the US Defence Department, law schools, education, the environment, and in organizations focusing on families, disabilities, and older people.

131

During this period the Carter Presidential Center and Martin Luther King Center were developed locally, and networking with these was continuous. As the work expanded, a new building was opened in 1990 by President Carter, and it was decided to rename it the Justice Center of Atlanta (JCA), to focus public attention on its prime purpose to promote justice through mediation for all people.

In 1989 the JCA was chosen to develop one of NIDR's nursing home mediation programmes in Atlanta, which involved training local ombudsmen, their professional workers and volunteers, most of whom were older people in mediation. This was needed as by 2010 Georgia's old people over 65 years are expected to grow by 61.1 per cent and those over 85 by 147 per cent.

The Atlanta *Ombudsman Newsletter* (1992) stated that in addition to nursing homes (which appeared to be unquantified then), there were 350 licensed board and care homes in Atlanta, and more than 1400 in Georgia, and many other unlicensed ones. These homes are generally of a very low standard, mainly used by very poor black and white old people, and cause great social concern, although leading to little reform. Although Georgia has over 100 people working in its LTCO agencies, most are volunteers, and it is difficult enough for them to monitor conditions in the nursing homes, many of which appeared to have nearly 400 beds.

The JCA appointed one of its staff, their special projects co-ordinator who had experience in family and parent mediation, with a social work degree, to run two 4-day training courses of 30–40 hours, for the ombudsmen and their volunteers. This included the production of a specialized training manual, *Mediation in the Nursing Home Setting* (1990), with additional material and a video.

Subsequently, the JCA also joined with the State Office on Aging (OoA) to offer mediation to senior citizens participating in the local Community Care Program, a home delivered services programme in which also nurses and aides provided supportive care. The *Elder Abuse Forum Newsletter* published an account of this work by the JCA co-ordinator who stated that 'disputes arising in this area generally involved personality conflicts between the client and the aide and the payment of the fee required for the continuation of services' (Blanton, 1992:2).

The JCA, and the Atlanta Council on Elder Abuse, viewed this mediation, offered by the visiting older volunteers, as a preventive contribution to the development of abuse, but as the programme had only recently begun, it was too early to evaluate results and incorporate them into the present research. However, one immediate advantage lay

132

in it raising awareness about mediation, and also about elder abuse, amongst housebound old people, who were known to keep their troubles to themselves.

It was this factor which the JCA evaluation of its programmes for old people suggested was partly responsible for the low number of respondents. Old people, especially in institutions, are often afraid to make complaints, and if they do, then withdraw from active involvement in the conflicts that ensue. It is another aspect of their passivity and dependency that they prefer to rely on the ombudsmen, their families and friends to pursue complaints for them.

A second reason for the low recorded rates of mediation was that the ombudsmen mostly used their mediation skills informally, and on the spot, and do not have time to write up results of this or the many other aspects of their work, which has to concentrate on reporting the necessary statistics on the material deficiencies for regulatory bureaucracies.

However, two cases illustrate the mediation work of the ombudsmen:

Case 1 involved a 73 year-old resident suffering from osteoporosis, arthritis and incipient dementia. As a result of her night wandering, bed rails were used to restrain her, but, as a consequence of these, she fell and hurt her hip and arm, began to scream constantly and attack staff. The doctor increased the restraints, but the resident's grand-daughter, who paid the bills, threatened legal action. The LTCO was invited by all to help mediate the matter. The result was a mutual agreement whereby the doctor would obtain specialized psychiatric opinion and treatment for the old lady, and remove the restraints, except at times when she might be a danger to herself or others. The manager agreed to arrange in-service training for her staff in handling such difficult cases, and to call the grand-daughter at any time that restraints were being considered, who also agreed to encourage the old lady to accept problems caused by her ageing, and to cooperate peacefully with staff in their care of her.

Case 2 was less typical in that the manager was suspected of having an *affaire* with the husband of the old resident, who had a broken marriage. Her twin daughters and a brother then complained about electric blanket burns on their mother, and her uneaten breakfasts. The ombudsman was invited to mediate as the manager denied neglect and said that it was the daughters' fault for bringing in an outside breakfast, and dressing the mother's burn against medical advice. The mediation resulted in the affaire diminishing, the manager apologizing for the accident and agreeing to monitor the resident's needs more closely, while the daughters promised to encourage their mother to cooperate peacefully in her treatment, and to eat the home's breakfasts which were set to improve.

In both cases mediation checked marginally abusive behaviour and appeared to prevent reoccurrences, and, in the second one, appeared to be the most appropriate process for the sensitive sexual issues involved.

However it is more difficult to prevent structural abuse, which is a special problem in Georgia where over the fifth of older people exist in poverty, as they also may in institutions. For example, in one 400-bed public hospital visited over three-quarters of the old residents had no dentures, and there was no money to provide or replace these.

It was due to public disquiet about this long term facility that it appointed a social worker who had formerly been a quality assurance consultant for one of America's largest nursing home chains. She described the acute pressures on inadequate numbers of poorly trained staff, which led to constant conflicts with residents, which made her want to take the JCA mediation training.

An example of this happened during a research visit to the hospital in the company of an ombudsman:

Case 3 concerned a distraught old couple watching the terminal treatment of their son dying from AIDS. They were angrily quarrelling with a male nurse about an intravenous intervention he was making. The ombudsman immediately offered his services, comforting the patient and old parents, and also the equally distressed nurse. Ensuring the patient was in no immediate danger, he listened to the parents' protest that the nurse was untrained for the procedure and was inflicting pain on their son. They also said that he wished for no further life support to be given, to which he nodded in agreement. The nurse immediately denied incompetence and called the charge nurse who confirmed this, but who said there were no other senior staff available to warrant the procedure being discontinued, especially as the patient had made no alternative Advanced Directives. After further listening to all view points, which helped all involved to understand other aspects of the situation, a provisional agreement was reached that the treatment would be accepted and that the parents would give their son calm support for this, but that the two nurses would bring a doctor and a social worker as soon as possible to discuss future intervention. The ombudsman might be asked to mediate such a meeting to ensure that the patient's voice was heard.

Another opportunity for seeing the ombudsman doing on-the-spot mediation in difficult circumstances came when visiting a board and care home for mentally ill homeless men which was no more than a doss-house situated in a small broken-down wooden plantation shack:

> Case 4 involved a black old man in a wheelchair, just discharged from a mental asylum into 'community care'. The man was sobbing, begging for water, which no-one gave him. The ombudsman found a tin mug by the man's bed in a small room with other beds, and found three live cockroaches swimming in some water. He called two aides who were eating in a small cooking galley, but they began to insult and blame the old man who had begun to swear at them. The ombudsman offered to sort out the problem, and the aides said that the old man had just brought the mug from the hospital, which he denied. The ombudsman reminded the aides of their duties under the regulations which said that at all times people should be supplied with clean water, but offered to speak to their manager to see if they needed more help. The old man agreed to stop swearing at the staff, and the ombudsman said he would call again to check that the situation had improved.

He said subsequently that if all such homes were closed down, Atlanta's population of elderly homeless people, then assessed at nine per cent, would greatly increase. This case, and many others described, indicated that ombudsmen have to play many roles, advocating for residents, monitoring regulations and also mediating in conflicts as they occur, although always in advance asking for consent to this course.

A more telling account of structural conflict was given at an LTCO case conference where the appropriateness and potential of mediation was discussed. An elegant new nursing home complex had been built, incorporating a day centre, where the food, treatment and washing facilities were located. The residential quarter had been built at such a distance that a trolley had to collect the old residents and take them to the centre, several times a day, or whenever they needed these amenities. No provisions existed for them to be cared for in their bedrooms, or if they were ill, and they had to dress warmly for winter journeys.

Planning permission had been by-passed through political influence with the State government, which would protect the owner from adverse LTCO surveys. It was decided that the choice lay between their professional reporting and pressure on the State OoA to withdraw the public funding involved, which could lead residents being made homeless, or mediating with the owner on their behalf, with the aim of giving him a period of time in which to instal adequate facilities in the residential block. The final choice would be made only after the LTCOs had networked as widely as possible to canvass better options, especially with the local Council on Elder Abuse and Neglect (CEAN).

CEAN was founded in 1986 by its director, aged 72, who cared for a mother of 90 in her own home, was a still active writer of plays, and introduced an *Operation Red Flag* programme involving police and business people in developing techniques to prevent the commercial and fraudulent abuse of old people. She also established good refuge homes to protect victims of elder abuse, and a human services team of visitors to support the local APS worker. An example of financial abuse follows, which mediation succeeded in ending:

> *Case 5* involved an elderly woman, living with a psychotic daughter, who had been found dehydrated and starving lying on the floor. The old lady was admitted to hospital and recovered. CEAN visitors found out that the psychotic daughter and a sister had earlier obtained Enduring Powers of Attorney (EPA) over their mother's money, arguing that this protected it from being means-tested so that she was eligible for free 24-hour community care. More distant kin were contacted, and everyone was represented by an attorney to ensure that legal rights were maintained, but it was CEAN which facilitated meetings and an agreement that the EPA would be cancelled, the money returned to the mother, and that a fair assessment would be made about the help that she, and her psychotic daughter needed to stay in her own home. The mother, of course, did not wish any criminal charge to be made against the only one of her kin who was prepared to look after her, and who herself needed help, as she could neither cook nor clean the home.

This case showed good working co-operation between the APS and CEAN in its varied use of processes, and had the mediative approach been sought earlier it might have prevented the traumatic emergency removal to hospital.

However mediation involving mentally impaired people is always difficult, although possibly no more so than in other social interventions, and this was discussed at a monthly meeting of the LTCOs with Formby (1992), a social work specialist on decision-making with mentally impaired residents. She argued for regular personal care planning reviews of resident decision-making capacity, preserving this in as many areas, even smaller ones such as meal choices, as long as possible. She thought that when conflicts arose, the mediation approach was valuable in

136

reinforcing resident autonomy and a related sense of self-achievement, and should be used where possible. She also pointed out that mental capacity can be fluctuating, so that a resident may be able to make lucid decisions one day, but not the next, so that gentle processes which did not rush them were recommended.

Another area of uncertainty in Atlanta was in respect to police work on elder abuse, although there was a designated police officer responsible for this. He was basing his police training on an earlier domestic violence training manual, in which mediation is recommended as an important option, depending on the circumstances. This officer, a member of CEAN, had previously been a social worker and had taken as well as given mediation training.

He saw mediation as an essential strategy with which police could control some abusive situations through structured negotiation and communication, and in which they act as transmitters and interpreters of processes of de-escalation. He also felt that police should not interfere with any resolution of the conflicts which the parties were deciding for themselves, unless any misdemeanour or crime was involved or threatening. This had to be met by arrest and removal of the suspect.

As he was considering designing a separate elder abuse training manual, an opportunity came for developing another aspect of the participative research mode in Atlanta, by linking him with the JCA and its senior mediation project, so that a joint publication might be produced.

This focus on the use of mediation at the earliest possible stage in relational conflict to prevent elder abuse made an important contribution to the research study in Atlanta, and its value was reinforced because the JCA was regarded as one of the premier American sites of conflict resolution services, with an international reputation for pioneering work which was subsequently followed elsewhere. Thus their development of senior mediation services is significant at every level.

The Kansas Mediation Service for Older Adults

Kansas, a major city of the predominantly white American heartland, has its cultural history marked by having been a boundary State in the Civil War and a site of spectacular conflicts. In comparison, the increasing social conflicts connected with the care of its ageing population may appear minimal, but many are also concerned with the abuse of human rights.

It was the Olathe Human Rights Committee which, receiving about 400 cases of conflict and complaints each year, asked the Kansas Legal

Services (KLS) to start an Olathe Dispute Resolution Service (DRS) in 1985. The KLS staff of lawyers gave free advice and assistance to older adults in civil cases, with an affirmative action policy targeting poor, minority, disabled and vulnerable populations.

The lawyers were also committed to using mediation when appropriate, as they found it more constructive than adversarial approaches which polarized people. The DRS list of disputes for which it was prepared to offer immediate mediation (instead of perhaps late-listed court hearings) was perhaps wider than that of most British mediation services. It included:

> community, organizational, educational, correctional, business, landlord/tenant, consumer, family and old adult conflicts … parent/ adolescent, divorce, custody, access and adoption … age and housing discrimination, nursing home placements, grandparent visitation, family conflict and work discrimination (DRS, 1992).

The DRS director, a retired school counsellor and mediator, with a Master's Degree, who had recovered from a stroke and taken paralegal training, noted increasing number of referrals of older people. The KLS encouraged her to apply for an American Bar Association (ABA) grant in 1989 to develop a Kansas Mediation Service for Older Adults (KMSOA), based on the fact that in that year 761 old people had been given legal advice and assistance by the KLS, and that as the local county then had 42,000 people aged over 60, mediation could usefully serve them.

In 1990 the KMSOA was started with four objectives:

> 1. to present informal programs about mediation throughout the county;
> 2. to train older adults to serve as mediators, in a voluntary capacity;
> 3. to offer a workshop on mediation to 'helping professionals' who work with older adults;
> 4. to offer mediation services to older adults to resolve their disputes (KMSOA, 1989).

The now KMSOA director accepted 16 senior citizen volunteers, 14 of whom became active mediators, receiving 20 hours' training, mediation observation and supervision, mediation manuals and publications describing the special physical, psychological and emotional needs of older people. Her volunteers had an average age of 66 years; most were retired and were from trade or professional backgrounds; one woman, aged 75, said that mediation was her most recent career, having taken a law degree when she was 65, after 40 years' work as an accountant.

One typical case illustrates the referrals that came from the Small Claims Court where the judge suggested that people should try mediation first, although this was not compulsory, and this case was observed:

Case 6 involved a nursing home conflict in which a deceased resident's Advanced Directive had not been followed, leading to extensive life support and substantial extra costs. The daughter refused to pay these, so to the management took her to court. The mediation took two hours and enabled the daughter to express her pain and anger at seeing her mother's prolonged suffering, which prompted the manager to apologize for having lost the Advanced Directive and starting resuscitation. He said he would withdraw the account for the extra costs if the daughter paid the rest of the care bill which was owed, and she agreed to this, adding that her mother had otherwise been very happy at the nursing home.

Another case was referred by a lawyer who felt that his client was inappropriately seeking legal action:

Case 7 involved an adult daughter who said that her mother was enticing her grand-daughter to visit her each day when she should be doing school homework. The mediation enabled the daughter to express her feelings of anger, and her concern for her child's studies, while the grandmother spoke of her isolation living alone. Agreement was reached about mutually acceptable visiting times, and, although the issues appeared minimal, the daughter admitted that mediation had not only prevented a law suit but also, the physical as well as verbal abuse that she had begun to show her mother.

Research visits were also made with the KMSOA director to nursing homes whose staff and ombudsmen she trained in mediation so that they could use their skills on site:

Case 8 concerned a resident with a difficult behavioural problem who always hit anyone approaching her. The ombudsman arranged a meeting with the staff, family and resident, who confessed that she had a failing sight problem, plus a past trauma when she had received an unwanted injection, which made her feel that everyone had to be pushed away. The agreement reached was that whenever staff wished to contact the resident, they would call her and their names loudly, giving the reason for their approach, and wait for her agreement before proceeding. The resident was relieved and the family said they would encourage her cooperation.

Many other nursing home mediations took place between residents who shared rooms and who quarrelled constantly. These were often residents with whom no other person wished to share, and mediations generally involved writing down detailed lists of each resident's complaints, and then enabling them to do trading, with a signed agreement about each one settled.

Research visits were also made to community mental health services, where some staff had also been trained in mediation as one case shows:

Case 9 involved a patient of 80 who had unexpectedly recovered from a major operation, and had remarried as his former wife had neglected and verbally abused him. She found out that he had made a new Will in favour of the new wife, and threatened him about betraying their daughter. He asked the social worker to mediate, and a very emotional and angry meeting took place, as the man said he could not face the rest of life losing the love of his daughter. It was agreed that the Will should be changed so that his first wife and daughter inherited the property, and the second wife received investments and cash.

Discussions were then held with a young adult protective services (APS) worker who was also saw the value of mediation skills in preventing elder abuse in her capacity as an authorized officer under the 1985 Kansas Elder Abuse, Prevention, Identification and Treatment Act. Yet although she was the only APS worker in the large county, she had no case conference system to support her, and was overwhelmed by her first job following a student placement.

As a result of pressure, she said that emergency removal of old people from their homes was too often a first rather than last resort, and there was as important a need for mediation between all the services involved, as there was between the families having conflicts. This view about the need for interdisciplinary co-operation will be re-echoed more strongly in the later account of the Norwegian elder abuse project, where mediating skills were used in this additional way.

The APS worker illustrated her views about the need to resolve family interpersonal conflicts by referring to one of her cases:

Case 10 concerned an old couple who had been visited by a community nurse for seven years, as she always suspected that the woman's continual bruising and lacerations were due to spousal abuse, and where the home was squalid and unhygienic. One day the nurse found the woman unconscious, having been hit by a heavy hammer, needing urgent hospitalization after which she insisted on returning to her husband. It was suspected that they were both alcoholics, who had no kin, and only each other for love and support.

The APS worker said that she would like to get training in mediation skills, because she did not feel experienced enough to help the old couple work out some constructive plan for either better home conditions, or joint entry into a care home, but it was difficult to help them confront the facts of abuse.

It was because so many old people found the concept of elder abuse threatening, that a Kansas multidisciplinary coalition renamed itself, and its telephone hotline, the Elder Rights Coalition (ERC). The ERC published a good guide in which it estimated that the ratio of reported to unreported cases was 1 to 5.5, that 1 in 20 older adults were victims of abuse, and that most abusers were related to the victims.

The research visit to an ERC monthly meeting included meeting Kansas and neighbouring Missouri police who then had no special guidelines on elder abuse, although they had an interest in starting a fraud control unit, asking banks to display leaflets about the improper use of accounts, and to co-operate in monitoring those of old people where amounts drawn raised suspicions. Otherwise police dealt with elder abuse cases on the same basis as domestic violence, but said that, if the inadequate numbers of officers had sufficient time, mediation training would be useful for them.

The area of unreported abuse was a campaigning issue for an 80 year-old community activist who was especially concerned about its occurrence in nursing homes. She started a pressure group, the Kansans for Improvement in Nursing Homes (KINH), which published monthly newsletters giving hard facts about elder abuse, which she said was then endemic in about 149 sub-standard homes of the Kansas total of 380.

One typical case reported were that of a man with bleeding bed sores tied to his bed, who had to be removed to hospital. The nursing home denied neglect, saying that the man had scratched himself, and, although the regulatory surveyors found nursing deficiencies, no penalties were imposed.

In another case a resident was over-sedated, leading to tardive dyskinesia, and eventually died from gangrene. Many cases involved residents not having a call bell, nor being given water, or toileting when

141

requested. Families had been afraid to complain, and there were insufficient and hurried ombudsmen visits.

KINH also exposed what they argued was structural abuse, in that employment legislation then gave subsidies to nursing homes for giving work to the unemployed, in return for training them. Unmotivated people with social problems were taken on, never trained, and then discharged after a year (after the subsidy ended) when a new intake of cheap labour took place.

It was also reported that although the majority of ombudsmen and their volunteers were highly motivated and dedicated to upholding the rights of old people in long term care, others used their status and training in a struggle for upward social mobility. Ombudsman work was poorly paid, but after a short time served, it enabled people to obtain better State employment in other sectors. So some ombudsmen did not wish to get a reputation as being troubleshooters, although this was their ideological function.

An Hispanic ombudsman, who had done the KMSOA mediation training, illustrated some of these issues by referring to a recent case:

> *Case 11* She was asked by a nursing home manager to mediate in a case in which they wished to discharge a patient with difficult behaviour, which had resulted in the family threatening to take legal action, as a violation of the elder abuse legislation. The ombudsman felt that mediation would be used to suppress elder rights to care in the home and to preserve its reputation. Although she received hostile reactions from the management about failure to do her job by mediating, she referred the family to the KLS lawyers, supported by the KMSOA director, so they could assist the court action. Firmness about this, resulted in the home deciding not to discharge the resident, but the ombudsman felt that she now had to leave ombudsman work, as being a Hispanic, she felt herself to be in double jeopardy of criticism.

Fortunately, the ombudsman was recommended for a job with the Kansas Institute of Biomedical Ethics which wished to employ an ombudsman trained in mediation to develop a new service related to Advanced Directives and nursing home ethics committees, where work was increasing.

Research discussions with University of Kansas Medical Center teaching staff indicated that complaints about nursing homes had trebled in the previous five years, and that they shared concerns to use mediation at sufficiently early stages of conflicts, before attitudes had hardened, or

142

practices had become abusive. Staff were trying to raise funds for a Social Work Fellowship to study this possibility.

All those consulted during the research tour co-operated enthusiastically in what they felt to be a participative project for them also, as British knowledge and experience was shared with them, although findings show how much more advanced are Americans, and Kansas in this specific study, in relating the use of mediation to the prevention of elder abuse.

However the work of the KMSOA suffered from the recession, and no further funding was obtainable for continuing the project. It had achieved pioneer status and important public credibility because it was situated in the KLS law office where people could see that they had a free choice of either legal or mediation remedies, or both.

Another achievement was the way in which the KMSOA director had provided a substantial group of senior citizens with a new social career that gave them all increased feelings of self-worth and fulfilment, as well as many important social skills which they could use in other walks of life. They all continued to mediate for the KMSOA director, who remained on the KLS staff, even though the project was in abeyance.

However, an admitted concern of the KLS and its KMSOA was that there had been fewer organizational and self-referrals than expected. One explanation, already noted in this book, suggested that many social agencies were trying to do informal mediation work themselves, although not trained in its specific skills, and that the amount of this was neither evaluated nor recorded. The second relates to the well-known hesitancy of old people to report family conflict, or that with carers, of those close to them. The majority of their complaints were about commercial, tenancy and such like issues, most of which needed legal advice and action.

In conclusion, it is significant that in both the Atlanta and Kansas mediation projects, they were situated in centres associated with justice and the law, where they were regarded as equal partners in the affirmative action that was promoted and practised. Also, in both areas, mediation was shown to be useful in some of the most sensitive social conflicts of interpersonal relations involving vulnerable older people, their carers and associates. It is suggested that the research findings reported, and the cases illustrated, support one of the main themes of this book, that mediation, especially at early stages of relational conflict, can contribute to the prevention of elder abuse.

Part III

THE SOCIAL DEVELOPMENT OF ELDER ABUSE AND MEDIATION SERVICES IN BRITAIN AND EUROPE

7 The British Elder Mediation Project (EMP): EMP for EMPowerment not EMPire-building

The preface to the book has already explained the genesis of EMP, and the earlier references to research ethnomethodology noted the individual casework aspect of EMP's activities. This chapter describes EMP's embryonic growth, and those of its empowerment principles, policies, practices, problems and potentials which are relevant to that aspect of its work concerned with contributing to the prevention of elder abuse. A following section includes illustrative individual casework and discusses at a deeper level the interpersonal issues involved.

A brief recapitulation shows that research in 1992–3 resulted in recognizing the many achievements and potentials revealed by American work in senior mediation, and these greatly influenced the gestation and growth of British EMP, as a self-help social empowerment project.

EMP voluntary workers chose the title of the project to reflect the aim of enabling older persons to strengthen their skills and affirm their rights in contributing to decision-making about their lives, especially that which involved them in conflict and potential or actual abusive situations. Related objectives were planned to increase associated feelings of empowerment, when people perceive themselves as having autonomy, independence, self-efficacy and self-worth: EMP workers had internalized the buzz words of popular gerontology.

This principle of empowerment, as has been discussed earlier, is especially important in working with and for older persons so that as many as possible of the disempowering processes of biological and psychosocial changes in later life can be prevented, delayed or ameliorated, and those of resistance to abuse strengthened. So EMP's organizational aim of empowerment has been a guiding principle from the beginning, and an essential experience for its workers who participate in EMP's developmental planning and in continuing education and training.

It has been this primary and preventive focus on *direct empowerment*, through holding *Coping with Conflict* workshops in old people's groups in libraries, for leaders of their general social groups, and in an ethnic clubs, etc., which has been a distinctive feature of EMP. It has generated self-referrals of elders with unresolved conflicts, some of whom are in abusive situations, although the promotion of EMP by the professional press, has encouraged others from social agencies.

Although the general literature on empowerment has been referred to earlier, here it is appropriate to mention that the *conscientización* work of Freire (1972) amongst stressed populations in Latin America was one of the idealist inspirations behind the workshops, which aimed to strengthen the survival, resistance and coping skills of old people. The workshops provide a practical example of offering older people the opportunity of developing *learned resistance* instead of learned helplessness (Seligman, 1975) in facing conflict, which is critically important if they are in potentially or actual abusive relationships.

EMP had also learned from the inadequate funding and time-limited restriction of the American projects, that employing paid staff and trainers of senior volunteers, had inhibited wider developments. So another important principle was to focus on developing a *volunteer* movement. This followed the model of Mediation UK and most of its member organizations. More importantly it visibly testified to the belief of EMP and others that many older persons have the experiences, skills and time to work with and for their peer group.

Mediation UK was primarily based on extensive and efficient networking, made easier because its national and local territories are so much smaller than those of America. EMP immediately adopted the same principle. This led to what was gradually constructed as a *social diffusion model* (Morhman and Lawler, 1984), rather than an empire-building one. This principle became an essential part of EMP policy.

Through extensive networking with ageing organizations and Mediation UK members, EMP was publicized not as a *service* but as a *project*. Instead of making an unfulfillable promise to provide later life mediation services on a national or regional basis, the message was given that EMP encouraged, and would enable, all social groups working with and for older persons to develop their *own* EMPs, in their *own* time, to suit their *own* organizational and local needs. EMP offered free consultation, information, training resources and support for this, as well as offering to mediate in individually referred cases.

In particular, EMP has always affirmed that most multidisciplinary workers in the caring agencies find themselves in mediating roles, and offered to help them increase natural skills through workshop trainings, so that they can be more effective. EMP has always sought to share, rather than restrict its growing knowledge and experience.

Developing this social diffusion policy from the principle of networking served many practical purposes. Firstly, EMP volunteers believed that small is beautiful (Schumacher, 1974), and that encouraging organizations to consider the excitement and potential of owning and developing their own EMP work, naming it as they wished, would better ensure the diffusion of mediation ideas and practices. It was recognized that *group identity* is as important as personal identity in establishing and furthering processes of empowerment. Similarly collective social action, like personal activity, is increased when there is collective *decision-making*.

Secondly, it was realized that financial viability of individual small projects is easier to stabilize than that of large ones, especially in an era of economic recession with competition for scarce public and charitable funding resources. Determined to act as a model of independent voluntarism, reliant on minimal funding, EMP planned its first year's work on a £500 grant from the New Horizons Trust, then a similar grant from the McCarthy Foundation, followed by its largest annual grant of £3000 from Comic Relief to develop work with disability groups. Administrative support and charitable registration was provided by Mediation UK.

Major British ageing organizations and charities, would have far greater access to funds, if they wished to develop their own EMPs, even to the extent of paying part or full-time co-ordinators of their volunteers, as is typical in that general area.

Thirdly, it was recognized that elder mediation is a new field about which we know little and have much to learn. One of the values of Mediation UK is its focus on the needs and interests of users, and its services have developed in a dialectical relationship with them through responding to their views and requirements. So EMP has similarly developed as a peer learning community (Reason and Rowan, 1981), cautiously watching how its ideas are accepted and utilized elsewhere, especially observing how these are being adapted to suit different environments and cultures, and noting when problems and failures occur. It can then learn from, and share these, through its social diffusion network.

149

The third major principle on which EMP was based derived from Mediation UK's foundation as an Equal Opportunities organization with a commitment to taking positive action with regard to working with and for multicultural people and their communities. EMP's concern for a vulnerable age group acknowledged the triple jeopardy which older ethnic persons face (Norman, 1985), and those of their family and informal carers (McCalman, 1991). EMP was therefore concerned to invite representatives from as many different cultural communities to join its working group; to learn traditional ethnic ways of coping with conflict; and to ensure that all its workshops and study days reflected this principle.

The volunteers included an Afro-Caribbean community worker, a Bangladeshi lawyer and magistrate, a West African teacher, an Iranian Zoroastrian United Nations interpreter, a European Jewish counsellor, all retired, and a Kashmiri Muslim Age Concern worker, a Malaysian nurse and an Indian Sikh college tutor.

EMP's volunteers, who were often referred to by using the empowering term, consultants, all brought valuable skills as well as rich life experiences from their varied backgrounds:

> J was a qualified and trained social worker, who had then entered the probation service and become a senior probation officer. In that capacity, and as an early member of Mediation UK, he founded a mediation and reparation project attached to his probation service, in which selected offenders, with the positive consent of victims, met them to apologize and discuss their preferred form of reparation. J was also an Anglican priest, and, on his retirement from the probation service, developed chaplaincy work with local nursing homes. It was here that he was constantly using his mediating skills, and very soon formed the idea that some kind of specialized elder mediation work was needed. He became an important founding member of EMP as he was also secretary of Mediation UK's executive committee at that time.

All the mediators were concerned that their work helped to prevent conflict escalating into abuse. This was also true of a Jewish drama therapist, who was a trained marriage counsellor. She was concerned to learn and incorporate mediation skills in her work as there was a possibility that this might extend to involvement in a project concerned with the psychosexual abuse of elderly victims.

Here it is significant to note that EMP was thus empowered by its associates, as well as empowering them through enlarging their visions

150

and expertise. This *reciprocal empowerment* is an important model of the assurance that is given to all people involved in conflict who are considering accepting invitations to mediation: it is offered as an experience of *mutual* empowerment. This is crucial in family, community and institutional conflicts involving older persons, and especially in mediation work involving people in abusive situations. Carers, neighbours and caregiving staff need to be reassured that their rights, interests and needs will be given full opportunities for expression and consideration.

The fact that EMP's working volunteer consultants came from different backgrounds also emphasized that the project was not an empire-building one which sought aggrandizement by establishing an agency which marketed a product of exclusive specialized skills. In contrast, through its funding, aided by support from Mediation UK, and with the help of its working volunteer consultants, it has been able to offer its resources freely and widely (travel and low-cost expenses excepted).

Neither has EMP an empire-building picture of the form future development might take. It could be that one of the major ageing organizations might be interested in taking over the work, either starting its own project, which would extend to its branches, or just integrating the teaching of mediating skills into its own training programme. Another possibility is that another voluntary organization might find it useful to adopt and adapt EMP's principles and methods as a specialized project within its own general work. Here it is noteworthy that the National Council of Voluntary Organizations and the London Voluntary Service Council are just developing their own mediation services, although not specialising in ageing issues.

This social diffusion may help EMP avoid the otherwise pressing problem that its aged volunteers are ageing, and although it is hoped that these will be replaced, it may be that welcome changing attitudes towards extending employment to old people will lead to fewer active and available retired people.

It would be ironic if EMP faded just as increasing social concern about elder abuse and the useful role that EMP can play in contributing to its prevention has led to more invitations from agencies to present its lectures, videos and workshops to conferences and study days, where academic, professional and practitioner response has been very positive. At the end of all sessions for nurse and nursing assistant staff, nearly all those present asked if free training workshops in conflict management skills could be given in their residential care and nursing homes.

Here another problem surfaced. Despite this staff request, no positive responses were received from *home owners and managers*. The reason, of course, is that home owners and managers seldom admit openly that conflict or abuse *exists* in their homes.

It is also interesting that although EMP stresses that all its training resources are offered on the basis of *co-designing* details with the organizations concerned, in order to ensure their ownership and participation in the work, this appears to provoke an ambivalent rather than enthusiastic response. The offer implies that respondents are invited to think deeply about their situation and assess needs for training. This is also a threat to many institutions which provide inadequate numbers of staff, with inadequate time, to undertake inadequate on-site induction and additional training. The fact that resources are freely offered may not offset the costs of giving staff time to take training.

Many of Mediation UK's associated community mediation services ask for EMP to provide training days with a view to them considering starting their own EMPs, and this is an ongoing development, which fulfils one of the main aims of the diffusion model.

A relevant welcome request from the Standing Conference on Ethnic Minority Senior Citizens (SCEMSC) to develop with them, and the support of the Commission for Racial Equality, a mediation project to prevent family violence in 32 London boroughs still awaits implementation due to SCEMSC organizational changes which led to the withdrawal of a Home Office grant. In the project, mediation was designed to be used in association with advocacy and counselling, as these triple services make an effective complementary combination in dealing with elder abuse.

Established professionals and practitioners may see boundary problems in such coalitions, particularly if they work within an empire-building agency. However, the chapter on American conflict management with older persons showed that many individual workers successfully use, and *have* to use, a combination of varied skills in certain situations. The ethical key to this is the recognition of when different services, or role changes should be made, explaining the reasons involved so that clients can freely consent to working with these. In elder abuse cases, constant consideration has to be given to decisions about the need to involve legal and police services.

In concluding this brief description of EMP's work it should be stressed that it still has to meet many unfolding critical challenges. Its preference for bridge-building with other organizations may not effectively ensure that EMPs are adopted and adapted as widely as hoped. Although many people approaching later life have become familiar with words like mediation and conciliation, other people may prefer to remain with their traditional survival skills and loyalties, rather than having open discussions of their conflicts. It will depend on how the experiences and perceptions of elderly people change in the coming decade, and how they respond to public education about elder abuse as to how EMP develops.

It is to some of these experiences and perceptions of old people in relational conflicts which involve abuse that the next section of this chapter turns, focusing on some of the individual casework with which EMP has been concerned, and the conceptualizations supporting it.

Individual cases referred to EMP

EMP has increasingly had cases of older people feeling trapped in situations of unresolved conflict referred by social agencies, and by individuals themselves. Some of the casework and mediation has been done within the aegis of community mediation services, in co-operation with their volunteers who share the visiting and mediation work.

This section of the chapter considers three cases in detail, relating these to some of the conceptualization on which the casework is based, supportive to its primary practical aim of relieving human suffering, followed by attempts to offer theoretical insights into the dynamics of abusive relations in later life.

This casework can be interpreted in various ways, and at different levels, but communications and relationships studies are especially relevant and helpful in suggesting explanations of interpersonal conflict and abuse.

These provide a background to the ongoing research generated by EMP, which can be linked with what Wood and Duck (1995) describe as situated accounts in a situated study within an unconventional framework. Casework conceptualization aims at unifying explanations with internal and external coherences and predictive simplicities, which McLaughlin et al (1992) argue belong to lay explanations: EMP's volunteer work is essentially a contribution from the laity.

However the research conceptualization for this book has been based on considering the literature on accounts episodes, decision-making, impression management, relational maintenance, self-disclosure, social judgements and associated aspects of communications and relationship studies. The research aim here is to understand how people, especially the old, can become involved in destructive social relationships, and to explore how they can be empowered to build constructive ones.

153

The mediation process of encouraging participants to listen to each other's account of relational disorder provides instances of what Schonbach (1990) calls account episodes, which enables them to reduce the conflict potential in a direct, unmitigated confrontation of claim and counterclaim, and thus restore their normative expectations of social order.

Mediation empowers people with a sense of self-achievement as they develop what he calls control competencies and coping attempts through being encouraged to turn competitive into co-operative negotiation, and transform past failure events through what Goffman (1971) calls remedial interchanges and strategic interventions.

This connects with Canary et al's (1994) work on relational justification, and the need for communication damage limitation with repair strategies to ensure relationship maintenance, through essential conflict management processes. His point about the need to reformulate and rejuvenate relational elements is relevant to the way in which mediators may reframe antagonistic communication to minimize misunderstandings and rebarbative retribution.

A case of rape and reparation

These insights were relevant to a recent case of the alleged rape of a white retired social worker by a black student, three times younger than herself, whose virginity she had initially seduced while she and her husband had given him prolonged hospitality. This son of a West Indian minister, who assisted the white rector of her church, had suffered two psychiatric breakdowns, diagnosed as schizophrenic episodes, catalysed by acculturalization pressures of living between the conflicting mores of his strict, fundamentalist parents and progressive academic liberals.

The social worker saw mediation as a repair strategy to limit the damage to the church's and her family's reputation (as she had two married sons older than the boy), whilst restoring the relationship with his parents who were hostile towards her competing influence over their son. They saw mediation from their Christian perspective of seeking reparation in the relationship, co-operation in ensuring their son's future mental health, and minimization of her future interpersonal contact.

Mediation enabled the participants to acknowledge the respective failure events of their inadequate parenting, and the social worker's perverted friendship. The parental relational justification was based on their restrictive tribal traditions, and hers was ego-defensively given as

154

spousal impotence. However the confidential and empathetic mediation process of self-disclosure (Derlega et al, 1993) helped the social worker reformulate her activity as a shameful transgression, for which she asked forgiveness from the parents, and God. This, and age-exhaustion, had led to her trying to control the boy's increasing sexual appetites, angrily alleging that he was raping her without consent. Anger is often utilized to protect the self from feelings of shame, and it is significant that, after her confession, and as a result of the mediation, her outrage dissolved.

The parents saw the conflict as due to what Rook (1989) calls the perceived violations of relationship norms, but acknowledged that the mediation had uncovered complex interactions of the situational and dispositional factors within their own family relational dynamics, and accepted the superordinate goal of relational maintenance for the sake of the church community. Rook also argues that it is the *manner* of handling conflicts which determines if they despoil relationships, and it is suggested that, in this case, the mediation restored those between the older adults. From the research perspective it also contributed to the prevention of what was perceived as incipient elder sexual abuse, whilst maintaining ethical principles of relational justice by enabling the woman to admit additionally that she had abused the boy.

This mediation also illustrated what Antaki (1994) described in argumentation theory as a stretch of talk which was bearable because it resolved a problematic state of affairs, and in which explanatory relations were a joint accomplishment.

It also relates to Martin and Tesser's (1992) work on the construction of social judgements which shows that attitudes can change if people become aware of, and then understand, the reasons for feelings and events, whilst being enabled to generate solutions for what is called relational microjustice. In this case mediation made manifest both impression formation and impression management, whilst reducing relational suffering.

It also vividly illuminated the often invisible changes of personal identity. As Wood and Duck (1995) say, we have no fixed identities but only relational selves that develop within a teeming mass of potentialities, which are continuously re-defined. The traumatic spurt of their son's *rites de passage* to manhood had to be assimilated, evaluated and integrated by the parents, and the mediation helped them to begin a less speedy adjustment of their own personal growth.

Sherman and Webb (1994), in their paper on the self as process in later life, note the spiritual importance to people of their self-concept, in which a sense of *being* can become more salient than that of *doing*. This insight might be borrowed to describe euphemistically the transition of the active sexual mistress to that of a passive penitent seeking a righteous retirement. She was trying to reconstruct her identity.

Hummert et al (1994) describe how the social identities of old people are continuously constructed through negotiative communication, which is a relational process. When it is creative, it can valorize or build up feelings of self-worth; when it is destructive, as it is in abusive relationships, it can destroy self-esteem.

Nussbaum et al's (1989) comment that the social construction of ageing relationships has an ecological perspective connects with the perspective of mediation that its process provides a safe path within a secure and serene environment for explicit negotiative communication to take place, especially when the situation or relationship is abusive.

Coupland et al (1991) refer to the etymological links between the word 'old' and 'to nourish', and show how important a good negotiative process is for morale and psychological well-being. They further suggest that idiosyncratic forms of 'elderspeak', in its forms of over and under speech accommodation, can be at the root of many intergenerational conflicts.

It is through the reflection, reframing and restructuring of conflict accounts in mediation that negotiative communication can become constructive rather than destructive in relationship reformation (Donohue and Kolt, 1992).

The need to help old people increase their communication competencies is more urgent when, as Giles et al (1990) show, linguistic deficiencies precede and accompany failing mental health. The work of Burleson et al (1994) on the communication of social support points to skills necessary for the protection as well as construction of self, and mediation can offer crisis and screening intervention processes which are simple and face-saving at times when old people are emotionally confused or suffering from fluctuating mental capacity engendered by unresolved situational conflicts, or precipitating relational ones as when senility threatens.

Barnes and Duck (1994) describe protective face-saving and facework as important communication constituents that lay the basis for the specific management of crises, when painful self-disclosures are made. Here mediation principles of providing continuing personal affirmation and impartial interpersonal support through communication skills, enable participants, as dispassionately as possible, to deconstruct their abusive relationship and situation.

This deconstruction might be conceptualized as a reverse form of the relational dialectics which takes place as people wrestle with the tensions of self-disclosure, and the reconstruction of their social selves. Baxter (1988) describes relational dialectics as conflict strategy in relationship development, suggesting that its integrative management of co-operative pro-social problem-solving as opposed to competitive approaches provides a useful early warning in marriage. This fits neatly with the commonsense hypothesis of this book that it is at early stages of relational conflict involving older people that mediation strategies have most potential for preventing elder abuse.

These collective insights are instructive in analysing the next case.

A case of racial and sexual verbal abuse

An old couple, living in a Council housing ghetto, had accused a schoolboy of threatening them with abuse and damaging their property, while his mother urged him on. She, in turn, accused them of vicious racial discrimination, as her son was of mixed race parentage, and verbal sexual abuse of herself. The old people asked for mediation, bitterly complaining that the police, lawyers, social workers and housing officers were unable to do anything about the neighbour conflict which they said had made their retirement years a 'living and dying hell'.

The initial pain of the old people's self-disclosure related to the fact that they had lived in the community for 20 years where they considered they had a good reputation, winning social esteem from neighbours. They felt that new ones (immigrants) were now arriving who did not speak the same way, or have equally good habits as themselves. Conversations and meetings became unpleasant, and the old couple felt that they were made to appear at fault because they criticized. Communication failed, then froze, and no-one took any notice of them when they complained.

Bromley (1993) points to the importance of interpersonal communication in determining social reputations, and to negotiation as an impression management strategy which can either be negative or positive. Part of the later mediation strategy was to enable the participants objectively to see the effect of negative or null communication on their reputations. It was also important for mediation to empower their positive self-presentation in the social environment of neighbourhood conflict, so that, to borrow Coupland et al's (1991) concept of communicative attuning, miscommunication problems did not escalate abusive relations.

It was also obvious from the limited vocabulary of the old couple that their linguistic deficits prevented them from finding more socially

157

acceptable ways of describing her son's behaviour to the mother. They called him evil, wicked and sinful, using generational Biblical references to judgement in ways that Martin and Tesser (1992) describe as constructing people in negative narrow categories.

The mental capacity of the old woman was also problematic as she admitted to receiving in and out-patient psychiatric care, and her husband confessed that he could not cope with her obsessions about the boy. When mediation clarified the factual base of her allegations that he had been spitting at and threatening her, it was proved that he was elsewhere at the time.

Following the view of Buttny (1993) that face-saving is a protective and co-creative strategy in relational control, mediation helped the old man to apologize for his age-based misunderstanding and misperceived assumption that the boy's mother was a single parent, after he was confronted by the fact that she was a hard-working widow whose black husband had been killed by the police. The old man had called her a slag and a prostitute, and her son a half-caste bastard, when the boy had climbed on the shared garden fence and damaged it. This was the cause of the mother's allegations of racial and sexual abuse, although the apology was face-saving for her also, so that she could withdraw them.

The dialogic process of the mediation was facilitated by the confidentiality and trust which it provided so that painful self-disclosures could be made and their angry relational dialectics were therapeutically synthesized. This involved them reaching an agreement about improving future communication, which would positively and politely address any issue of potential conflict.

This case also illustrated the importance of locus of control issues. The old man admitted he could not control his wife's moods, nor his own angry frustration at being unable to cope with neighbour conflict, nor in persuading the police to use their powers. The mother was concerned about controlling her son, who she was fearful about getting a police record because he was a black boy. Mediation, which aims to be a rights based process, balanced the power relations between those involved in the conflict, and encouraged them to use early co-operative communication problem-solving to prevent any future abusive situation developing.

However, as suggested by earlier indications of the infrastructural causes of conflict, and EMP's focus on areas of social deprivation, these brief references to selected communications and relationships theories are not made to skew attention away from the sociological construction of abusive relations in later life (Townsend, 1961; Phillipson and Walker,

1986). In most of EMP cases, as in the case of the old couple, and the next case, the aged poor feel exhausted and humiliated for having to struggle through *social* conflicts about access to resources and services, fearful for their reputations as welfare spongers. Self-esteem fades, and hostility is projected on to others over whom it is determined to win battles of *personal* conflicts, utilizing abuse if this is necessary or natural.

Relationship studies point to the centrality of conflict (Argyle, 1973; Duck, 1988; Gudykunst, 1994), as does decision-making research (Cicerelli, 1992; Grimshaw, 1990; Janis and Mann, 1977), while Klein and Milardo (1993) show the importance of third party influence in its management, referring to the seminal work of Deutsch (1973) on the subject.

External intervention in relational conflict is often inimical to what Brubaker (1990) calls the concept of family ethos and its repertoire of adaptations, although Burr et al (1994) list coping strategies for family stress which fit well with the ethical aims and practices of mediation, that also take account, as they do, of metalevel relational changes.

One of these is the relational formation of metarules about decision-making, and another is about systems of values and the search for meaning which the gerontologist, Moody (1992), focuses on in his Habermas-based theory of communicative ethics. Although he develops this largely about later life decision-making with regard to institutional and terminal care where abusive relations and situations develop (Craig, 1996), he upholds the Cicerelli (1992) view that shared rather than direct autonomy may emerge as a higher ethical ideal. Moody (1992) also sees the positive use of mediation in relational conflict, especially as it models a non-coercive communicative process for talking about sensitive subjects.

Kreisberg (1982) also notes the protective function of mediation in upholding ethical ideals of relational justice, although Kressel and Pruitt (1989) warn that, like other social interventions, it is often unable to alter chronically dysfunctional patterns of relating and communicating. However Gubrium et al (1994) refer to the importance of communication collaborative accomplishments in keeping alive Alzheimer patients' sense of personhood, and mediators respect people with mental health problems who wish to co-operate in relational conflict management. Burgoon et al (1994) add their own cautionary note that improving communication can, in some marriages at least, be counterproductive in that irreconcilable divergences are exposed, instead of avoided, and relationships consequently dissolve. These observations are pertinent to another case.

159

The case of the angry tenant

An old man of 80 lived on his own because his family considered him to be a very difficult. Not only had he created conflict in his family, but also continuously for over ten years with the Council in the sheltered housing they provided.

He maintained his strong sense of self-identity through the autonomous management of his own tenancy arrangements and paternalistic decision-making on behalf of other residents, boasting that he based this on his professional identity as a retired housing officer. He constantly complained about poor accounting, inadequate managing and bad communications. A heavy file of these complaints, with photocopies of his copperplate minutely written letters to every relevant central and local government official over the years was sent to EMP with a request for mediation, after the relevant ombudsman became the last of all the rest who had refused to consider his case.

The reason was because his impeccable syntax was laced with invective: in abusive terms he accused the Council of elder abuse. It was attacked in libellous terms of fraud, deliberate dishonesty, professional incompetence, using additional adjectival swear words. Social agencies appeared to think the old man was obsessional: his negative communications were dysfunctional and escalated his relational conflict with the Council. Yet his anger and vituperation was the way in which he maintained his identity of independence, power and virility, while his sense of self-esteem was bolstered by campaigning on behalf of other residents who he said were soft, stupid and senile.

The mediation resolved some long-standing misunderstandings about the accounting, and the Council officer offered to make an apology, and, as a goodwill gesture, financial reparation for the distress caused to the old man through two genuine mistakes in the past (although these had been rectified at the time). In return the Council wanted him to stop his offensive verbal and written complaints about alleged elder abuse.

Here the mediation failed to help the old man see the necessity of a change in the communicative aspects of his personal and social relationships. His offensive language continued despite the mediator's presence as he tried to overpower the proceedings with continuing abuse of the Council. He became so excited that he fell over, quickly picking himself up. Although he was urged to call the doctor, and take advantage of an adjournment, his autonomous decision to continue was belligerently made, and had to be respected, due to the ethical basis of the mediation contract as it was then formulated. There were failed efforts at shared decision-making with the Council officer who offered to take the old man to the local hospital for a check-up.

However there was a collaborative achievement in persuading the old man to take a lunch break and rest in his home, where the mediation had taken place. Sadly, an hour later, he was found on the floor, having had what was then realized as being a second stroke, although his mental and communicative competence was intact and as active as ever. Yet there was an extraordinary relational change: gently, he expressed the deepest gratitude for all the tender loving care which was immediately given to him; he became apologetic for all the trouble he had caused, and gave the impression of being the most appreciative of gentlemen as arrangements were made for him to leave his home by ambulance. Anger and abuse was no longer needed to gain him the kind of attention he had needed.

The mediation process had certainly not been protective in the literal sense, and revised practice guidelines focused on mediators' increased responsibility to adjourn proceedings when necessary, but it had provided a positive experience of nourishing communicative concern and relational care which had inadvertently transformed a negative crisis. Fortunately he made a good recovery in hospital where he had a reputation of being as charming to the nurses as they were to him, and telling them stories about all the important work he had done in his life.

The stories we tell are embedded in a cultural matrix, and we have inadequate understanding of how narrative features in the multicultural abusive relations of later life. As unresolved conflict is as prominent a feature in elder abuse theory (Pillemer and Wolf, 1986), as in relationship studies, there is a need for interdisciplinary co-operation to initiate the many more detailed research studies which are necessary to illuminate this dark area of interpersonal conflict, the social importance of which will increase.

Understanding the social accounts of old people, and the construction of abusive relations in the later life with its associated conflicts, is a critical aspect of the work of EMP, as these cases have shown.

In many cases the conflict and abuse may appear minimal, especially in long-standing disputes about loud noise levels, late night visits, disruptive children, privacy invasion, and bad language between quarrelling neighbours, but old people are often desperate in their referrals to EMP as they can no longer bear the violation of their retirement years in the much loved nest of their homes. Their perceptions of abuse may be heightened, but they are real and deeply felt, and are too often responded to, or provoked, in destructive and sometimes abusive ways.

This may uncomfortably stretch the definitional boundaries of elder abuse, which theorists and practitioners understandably wish to restrict to avoid labelling and other counterproductive tendencies. Nevertheless such experiences have to be accommodated by academics and social agencies involved in considering the impact on community care of increasing numbers of old people choosing to live alone, especially if their isolation and restricted social networks provide no constructive defence and management in neighbour conflict.

In conclusion this is where EMPs can play a useful contributory role in empowering old people to cope with conflicts, and stop or prevent abusive relationships from developing. This is a vital part of the present EMP's evolving services, and the casework component of this chapter has illustrated the person-centred approach which is the base on which its earlier description of organizational aims and structure was founded.

The next chapter shows how a more formally structured organizational approach to using mediation in an Oslo elder abuse project, which has attracted considerable European and international social attention, has also been concerned to match theory and practice in its developing work.

8 Elder abuse and mediation work in Norway

There is no existing body of literature on the role of mediator as informally used by the many multidisciplinary workers who are involved in caring for older persons, and those with whom they have interdependent relationships. However most workers consciously or unconsciously feel that one element of their complex tasks is to act as a go-between between people, when appropriate.

This chapter[1] continues the dialogic interplay between theory and praxis which has characterized this book, perhaps uncomfortably for some readers, but necessary to validate the ideas of the research through seeing how they relate to real life issues and developments.

It points to the importance of communication in all go-between or mediation activity, especially as one of the many effects of the British National Health Service and Community Care Act 1991 has been to increase the necessity for mediating skills, especially in elder care. In Norway this has been given major social recognition through the pioneer work done by Johns and Juklestad (1994a), from the University of Oslo Department of Geriatric Medicine. They formally conceptualized the role of mediator in social care terms, and operationalized it in their elder protective project work, supporting by important theory.

Before their work is discussed it may be helpful to precede it by introducing some relevant findings from British communication studies, and follow it with concluding brief references to evolving Scandinavian and European perspectives about the importance of empowering older people in constructive decision-making when confronted by later life conflicts and abusive, or potentially abusive situations.

Metacommunication and miscommunication in elder care

British communication studies have only recently dealt in depth with their subject as related to old age, with Giles et al's edited book, *Communication, Health and the Elderly* (1990), following the more general work of Argyle et al (1983; 1991) which has sections on situations of later life which contribute to misunderstandings. Hummert et al's *Interpersonal Communication in Older Adulthood* (1994) and Duck's *Relationship Challenges* (1995) add notable American contributions to this literature.

Giles et al's concern is to focus on the centrality of 'the need to establish good communication ... in order to reduce social conflict' (1990:1), and their book gives detailed descriptions and analyses of how elderly people suffer from depersonalization and social controls through the linguistic modes of, especially, professional caregivers. Although their study provides valuable material which can be used to reinforce the aim of mediation to be an egalitarian process using clear jargon-free language which respects the understanding and abilities of older persons, in this chapter, another aspect of their work is developed.

This quotes from an 1988 Fullbright Colloquium:

> We believe communication forms the linchpin to providing an understanding of the complex and controversial interrelationships mediating forms of social support, various measures of psychological well-being, and physical health (Giles et al, 1990:6).

There is then a reference to Albrecht and Adelman's *Communicating Social Support* (1987) which shows how the way in which people perceive and accept social support is dependant on the level and quality of the communication. Giles et al follow this by introducing the concept of 'high attuning', a skill to be recommended for professional caregivers, based on active listening and empathy with the feelings of people. They add that 'our model highlights the psycho-social-linguistic armoury individuals bring to different situations: our so-called "pre-interactional mediators"' (1990:15).

This phrase, resonant with the subject of this present book, might also be borrowed to illustrate the problems of metacommunication which exist in this social area, which the authors suggest might be

164

called 'gerontocommunication' (1990:21). Leaving aside the critical importance of active listening and empathy to people in later life, especially the very old, such pre-interactional mediators of good communication and social support are equally vital in establishing constructive interrelationships between the supporters.

Ironically, it is within the skilled and specialized health and social services, with their extensive professional knowledge of the *meaning* and *significance* of active listening and empathy at the deepest psychological level in mediating social relationships, that controversies and conflicts have a destructive influence. Whereas a positive philosophical view of the human services might suggest that their shared aims of contributing to the welfare of people would be associated with the metacommunication of a shared understanding of principles and policies, the advent of community care is professionally and publicly perceived to have produced extensive miscommunication and conflict.

Although authorities writing on the development of British community care (Bulmer, 1987; Willmott, 1989) have always stressed that its success depends on effective partnerships between the health and social services, and the statutory, voluntary and private sectors, in practice there has been as much conflict as co-operation.

Here it is not proposed to digress further by discussing the principles and values of community care, which are upheld in this book, and which are entirely consistent with those of the mediation movement, but, rather, to note that the well-rehearsed rhetoric about partnership has not been reflected in the discord and disputes which have surfaced at various levels. This is clearly seen in Britain, has been reported about appearing in Europe (Jamieson, 1991), and is commented on by Johns and Juklestad (1994a) in the work for old people in Norway.

The point being made is that community care, at least in its early stages, has been an experience of conflict in many instances, and situated at structural, inter-agency, professional and direct caregiving levels. The conflict has been compounded by miscommunication, partly from the accidental or intentional obfuscation of legislation and regulations, partly by the promotion of unilateral agency and professional perspectives, and partly through the misreporting of relevant events by the press.

Although Government spokesmen, as partisans for the policies they have promulgated, have sought to pacify conflict, there has been a real need for the deployment of communication and mediating skills, at the different levels indicated, to reconcile relationships which have become fragile, and to encourage practical problem-solving approaches to the difficulties of community care.

These ideas of workers having a mediating capacity, and of using communication skills are increasingly if insufficiently spreading, and the pioneer work at the University of Oslo Department of Geriatric Medicine by Johns and Juklestad (1994a) has now given them stronger visibility in Norway and Scandinavia, specifically in their Oslo elder abuse project.

Breaking down barriers in Norwegian elder care

There is no APS (adult protective service) agency in Norway, but there is a well developed health and social services program for the elderly in general. Our experience with elderly victims of family abuse indicates that numerous institutions and resources should be able to help, but that professional and administrative barriers complicate it seriously. Elderly victims of family abuse are a group of clients who need help from several different agencies simultaneously. The lack of flexible, client-oriented and inter-disciplinary action is the basic problem, that also affects other groups of elderly at risk. By focusing on victims-support, mediation and co-ordination, our project is designed to deal with this problem in particular (Johns, Juklestad and Hydle, 1992:1).

This extract from a 1992 draft conference paper links the references already made to British partnership problems between its programmes for elder care with similar difficulties in Norway as related to the special area of elder abuse.

It specifically identifies mediation as a working principle and practice to be developed in the approach made to developing adult protective services in Norway, even though there has been no national legislation to initiate and support these. The extract goes further in stressing the embeddedness of mediation and the regularity with which it will be used, as will be other helping processes:

The project is directed towards developing methods for future work on an extended scale. Based on the various methods of social work, we aim at developing community-work, (networking) and advocacy towards more systematic mediation between client and professional helpers (Johns, Juklestad and Hydle, 1992:1).

Johns is a social anthropologist, working in 1992 at the University of Oslo Department of Geriatric Medicine, which has a location at the Ullevaal Hospital, Oslo; Juklestad is a social worker with practical experience of the social services, hospitals, and a senior citizen centre, who was appointed to develop the project; Hydle, a geriatrician, was the director of the project, named the Elder Protective Services, for which the Norwegian Ministry of Social Affairs granted funding in 1988.

In a 1994 conference paper Johns gives a brief account of Norway's discovery of the problem of elder abuse in the 1980s, and describes the powerful effect of *naming* the problem. He played a prominent part with Hydle in developing Norwegian research on the subject, and in establishing good communication with Sweden and Finland in a Nordic network of researchers. However, he and Juklestad state that 'excepting Norway, the Scandinavian governments have been very reluctant to engage in the problem of elder abuse', adding, in a footnote, 'we have no simple explanation of how it has been possible to mobilize the Norwegian Government' (Johns and Juklestad, 1994a:3).

An outside observer, aware of the importance of metacommunication as mentioned above, and noting the significance of Norwegian researchers' success in raising public consciousness in the naming of the problem of elder abuse, might offer this as a possible explanation. From the extracts already quoted it can be seen that good communication and networking has been a hallmark of the Norwegian project.

Although this chapter is not the place to describe the details of the Norwegian research, it is relevant to remark on the theoretically innovative introduction of the role of the 'witness' in elder abuse situations, which has been developed from its use in Riches' study, *The anthropology of violence*, (1986). This recognizes 'a social triangle of violence, involving not only victim and perpetrator, but also others (directly or indirectly) witnessing the act' (Johns and Juklestad, 1994a:5).

This research has led to the following definition of abuse:

> Abuse is a social act involving at least two actors, one of whom is violating the personal boundaries of the other. This is abuse insofar as it is interpreted and morally evaluated as illegitimate by a third party, the witness (Johns et al, 1991).

This interpretation raises interesting issues, especially in the British criminal justice context, where the term witness has specific legal and court connotations, although its Norwegian usage cannot be further discussed now. However the welcome wide Norwegian criteria for defining abuse as based on the violation of personal boundaries, reflects a concern for the effects of miscommunication and mistrust, and is consonant with the broad approach of this book. Johns et al write of the effects of personal boundaries being threatened or even completely broken:

> This fear leaves deep psychological marks and creates in the abused fundamental mistrust towards the world which they once thought to be a safe place ... We need to know that we have the independence to make our own decisions. We need to control our personal boundaries (Johns et al, 1991:57–8).

In passing it may be suggested that it is the similar painfulness of professional boundary disputes which has appeared so threatening and stressful to the multidisciplinary workers and agencies whose conflicts over community care have already been noted. Miscommunication and mistrust can be as damaging in general elder care as they are in the special area of elder abuse, which is why mediating skills can be used constructively to prevent this.

However another aspect of this conceptualization of the witness is developed further:

> *The witness*, shorthand for the person labelling an act as abuse, is crucial in this definition. When analyzing problems of diagnosis and intervention, this term serves the important purpose of explaining the role of the professional helper (Johns and Juklestad, 1994a:5).

Here there are indications of the ambivalences and ambiguities for professional helpers about identifying and labelling elder abuse, and these are also related to communication difficulties, the breaking of professional boundaries, and barriers to inter-agency partnerships in coping with the conflicts of later life:

> This points towards the third set of barriers, those complicating cooperation, coordination and information within the bureaucracy of care. The barriers partly arise out of the division between professional groups, working with different and sometimes conflicting clients, and being located in different, rather self-

contained institutions. The lack of flexible, client-oriented and inter-disciplinary action is a major problem in the Norwegian welfare system (Johns and Juklestad, 1994a:7).

The discourse continues:

The problem amounts to connecting client and helpers in a fruitful coalition. We wanted to find means to build bridges over the administrative gaps and unlock doors in the barriers of privacy and bureaucracy. Adopting a central task of the APS worker, we found a possible procedure in the role of a specially trained *mediator:* a social worker who can skilfully relate to the needs of the victim and negotiate coordinated service plans (Dolon and Blakely, 1989; Hwalek et al, 1991; Johns et al, 1992). By focusing on victim-support, mediation and coordination, a project was designed to provide this kind of assistance to victims and professionals (Johns and Juklestad, 1994a:7).

It was Juklestad who was recruited to do the casework and develop the process and techniques implicit in this design using mediation, and her comments form the second part of the 1994 conference paper.

Mediation in Manglerud

Juklestad described her responsibilities 'for the day-to-day running of the "Elder Protective Services" project, localized at the Senior Citizen Center of Manglerud, one out of twenty-five communities and administrative entities, in Oslo' (Johns and Juklestad, 1994a:8), which had a population then of 500,000, out of a national Norwegian population of about 4.5 millions. Out of the 12,000 inhabitants of Manglerud, nearly 2,500 were over 67 years old.

During the first 36 months of the project 67 suspected cases of elder abuse were reported to her, 56 (86 per cent) being substantiated, most of them involving family conflict.

Juklestad lists 11 local supportive agencies, including home nurses, sheltered housing and social services, and an additional seven Oslo services, including a women's shelter and addiction clinics, which provided available resources for her clients. She describes her role as mediator between these agencies:

From my free position at the Senior Citizen Center I functioned as a key person, reaching out to victims and collaborating with

169

the health and social service professionals. I have a wide-ranging mandate to contact, motivate and coordinate all relevant resources and services who could contribute (Johns and Juklestad, 1994a:9)

In one particular case an addict and perpetrator of abuse was a long-time client of the social services, which therefore had problems of confidentiality and prior responsibility in his individual case. He had threatened to kill his parents, stolen their valuables and caused them crippling debts. Juklestad was concerned that in such situations, 'approaches by both the social services and family counselling can therefore be downright dangerous, if the victims cannot be given protection' (Johns and Juklestad, 1994a:15). She therefore worked to motivate the parents to contact the police, and acted as a negotiator with the parents' bank to ensure their financial security.

Juklestad saw her role as empowering the parents to take as much control as possible of their situation, and enabling them to make their own choices and decisions as far as possible. 'In this kind of case it is necessary to follow the couple through a process. They need support and help to see possible solutions, alternative actions and assistance.' It is these skills which are essentially those of mediation, as Juklestad goes on to say. 'It is through being available and backing them up through the process that I can help them change their situation. Giving good advice is just not enough' (Johns and Juklestad, 1994a:16).

Through Juklestad's mediating skills, both with the family and with the social services, the son was encouraged to admit to the abuse and to agree to a treatment programme, whilst the parents' situation greatly improved.

In concluding her casework contribution to the conference paper, Juklestad commented that the project had demonstrated significant practical and positive results and that the local authorities planned to incorporate it into their permanent services. She also made a further comment:

Relying on support from well-developed public health care and social services, one person has been adequate to work practically as a mediator and taking care of education and information in a community of this size. It has not been necessary to discuss whether or not we should have laws to regulate this activity. We have been able to work within the existing framework (Johns and Juklestad, 1994a:16).

This last sentence is of especial significance to the present considerations of the currently formulating British social policy on elder abuse. There has been a concern to avoid some of the difficulties which have been connected with American legislation for adult protective services. The consequences of this have often worsened family conflicts and dependant elders' situations rather than having provided constructive solutions which have healed tragic lives.

Thus, in Britain, there has also been multidisciplinary preference for focusing on establishing appropriate services which work within the existing framework. Johns and Juklestad's experience of mediation, and mediating skills, and their work showing their value in a widely developed context is a salient recommendation, as Norway and Britain are approximately at the same stage with regard to recognizing and responding to the problem of elder abuse in elder care situations.

Another important aspect of this Norwegian approach is referred to in the 1992 conference paper referred to earlier, and relates to the real value of mediation work to clients:

> ... the suffering person has to convince the doctor, nurse or social worker that he is sufficiently in need of their help. For most people, this is not a serious problem. But elderly victims of family abuse are generally very weak clients. They need help from several different agencies simultaneously, and do not know how to define and prove their needs in a convincing manner., (Some of them are too ashamed to even try). Professionals, on the other hand, claim it is hard to find out about conflicts in the family, and even harder to intervene in the privacy of people's homes. So, in spite of welfare, it does not follow that the victims receive the necessary help (Johns, Juklestad and Hydle, 1992:3).

Thus the University of Oslo Department of Geriatric Medicine found that mediation and advocacy were, more importantly, useful direct benefits to their clients, and a significant reference made in personal correspondence appropriately ends this chapter's appreciation of their work:

> We find that the elder protective worker must be a mediator in a very wide sense of the term: first, there is the problem of establishing contact with the victim, then there is the problem of mediation between victim and perpetrator, thirdly there is the problem of mediating a good helping relation between the victim and relevant professionals, and finally, there is the problem of

mediating good cooperation between different professionals from different agencies (Johns and Juklestad, 1994b:1).

However it is interesting to note also that Daatland of the Norwegian Institute of Gerontology, writing in the *European Journal of Gerontology* (1/3, 1992), sees the importance of the role of mediation in a similar context to that of the British Elder Mediation Project:

> In fact, in some circumstances and settings, old persons with strong family members act as mediators between the elderly and the public care system (1992:177).

His article reinforces the views of Johns and Juklestad described above, in that Daatland also sees the delivery of needed services depending on go-between activity and negotiation. However he additionally suggests that mediation by family members has been necessary in Norway because the family has traditionally been responsible for the welfare of its members. Daatland conceptualizes a process of replacement, transference and partnership of welfare responsibilities: those of the family are being replaced by the state; the transference leads to conflict and overlapping of provisions; the need is for positive practical partnerships between the family, the state and its voluntary and statutory sectors to be worked out.

This is also a principal concern of two authoritative texts on elder care in Europe, relevant brief references to which conclude this chapter.

European perspectives of the social go-between

Jamieson's landmark edition of contributors to *Home Care for Older People in Europe: A Comparison of Policies and Practices* (1991) is introduced by her comment that community care, as a term, does not exist in other languages, and that, generally, in the nine European Community countries studied, there were inadequate and inappropriately used services. The need for co-operation in establishing effective partnerships between all the services is continually stressed, as it has been throughout this chapter.

Jamieson, in a penultimate general chapter about European provisions for elderly persons, also comments that 'the exclusion of the elderly people from the whole decision-making process is characteristic of most of the countries studied' (1991:262).

In an earlier volume, *Contrasting European Policies for the Care of the Elderly* (1990), Illsley and Jamieson say specifically that some professionals 'tend to exclude the elderly from participation in the decision-making process' (Jamieson and Illsley, 1990:13).

Nothing in Kosberg's worldwide edition, *Family Care of the Elderly* (1992) dissents from the points made in this chapter, while Horl, describing the metalevels of family conflict in Austria, points to what he calls the 'superindividualization' (1992:247) which threatens normative concepts of the family. He suggests that 'losses in the intergenerational and intragenerational social network will have to be compensated by installing even more organized professional social services, unless new interaction and household patterns develop based on nonkin relations' (Horl, 1992:248).

This, he goes on to say, is problematic because their communication systems and processes may not agree:

> Knowledge concerning interaction effects between family and social service organizations is salient for social policy planning, because coordination and cooperation between the family and the state is only possible as long as competing, conflicting, or otherwise disturbed relations between both parties are anticipated and comprehended (Horl, 1992:248).

These comments reinforce the introduction to this chapter on the imperatives of good communications in elder care, and an extract from Saveman's 1994 Swedish study of elder abuse offers a relevant conclusion. She refers to Logstrup's ethics (1971) with regard to any difficult situation:

> by stepping outside it, watching from a meta-level, solutions may become visible ... To be able to reflect on a meta-level formal carers might need to distance themselves from the family ... there must also be a balance between closeness and distance (Saveman, 1994:61).

This concern for appropriate and effective metacommunication follows her earlier reference to Phillips' and Rempusheski's 1985 study of decision-making, which describes the conflicts within those made about diagnosis, values and intervention, in which 'formal carers seem to be trapped in an indecision cycle' (1994:53). So Saveman sees there is a need for meta-level conflict resolution for family members and professional caregivers.

She then goes on to recommend that there should be 'municipal mediator(s)' (1994:64–5), saying that action research is needed in Sweden to establish the best bases of intervention and communication.

All of these Scandinavian and European references point to constructive intercommunication as being a prerequisite for good elder care, and support the major work of Johns and Juklestad, and the informal initiatives of the British Elder Mediation Project in using mediation skills to prevent elder abuse and to encourage effective co-operation between the protective multidisciplinary services.

The last chapter of Part III considers further developments and future possibilities in improving public attitudes, policies and plans concerned with the prevention of elder abuse, arising from widening perspectives and insights generated by international research and social agency co-operation. In these mediation processes and services may be able to make a contribution.

Note

1 Grateful acknowledgements are given to Sigurd Johns and Olaug Juklestad for their review of references to their work in this chapter.

9 Insights and initiatives with European perspectives

Although this book began with acknowledging its debt to American research into elder abuse and conflict resolution theories, and its pioneer work in practical mediation projects, a principal aim of these present exploratory studies has been to describe and comment on the related developing work in Britain specifically and, to a lesser degree, in Europe generally, where it is difficult to trace relevant insights and initiatives which are not yet publicized.

This chapter will thus reflect an undesired disparity in description and discussion of these insights, initiatives and perspectives, especially as there will doubtless be European developments in the area of research taking place as the writing of this present book ends, and while it is in press.

Nevertheless it is significant, at this juncture, to note that recently a French social researcher was considering doing a study to explore why family mediation in France was still undeveloped, in comparison to its legislative institution in Britain through the new divorce bill, which was mentioned in the first chapter of the book. This is hardly evidence for speculating that Europe, in general, may be as behind Britain in developing initiatives in areas of elder abuse and mediation, as we were in following America, but it supports the previous apologia for presenting perspectives in this chapter which may appear unbalanced.

Therefore it is not divided into British and European sections, but links relevant social experiences in the areas of elder abuse and mediation, these being dealt with under separate headings.

The chapter begins with discussing some of the most relevant and important insights in respect of elder abuse theory, research and practice which have developed in Britain, and then turns to further consideration of mediation initiatives that are of especial interest to older people. These two areas are then briefly reviewed in terms of their implications for public policy and planning.

The social development of elder abuse theory and praxis

Elder abuse, or 'granny battering' as it was often called then, first began to attract medical attention in Britain in the mid to late 1970s, as recorded in the first major survey of the subject done by McCreadie (1991), although Robb (1967) wrote an important indictment of it taking place in institutional care.

McCreadie, a researcher at the newly formed Age Concern Institute of Gerontology of Kings College London, supported by its director, Professor Anthea Tinker, and Sally Greengross, director general of Age Concern England, gathered together interested gerontologists, geriatricians and professional and practitioner members of the multidisciplinary statutory and voluntary services concerned with the care of old people, to consider what social action could be taken to prevent elder abuse.

Shortly after, following television programmes and media coverage, Action on Elder Abuse (AEA) was formed in 1993, situated within the central Age Concern England office infrastructure, but having its own separate charitable registration. It is the work of (AEA), vigorously promoted by its first director, Ginny Jenkins, which has been principally responsible for advancing the social confrontation of elder abuse.

It is not the intention of this chapter to give even a brief history of its research committee, publications, conferences, telephone hotline and other ongoing developments, as its address, noted in the references, can be contacted for networking purposes (AEA, 1996).

Dr Gerry Bennett, Chair of AEA's Council of Trustees, and geriatrician of the Royal London Hospital Trust, conducted a major elder abuse study there, recorded in a subsequent book (Bennett and Kingston, 1993), where research and theory substantially followed that evolving in America, which had begun to move the focus of attention from the abused to the abuser.

This study also stressed the importance of improving the search for, diagnosis and care of the old people suffering from elder abuse, principally through raising its profile in primary care services. However it also led to a much stronger drive than in America towards its practical prevention, based on striving to support adults who were either vulnerable through age and dependency, or equally vulnerable as carers unable to cope with undue external stress or their own potential pathologies.

It has been this British combination of theory and praxis, supported in other notable publications (Biggs et al, 1995; Decalmer and Glendenning, 1993; Kingston and Penhale, 1995; Phillipson and Biggs, 1992) that has been the chartermark of national and local developments, in the area of elder abuse. A similar attempt to combine theory and praxis about the interface between elder abuse and mediation has also been the aim of this book, although the problems of correlating and compressing two different sets of knowledge and experience are difficult to overcome.

However, the interdisciplinary co-operation between academics, researchers and practitioners involved in elder abuse work has resulted in many shared insights and initiatives, one being especially relevant in the context of this chapter. It concerns the role played by AEA in encouraging the first Support and Advice For Vulnerable Elders (SAVE) project, located in a London Local Authority's social service department in Lewisham. Part of the shared achievement is that it was set up in 1993 at the same time that AEA was initiated, reflecting the rapid response to situations requiring social action, which has also characterized the work of the Elder Mediation Project (EMP).

There were also similar shared approaches to participative consultation in that AEA has always encouraged and supported initiatives after joint decision-making with the agencies concerned. Prior to the development of SAVE, AEA's inter-agency discussions reached a consensus in their insights into the need to provide vulnerable adults with advisory and supportive services which were named so as to be non-threatening to old people and their carers.

It was hoped that within this compassionate, caring and helping framework that the tragic problems of elder abuse could be sensitively confronted and prevented from occurring again. The associated aims of SAVE and AEA were that the service would become a valuable prototype for the development of similar services throughout Britain, so that a reliable and responsive infrastructure was constructed to save old people from elder abuse, yet prevent it from becoming politically problematized (as has child sex and satanic abuse for instance), in ways that would expose vulnerable adults to even more suffering.

However, there is no wish for such a network of supportive services to follow the specific pattern of SAVE, as it is recognized that every area will need to develop projects which suit its own cultural pattern, so that some may be initiated by voluntary organizations, or coalitions of these, while others may be based in statutory agencies.

Nevertheless, while there is no intent now to describe SAVE's work in detail, as an evaluation by McCreadie should eventually be available from AEA or the Age Concern Institute of Gerontology, it is instructive to list briefly SAVE's achievements so far.

Although directed by only two paid workers, by 1995 SAVE had developed access to 12 social workers, about 10 institutional staff, 4 police officers, a district nurse and a number of volunteer visitors. SAVE also provided many multi-agency trainings and education in local colleges, with specific seminars on using the law to protect vulnerable elders. It also provided workplace training for over 700 workers in home care, housing departments, district nursing, medical and paramedical staff. At the same time it has published newsletters, articles, quarterly and annual reports, and attracted international interest.

These achievements of SAVE also have a structural importance in that it was initially funded by the Home Office which is a key government department in contributing to the development of any legislative changes affecting the criminal justice system.

Here it is significant to note that SAVE's acronym was chosen on the basis of highlighting the word vulnerable, when it might have stressed victims. Although SAVE networks with Victim Support, the established national voluntary organization working with victims, a prime focus is on helping those old people who suffer from abuse in families and institutions, leaving Victim Support to continue its work for those people, including elderly persons, who are the subject of crime as defined by law and the police. At the moment, elder abuse is not categorized as a crime by British law, as it is in most States in America, for the reasons already advanced.

The work of SAVE may thus be critical in influencing the Home Office away from criminalization of one of the most sensitive and complex areas of human pathology if it is shown that a developing infrastructure of advisory and support services can contain and prevent elder abuse.

However there could be mutual advantages from an interdisciplinary discourse between elder abuse theorists and those working in the fields of victimology and criminology, where literatures are generally not combined in research studies.

It could be of special benefit for elder abuse theorists to take account of the increasing interest shown by victimologists and criminologists in the use of mediation in victim–offender reparation projects, about which

Wright (1982; 1991; 1996; Wright and Galaway, 1989) has pioneered the major British research.

This research has consistently advocated principles of rehabilitation and restorative justice, which are not only consonant with the theme of relational justice noted in this book that will re-emerge again, but are significantly related to one of the main aims of elder abuse prevention, especially as demonstrated by SAVE, and similar projects.

Although not specifically conceptualized in terms of the protection of victims, the rehabilitation of offenders and their reintegration into the community, these identification and supportive services do aim to prevent victimization by reforming potential or actual perpetrators of elder abuse, where appropriate and possible, so that broken families may be healed, institutional staff can be trained and supervised more responsibly, and the community care of old people greatly improved.

Nevertheless it is important to stress that in elder abuse and mediation theory, as in victimology and criminology, the safety of possible or actual victims is of paramount importance. However, designating some sufferers from elder abuse as victims may not always be helpful, or accurate, as some of the EMP case references have suggested, and also as shown by studies of violent episodes in institutions where staff have restrained aggressive dementia patients who have attacked them (Stokes, 1987). Also, from the empowerment perspective, there is the alternative term, survivor, which some sufferers from abuse, notably many Jewish people, prefer.

Thus in all of these areas there is ongoing debate about the aetiologies and terminologies of elder abuse and crime, their differentiation and their common ground, and, more contentiously, questions about the varied remedies available, as to who chooses these, and when and how they are applied in individual cases.

Here is another area for academic, professional and practitioner boundary disputes, and mediating skills will be useful in moderating these, as has been shown in the last chapter's references to experiences in Norway. It is hoped that EMP, and its relevant EMPowerment not empire-building approach may play an appropriately modest but constructive role in facilitating such interdisciplinary co-operation. The chapter about EMP, and its constant references to communication and relationship studies in relation to mediation and elder abuse work, is a present example of how connections are being made between different research domains.

One immediate benefit of furthering such interdisciplinary discourse is that there appear to be shared concerns to avoid counterproductive labelling and problematizing in the social construction of deviancy (Downes and Rock, 1988). As has already been noted, one of the reasons why some old people do not report abuse is that they fear stigmatization of their families and labelling of relevant members as criminal. Such labelling in elder abuse cases may be doubly distressing if the perpetrator has poor mental or physical health, or acted uncharacteristically due to pressures of caring.

This is where mediation can provide a useful early screening device, where unresolved conflicts are noted in the social care of vulnerable adults. The accounts given in mediation often surface underlying difficulties and hostilities, which prompt mediators to offer referrals to social support agencies like SAVE, and which similarly, by their code of ethics, would require them to report any active abuse or crime to the police, and possibly discontinue the mediation. Participants would be consulted about this at every stage, and before mediation begins they would be warned about any ethical obligations of the mediator.

However elder abuse workers may be as reluctant to trust mediation as either a screening device, or as a conflict management and peacemaking process, as have been many people involved in domestic violence projects. There is an understandable fear that mediation could be used to suppress conflict and divert people away from stronger social interventions. In domestic violence work, there is a vast popular and research literature which urges immediate police intervention with arrest, removal and possible charging with offences, details of which will not be given here to avoid enlarging the reference list even further.

This literature, plus feminist political lobbying, has succeeded in changing public policy in this area, so that active police intervention has now become the norm, although the subsequent prosecution and court processes have not, for various complicated reasons, been as successful in proving that offenders are guilty, or finding appropriate sentences for the few that are convicted.

Therefore this criminal justice approach has not yet been found adequate for victims, their children, and their domestic life, the viability of which often depends completely on having the spousal breadwinner return home, which is why many charges are dropped by the victims. So here again, mediation can play a useful post-police intervention role, by helping those concerned to fashion a mutually acceptable agreement for this return home, provided that there will be no more violence, although, unfortunately, such promises are too often violated.

In America mediation has been used formally, if occasionally, in both the early and late stage of domestic violence conflicts, sometimes on the

180

recommendation of courts, but British experience in this sphere is so far generally limited to its informal use by probation and social workers.

As some elder abuse theorists conceptualize it as being part of family violence, the previous comments are relevant to the way in which insights and initiatives in domestic violence may influence future developments in the prevention of elder abuse, depending on how perspectives about using major or minor forms of social intervention evolve and change. It should be said, however, that some police authorities have officers especially dedicated to work on elder abuse (Craig and Woods, 1993), including those who have experienced the value of mediation in negotiating hostage or suicide situations, and in public disorder crises (Craig, 1992).

Discussion of these important topics cannot be further extended here, although a closing comment must re-emphasize a dominant theme in this book that the tragic area of elder abuse is complex and sensitive, and that we know too little about it, or about other aspects of domestic and family violence.

However, despite consensus views amongst voluntary and statutory services about broad general aims in preventing elder abuse, it could be speculated that central and local government agencies may develop a greater use of law enforcement, partly because of already established links with the police, but also to ensure their workers' safety, and to safeguard professional and agency reputations for not leaving vulnerable old people at risk.

This is illustrated by mentioning one aspect of a local authority social service department's guidelines on elder abuse, on which general subject this chapter now more briefly focuses. The guidelines in question specified that if any worker entered a home in which active abuse occurred, or was threatened, the worker had to leave immediately and call for police help, or, if uncertain, check with a staff manager. No discretion was allowable for trying to mediate or negotiate in the situation. Unfortunately, this elder abuse unit of the social services department, did not have the financial resources to provide its workers with mobile telephones, which can be protective and supportive devices in such visits, although their visibility could be counterproductive in non-threatening cases.

However this elder abuse unit did have an excellent 3-day training, at which the roles of advocacy, counselling and mediation were discussed, with very experienced social workers who wished to specialize in elder abuse, and who were ready to introduce supportive volunteer visitors, also to be trained.

181

As is general in British local authority social service departments, each has the freedom to shape its own policies and plans to suit the social context of their differing citizen populations, subject to conforming to broad central government directives, and to available financial and personnel resources. Due to pressures on these, there has been an irregular and non-standardized approach to developing both local authority and health authority guidelines, as well as to implementing them. For instance, there is no agreed diagnostic medical category of elder abuse for raising general practitioners' awareness of the problem, while multidisciplinary case conference procedures are not yet institutionalized, or operationalized, in every area.

Nor is there yet sufficiently firmly established internal co-operation within social service infrastructures so that new elder abuse units network regularly with the independent local authority inspectorates of residential care who have responsibilities for seeing that the homes visited under the 1984 Registered Homes Act, and its subsequent amendments, do not mistreat their residents. The two departments may have shared values about elder care and elder rights, but there may be more pressure on inspectorates to lower their definitional perspectives of abuse, if closure of homes leaves residents with no where else to go. This is a possible danger in some poor inner city areas, similar to that which was noted to be regularly occurring in Atlanta.

Within the national voluntary organizational ageing network, there are those especially concerned to act as watchdogs for old people in institutional care, notably the Relatives Association and Counsel and Care, which has produced publications about the abusive use of restraints and residents' rights in general.

The British government has also responded to public disquiet by introducing a system of lay assessors, who visit with the inspectorate, with a special responsibility to see that residents are content with their care. There is professional staff ambivalence about the use of volunteers which, from one perspective, is seen as a cheap and inadequate form of labour which also causes more work for inspectors, although other officers welcome working with caring enthusiasts who can give more personal listening to individual residents, and watch more closely for abuse.

Yet again, there is no standardized payment to the assessors, some of whom are only given minimal expenses, others of whom receive comparatively larger fees per visit made, which is a source of conflict when opposing practices are used by bordering boroughs, and remuneration and training depends on what side of the road a lay

182

assessor lives. For the training is also not standardized, and is sometimes done by local authority in-house staff, and sometimes contracted out to voluntary organizations like Age Concern or independent agencies.

The quality of training from Age Concern, independent agencies, and bodies like the British Association of Services to the Elderly (BASE), is of a high standard in their developing expertise in working on elder abuse, which is concerned equally for that occurring in the community as well as in institutional care.

Similar developments in Scotland and Ireland are also taking place although these are not recorded here.

In returning to the role of AEA in monitoring, and resourcing or co-ordinating where possible, all of these and other initiatives, it can be seen that a great deal has been accomplished in the last five years since earlier insights into elder abuse gradually became instrumental in leading to so many developments. It should also be noted that another leading ageing organization, Help the Aged, has started a Senior Line which, especially usefully, provides a free information call system to old people for any problem, not just that of elder abuse.

One of the individual key workers who has contributed greatly to understanding, and dealing practically with elder abuse is Eastman (1984), author of one of the first British classic texts on the subject, who also constructed one of the first set of guidelines for Enfield social service department of which he is assistant director.

It is therefore particularly apposite that his department has now received funding from Europe for a European Exchange Project to explore the care of elderly people in residential care, and the factors leading to their mistreatment. This appears to be the first practical partnership with Europe on elder abuse, and Kalmar in Sweden, and Murcia in Spain are involved. It is hoped that by 1997 a set of pan-European guidelines will be produced, and that any other elder abuse initiatives will become more visible and extensive than they seem to be at the moment.

Meanwhile great progress continues to made through the major European coalitions concerned with elder care and intergenerational solidarity in general, with Eurolink Age and its Council actively campaigning on many issues raising the social profile of old people, including that of elder abuse. Age Concern England continues to play an influential role in this and also facilitates the UK European Resource Unit.

In addition, references to some of these and other European developments, in a special issue on elder abuse *(Social Work in Europe,* 1995, December, Vol. 2, No. 3), show that it is primarily situated in the existing or expanding welfare framework, rather than in the criminal justice system.

A connecting link between this section of the chapter and the next involves one central London local authority setting up a Vulnerable Old People's Initiative with a walk-in co-ordinating centre of services which will attempt to repair some of the social and cultural deficits of community care. In addition, it acknowledges that some vulnerable old people can disrupt people's lives, as well as having their own threatened (Craig, 1996). This recognition is consistent with the findings about the mutually abusive relationships noted in the mediation casework described earlier.

It is to developing insights and initiatives in mediation that this chapter now turns.

Mediation moralities, measures and perspectives

The definitive history of Mediation UK has yet to be written, and it is not the purpose of this chapter to attempt even a potted version, but rather to concentrate on how the present and future developments most relevant to EMP and its concerns about elder abuse, are being shaped by issues of mediation morality, and the measures taken in response to these. It should be added here, however, that Mediation UK produces many important publications and videos about its practical work, its *Training Manual in Community Mediation Skills* (1996) being the most widely acclaimed, in which it can be seen how its ethical standards are operationalized in practice.

One of the consequences of Mediation UK's success in becoming a recognized part of the socially established national voluntary organization infrastructure is that it is always being asked to play a role in the increasing number of mediation or conciliation services which statutory and other independent agencies are developing. This takes the form of either publicizing criteria and specifications for such services to its member organizations, to which any can respond, or being asked to tender directly from its central office.

An example of the former relates to one community mediation service now providing the training and protocol for a Health Authority Medical Conciliation Service to deal with patient–doctor conflicts and complaints. The second illustration is a recent request for the Mediation UK national office to contribute to the government's proposed Advice, Information, Training and Conciliation Service (AITCS), which it wishes to set up to deal with disputes arising from the 1995 Disability Discrimination Act.

This issue, which also closely concerns EMP because the majority of disabled persons are old, raises moral questions about mediation, dealt with on a theoretical basis in Part I of this book, but re-emerging here as future developments are being charted.

It must be stressed that the following discussion has a personal bias, which other members of EMP and Mediation UK might not share, so the views expressed should not be considered as necessarily representative. Also, although every effort has been made to check the accuracy of factual statements, the substance of these may change while this book is in press.

Firstly it is relevant to remind readers that one of the moral principles on which mediation is based is that of enabling people to contribute to decision-making affecting their lives, through its own voluntary and non-coercive empowerment processes. Therefore social opportunities which are offered to, and through Mediation UK for contributing to increasing options for personal and interpersonal participative decision-making are welcome.

However, as has been stressed throughout this book, mediation is also based on the twin principle of upholding people's rights, including access to the law and other needed services. There may thus be morality in using mediation to complement these other services, but not to act as a substitute for them, especially if they were they were the declared first option of those involved.

It can be seen that understandable conflicts of interest can arise here, just as they can in the field of elder care, when the principle of maintaining a patient's autonomy in decision-making clashes with the principle of beneficence, as doctors feel that actions must be based on what they think is best for the patient.

In the case cited involving procedures for resolving disputes arising from the 1995 Disability Discrimination Act, Mediation UK modelled its basic moral position by trying to ascertain first what the feelings and attitudes of disability groups were to the proposals. In particular, comments were invited from EMP, as it was known that EMP networked with these groups, and was organizationally associated with one regional coalition of local grassroots disability consortiums. It was hoped that EMP could therefore take soundings on the ground from disabled individuals as well as disability groups.

This was done, and although the local groups were consulted came from poor inner city areas in which there might be some expectation that government proposals would be viewed cynically as providing cheap and inadequate remedies for grievances long felt about lack of political will and commitment to eradicating disability discrimination, it was found that this reaction was widely held throughout Britain.

It also resulted from the fact that the major disability coalition, the British Council of Organizations of Disabled People (BCOD) and the influential Royal Association for Disability and Rehabilitation (RADAR), had actively initiated the RIGHTS NOW Campaign, which urges that a Disability Commission (DC) should be established rather than a body like AITCS. It is argued that a DC (like the Commission for Racial Equality) would have the power to enforce the provisions of the 1995 Act and provide free legal representation for people making appeals, whilst AITCS would merely serve as a monitoring watchdog without any teeth, in which appeals to law and regulatory bodies would have to be individually funded.

Therefore, it has been argued, individual decision-making would be inadequately enabled and empowered, and this would make the substitute agency a spectacular failure for some of the most socially vulnerable citizens. Consequently, at this time of writing, the organizations mentioned have decided not to co-operate organizationally with the government in setting up AITCS, although of course giving their members full access to the proposals and any eventual services, to ensure the rights of those individuals who wish to use them to do so. In this way these disability coalitions can be seen to reconciling their own moral principles.

However, there may not be only one way of doing this. The RIGHTS NOW Campaign is supported by all British disability coalitions, including major established national voluntary organizations specializing in particular disabilities arising from both physical and mental illnesses and impairments. Some of these other bodies have yet to consult their vast memberships before reaching policy decisions about this issue. It may be that their members, branches and councils will more cautiously consider the pragmatics of individual interests in making the most of what is practically on offer now through the proposed AITCS, whilst continuing to campaign for DC. It can be judged equally immoral to deprive people of possible early benefits which they could derive from AITCS.

Unfortunately, this division in the protest lobby could prevent or delay the government agreeing to a DC, which it might have to do if there was a united stand by disability coalitions that they would not co-operate in legitimating AITCS.

It was this moral issue, together with the others raised, which Mediation UK had to consider in making its own response to the government

186

invitation to contribute to AITCS. An EMP memorandum on the subject to its parent body suggested that an alternative it could consider would be offering a press statement saying that, as an Equal Opportunities organization, its group membership already offers mediation to disabled persons, where they prefer their disputes to be dealt with in this way rather than by legal representation. After considering these issues, the Mediation UK executive committee decided not to support AITCS.

This lengthy focus on a current issue of moral principles which need reconciling is relevant to the subject of abuse as the majority of academics now writing about disability, many of whom are themselves disabled, consider that discrimination is a major social form of structural abuse which must be prevented (Barton, 1996; Swain et al, 1993). However, contributors differ between radical, liberal and conservative approaches to this.

It is always the tension between these approaches, which may vary at different stages of opinion formation, within individuals and groups, and between them, which contributes to the dialectical progress of organizational development. Here the mediation process, and its members who are disciplined in practising it, are used to testing each evolving stage by openly confronting issues, eliciting as many different individual and group responses to these, and constructing appropriate decision-making processes to discuss options for reaching agreements about future progress.

Thus there is always an ongoing dialectical discourse between those in the mediation movement involved in working with victims and offenders, where impartial and independent rights-conscious processes in sensitive and complex cases are especially valuable. Reference has already been made to Wright's early and recent writing (1991; 1996) about this, and this area is best explored by consulting his work.

However EMP has continuously experiences this tension in reconciling its own moralities based on working to empower older people in decision-making and resisting abuse, while also searching for ways of practically applying its principle of relational justice, through upholding the rights of others involved in conflicts.

Another example of this tension in its work arises from its multicultural team of volunteers, in which one of its most able and committed male Muslim mediators is not viewed by some outsiders as being impartial. Islamic stereotypes are projected upon him, and, although he works with women volunteers, some people feel he is bound to have a gender bias. As he also comes from Kashmir, he is regarded as a political fundamentalist, and this has led to the prejudiced view that he is

187

unacceptable for appointment as a local magistrate, and to other forms of employment which he has sought.

People who are sympathetic to him personally have differing radical, liberal and progressive views, because he is associated with Muslim extremism. This is complicated by the fact that although he speaks five Asian languages, and thus is of great value in EMP's multicultural outreach, his written English, in contributing to debates in the local press, may reinforce fundamentalist stereotyping, although he tries always to reconcile opposing viewpoints. The sad irony is that he is a deeply religious man trying to follow Koranic teaching about peacemaking, yet his faith makes him suspect.

An EMP Christian volunteer has also been found to be unacceptable as a mediator in a conflict involving a committed atheist.

Here the ethics of impartiality and independence vie with those of neutrality in the social construction of the morality of rights and values. Many mediators refuse to identify themselves, or their services, as neutral on the basis that they uphold positive action against all forms of discrimination and abuse. This view has already been discussed extensively through this book, and it is good that it will always be the subject of debate, because the ethics of mediation demands that its practitioners continuously question themselves as to whether they can work in particular situations if a neutral stance lends legitimacy to continued or future activities which are perceived to harm others, or if they cannot be neutral because of this possibility.

Problems of perception are once again critical here, as our Muslim and Christian volunteers found, which is why mediation services in general try to resolve these value conflicts, by inviting its users to decide whether or not particular mediators are acceptable when they have known personal affiliations, and whether they agree to service contracts including warnings about any need to report incidents to the authorities.

Emphasizing that mediation is only undertaken after users have given informed consent to it, and after volunteers have been given a choice of whether they wish to work with specific conflicts, helps to resolve some of the inescapable questions which, rightly, continue to concern the developing mediation movement.

Uncertainties in policy planning

The competitive market economy approach to public funding of its services for older people is as dominant here as it has been in America

(Minkler and Estes, 1991), and Walker accurately terms it as being based on a new generational contract (1996).

Although this contractual theme has a different usage in the mediation context, there is a shared focus on the negotiation and bargaining that has to be done in the social conflicts of later life. Cost is a driving factor, especially in recessionary periods with uncertainties about future political changes in British and European governments. The one certainty is that it will be services that are deemed to be essential in the care of older people which will receive public funding and support, and this is, of course, right.

So far mediation is not conceptualized as being essential, however needed, while advisory, advocacy and counselling services understandably follow the health, welfare, social insurance and retirement priorities for public spending. The first group of services even appears to be increasingly relegated to the voluntary sector, with often only inadequate subsidies from central and/or local government.

Although public awareness and pressure about elder abuse, as discussed above, may be instrumental in increasing public funding of the services already found to be necessary, which need universal development, this branch of family violence will have to compete with others concerned with child and spousal abuse, in order to attract financial support. Supplementary charitable funding will also be faced with similar competition for shrinking income and resources.

However, Age Concern England has a high social profile in Europe with regard to its elder care work, and may attract increased funding of specific projects from this source, which enables it to continue and extend its support of preventive policies and evolving strategies with regard to elder abuse.

Mediation is also enlarging its profile in Europe, which Mediation UK has led through the contributions of many of its individual members to two European conferences on the subject in recent years, the European Network for Conflict Resolution in Education started in Brussels in 1990, and the 1996 European Committee of Experts on Mediation in Penal Matters. However, these do not appear as yet to encompass any specific focus on old age or elder abuse, or to have followed the pattern of relevant networking which EMP pioneered in Britain. Thus the many exciting initiatives in other areas are not discussed here.

It is possible that as the older members of the public become more educated, and empowered, with regard to their rights and responsibilities in contributing to self-help services, as well as to those which encourage intergenerational solidarity rather than conflict, that mediation as a relatively new volunteer movement, may become more popular on account of its voluntary processes and minimal social interventions. However, Biggs et al (1995) briefly observe that elder mediation is still too unknown and marginal to be effective in any major way, and that there is uncertainty about its potential for future policy development.

It is this potential which the conclusion to this book next reviews, as it summarizes some of its themes, and evaluates their salience for contributing to the quality of elder care and the prevention of elder abuse.

However, it is difficult to assess the directions in which mediation is moving in Europe. Two European mediation conferences have been held since 1990, planned by a European team, but initiated by a Turkish scholar, and these developments were welcomed, even though they appear to have seeded ideas rather than led to any organizational structures for future large scale co-operation. This reflects the fact that mediation services in Britain, and apparently in Europe also, progress through local rather than central initiatives, and there is still no European umbrella organization, comparable to Mediation UK, which is able to co-ordinate developments.

It is principally in Germany and Austria, but also in Scandinavia, that major social developments in mediation have taken place, and these have been in victim-offender relations, rehabilitation and restorative justice areas, about which Wright (1991; 1996) has written with most information. It is highly speculative to consider how far the history of the holocaust has contributed to creating the social will and climate in the first two countries for developing progressive measures with regard to victims and offenders, and, in any case, there have been no movements there, or in Europe generally, comparable to the British Elder Mediation Project.

So the concluding section of this chapter on implications for policy and planning, must reflect the uncertainties which are apparent in wider European perspectives of the even more specialized area of this book.

Conclusion

This book has attempted to chart the social confluence of the subjects of elder abuse and mediation, how these were socially constructed in America, and then socially developed through practical services in Britain and Europe.

Thus these exploratory studies have endeavoured to maintain a critical and dialectical tension between theory and praxis through focusing in Part I on the main theme of mediation as a form of minimal social intervention and relational justice in the complex and sensitive area of elder abuse, leading to looking at the social relevance of developing participatory action research. In Part II, fieldwork was described relating to American elder care and mediation services in California, Atlanta and Kansas. Part III described the Elder Mediation Project (EMP) in Britain, illustrated by relevant cases, followed by a focus on a Norwegian elder abuse service using mediation, with a final chapter on emerging issues, insights and perspectives, including references to Europe.

Although these suggest the potential of mediation for contributing to the prevention of elder abuse, especially when developed by older trained volunteers as a form of collective social action and peer group self-help, no wider claims have been advanced because the need for more extensive and detailed research in the area has been consistently acknowledged.

Also global and national developments, in confronting the challenges of ageing populations, are in a state of flux, with ongoing negotiation over conflicts between governments and their statutory, independent and voluntary sectors with regard to the provision of social insurance and services for long term care. So there will be shifting social and cultural contexts in which the value and cost-effectiveness of mediation will be balanced against that of other more established types of social intervention in the area of elder abuse. Also no assumptions can be made about the changing power infrastructures which will influence, or determine, decision-making on the allocation of public resources.

So the previewing and reviewing of the subject share similar limitations in the effort to condense a necessarily uneven mix of theory and practice into a concrete formula compressing its elements of elder abuse and mediation. However, the unique and precious individuality of elders, each person having special abilities, needs and problems, offers a living template against which all theory and praxis has to be measured. Thus both are significant, but not dominant, and both are in constant construction, deconstruction and reconstruction.

Here the book has made a conscious attempt to model participative co-operation in research by acknowledging traditional references, but also advancing the argument for the benefits of theoretical integration, by introducing those from the literature of communication and relationship studies, so far generally unassimilated in the academic domains of elder abuse and mediation.

Renewing emphasis on the incompleteness of our knowledge and practical experience of work in these two complex and sensitive areas, stresses that any findings presented in this book are at best suggestive or provisional. Also highly relevant research is still incoming, and will modify past explanations, contribute salient present ideas, and re-chart future research issues. So it is important to consider some of these briefly in order to create a continuum through an open-ended conclusion, and to maintain the books's ethical stance of according value to all those who are furthering the constructive consideration of the issues with which it is concerned.

For instance, several current readings are rich in references which illuminate the ideas of this book. The first from a symposium edited by Stephens et al (1990) on *Stress and coping in later-life families* challenges loose labelling of words like conflict, crisis, stressor, negative exchange, friction and hassle, because they mean different things to different people in different situations, so future research must endeavour to overcome such definitional difficulties more adequately than has been done in these present studies.

However, Rook (1990), a contributor to the symposium, provides one of the missing pieces to the present book's findings about community abusive relations in later life, when she says that the more distanced old people are from kin (geographically, and perhaps psychologically also), the more they are likely to rely on, or have friction with neighbours, who can provide a relief from emotional intensity. She adds that high density, as in poor housing areas, leads to increased frequency and reactivity to negative social exchanges.

Two of the editors of the symposium, Stephens and Hobfoll (1990), then offer an ecological paradigm which well illustrates the perspectives from which this book has been written which also views the individual older person as situated in a social network in the context of a wider cultural background; in their terms, the microsocial, mesosocial and macrosocial domains of an interrelated ecosystem.

Another new book edited by Thurz et al (1995), *Empowering older people,* which illuminates the ongoing work of the Elder Mediation Project (EMP), has a chapter by Myers on the psychological basis for empowerment which defines it as 'a process of helping people gain, regain or maintain personal power or control over their lives' (1995:111), and then describes the different ways in which individual locus of control changes through the life course in confronting conflicts.

Myers then differentiates between internal and external locus of control showing that the former enables people to feel competent about being responsible for coping with conflict themselves, whilst the latter indicates dependency on others for decision-making and action. Myers advocates 'empowerment through social reconstruction: reversing breakdown ... by helping older persons experience a sense of control in the management of their lives, and by promoting older persons as capable and self-determined' (1995:116–17).

Not only do the ideas of Myers reinforce those of these present studies, but they lend legitimacy to the hopes on which EMP's practical work has been based when he concludes that 'it is possible to reverse the cycle, so that it may be self-perpetuating in a positive direction ... empowerment is self-perpetuating' (1995:117). Thus EMP has a long term aim of empowering old people to become more self-determining and resistant to elder abuse in general, as well as focusing specifically on the short term objective of enabling them to resolve present conflicts.

From this perspective EMP can be seen as contributing to what Wilson (1994), in another context and with reservations, has called the co-production of community care. However the ambivalence with which community care is regarded by users and providers alike is a necessary constraint on any idealism which has percolated through these pages, despite the realism which the book has espoused. For Biggs et al (1995) warn us that we live in an abusive society, with abusive families and abusive situations, and that there is an urgent social need for a stronger vision of old age.

This book has tried to enhance this vision by pointing to the value and achievements of the old people who have developed EMP as their own small contribution to the prevention of elder abuse and the promotion of elder rights, in which they seek relational justice for all those involved in the challenges and conflicts of later life.

References

Abel, R. (1982a), *The Politics of Informal Justice*, Vol. 1, Academic Press: New York.

Abel, R. (1982b), *The Politics of Informal Justice*, Vol. 2, Academic Press: New York.

Abramson, J. (1990), 'Enhancing Patient Participation', *Social Work in Health Care*, Vol. 14, No. 4, pp. 53–71.

Acland, A. (1990), *A Sudden Outburst of Common Sense*, Hutchinson Business Books: London.

Action on Elder Abuse (AEA), Age Concern England, 1268 London Road, London, SW16 4ER.

Action on Elder Abuse (AEA), (1995), *Bulletin*, No. 11, May/June.

Adams, R. and Blieszner, R. (1989), (eds), *Older Adult Friendship*, Sage: London.

Albrecht, T. and Adelman, M. (1987), (eds), *Communicating Social Support*, Sage: London.

Alper, B. and Nichols, L. (1981), *Beyond the Courtroom*, Lexington: MA.

American Association of Retired Persons (AARP), 1909 K Street NW, Washington DC 20049.

American Association of Retired Persons (AARP), (1988), *Helping Seniors – Seniors Helping,* Monograph, AARP: Washington DC.

American Association of Retired Persons (AARP), (1991), 'Long-term Care Ombudsman Program', *Fact Sheet on Nursing Homes*, AARP: Washington DC.

American Association of Retired Persons (AARP), (1992), Report on Health Care Administration, AARP: Washington DC.

American Association of Retired Persons (AARP), (1993), *Bulletin*, Vol. 34, No. 6, (Issue on Medicare Bills), AARP: Washington DC.

American Bar Association, (ABA), 1800 M Street NW, Washington DC 20036.

American Bar Association (ABA), (1990), *Family Dispute Resolution*, ABA: Washington DC.

American Bar Association (ABA), (1991), *Patient Self-Determination Act State Law Guide*, ABA: Washington DC.

American Bar Association (ABA), (1993), *Advanced Directives*, ABA: Washington DC.

American Society on Aging (ASA), (1991), Report on Homelessness, *Aging Today*, June/July 1991: San Francisco CA.

Ammerman, R. and Hersen, M. (1991), (eds), *Case Studies in Family Violence*, Plenum Press: New York.

Andrews, M. (1991), *Lifetimes of Commitment*, Cambridge University Press: Cambridge.

Antaki, C. (1994), *Explaining and Arguing*, Sage: London.

Argyle, M. (1973), *Social Encounters*, Penguin: Harmondsworth.

Argyle, M. (1991), *Cooperation and the Basis of Sociability,* Routledge: London.

Argyle, M. and Henderson, M. (1983), *The Anatomy of Relationships,* Penguin: Harmondsworth.

Auerbach, J. (1983), *Justice without Law*, Oxford University Press: New York.

Baldwin, J. (1985), *Pre-Trial Justice*, Blackwell: Oxford.

Barglow, R. (1994), *The Crisis of Self in the Age of Information*, Routledge: London.

Barnes, M. and Duck, S. (1994), 'Everyday Communicative Contexts for Social Support', in Burleson, B. , Albrecht, T. , Goldsmith, D. and Sarason, I. (eds), *The Communication of Social Support*. Sage: London.

Barton, D. (1996), (ed), *Disability and Society*, Carfax Publishers: Oxford.

Barusch, A. (1991), *Elder Care*, Sage: London.

Baxter, L. (1988), 'A Dialogic Perspective on Communication Strategies in Relationship Development', in Duck, S. (ed), *Handbook of Personal Relationships*, John Wiley: New York.

Bennis, W, Benne, K. and Chin. R. (1984), *The Planning of Change*, Holt Rinehart and Winston: New York.

Bergeron, R. (1989), Book Review of 'Older People and their Families' by Gwyther, L. , Gold, D. , and Hinman-Smith, D. , in *Journal of Elder Abuse and Neglect*, Vol. 1, No. 4, pp. 91–4.

Biggs, S. , Phillipson, C. and Kingston, P. (1995), *Elder Abuse in Perspective*, Open University Press: Milton Keynes.

Bitten, J. (1990), 'Spiritual Maturity in Psychological Development', in *Journal of Religion and Aging*, Vol. 7, Nos. 1–2, pp. 41–53.

Blanton, D. (1992), 'Mediation and the Elderly', *Elder Abuse Forum*, Vol. 6. No. 3, pp. 5, 7.

Blanton, P. (1989), 'Zen and the Art of Adult Protective Services', in *Journal of Elder Abuse and Neglect*, Vol. 1, No. 1, pp. 27–34.

Block, M. and Sinnott, J. (1979), (eds), *The Battered Elder Syndrome*, University of Maryland Press: MD.

Bonnyman, G. (1992), 'Moral Malpractice', Paper Presented to the Annual Meeting of the National Citizens' Coalition for Nursing Home Reform (NCCNHR), Washington DC.

Bornat, J. (1993), (ed), *Reminiscence Reviewed,* Open University Press: Milton Keynes.

Bottomley, K. (1979), *Criminology in Focus*, Robertson: Oxford.

Bourlet, A. (1990), *Police Intervention in Marital Violence*, Cambridge University Press: Cambridge.

Breckman, R. and Adelman, R. (1988), *Strategies for Helping Victims of Elder Abuse*, Sage: London.

British Association of Services for the Elderly (BASE), 119 Hassell Street, Newcastle-under-Lyme, Staffordshire, ST5 1AX.

British Council of Organizations of Disabled People (BCODP), De Bradelei House, Chapel Street, Belper, Derbyshire, DE56 1AR.

Bromley, D. (1993), *Reputation, Image and Impression Management*, John Wiley: New York.

Brubaker, T. (1990), *Family Relations in Later Life*, Sage: London.

Bulmer, M. (1982), *The Uses of Social Research*, Allen and Unwin: London.

Bulmer, M. (1987), *The Social Basis of Community Care*, Allen and Unwin: London.

Burleson, B. , Albrecht, T. , Goldsmith, D. and Sarason, I. (1994), (eds), *The Communication of Social Support*, Sage: London.

Burnside, J. and Baker, N. (1993), *Relational Justice,* Waterside Press: Winchester.

Burr, W. and Klein, S. (1994), *Re-examining Family Stress*, Sage: London.

Burton, J. (1990), *Conflict Resolution and Prevention*, Macmillan: London.

Butler, K. , Carr, S. and Sullivan, F. (1988), *Community Advocacy*, National Citizen Advocates: London.

Buttny, R. (1993), *Social Accountability*, Sage: London.

Cain, M. (1988), 'Beyond Informal Justice', in Matthews, R. (ed), *Informal Justice*, Sage: London, pp. 51–86.

Cain, M. and Kulscar, K. (1983), (eds), *Disputes and the Law*, Akademiai: Budapest.

Californian Association of Area Agencies on Aging, (1995), *An Aging Agenda, 1993–1995*, San Francisco CA.

Callahan, D. (1991), 'Distributive Justice', in Jecker, N. (ed), *Aging and Ethics*, Humana Press: Clifton NJ, pp. 219–26.

Canary, D. and Stafford, L. (1994), (eds), *Communication and Relational Maintenance*, Academic Press: New York.

Castells, M. (1983), *City and the Grassroots*, Arnold: London.

Chadwick-Jones, J. (1976), *Social Exchange Theory*, Academic Press: New York.

Cicerelli, V. (1992), *Family Caregiving*, Sage: London.

Clark, P. (1991), 'Ethical Dimensions of Quality of Life in Aging', *The Gerontologist*, Vol. 31, No. 5, pp. 631–9.

Cloke, C. (1983), *Old Age in the Domestic Setting*, Age Concern: London.

Coalition of Adults for the Rights of the Infirm Elderly (CARIE), (1992), Mission Statement: Philadelphia MD.

Collopy, B. (1992), *The Use of Restraints in Long Term Care*, American Association of Homes for the Aging: Washington DC.

Coser, L. (1956), *The Functions of Social Conflict*, Free Press: New York.

Coupland, N. , Coupland, J. and Giles, H. (1991), *Language, Society and the Elderly*, Blackwell: Oxford.

Counsel and Care, Twyman House, 16 Bonny Street, London, NW1 9PG.

Cox, B. and Waller, L. (1991), *Bridging the Communication Gap with the Elderly*, American Health Association: Chicago OH.

Craig, Y. (1991), *Community Conflict and Community Conciliation*, MA Dissertation, University of Leicester: Leicester.

Craig, Y. (1992), 'Elder Mediation', *Generations Review*, Vol. 2. No. 3, pp. 4–5.

Craig, Y. (1994), 'Elder Mediation: Can it Contribute to the Prevention of Elder Abuse and the Protection of the Rights of Elders and their Carers?', *Journal of Elder Abuse and Neglect*, Vol. 6, No. 1, pp. 81–96.

Craig, Y. (1995), 'EMPowerment: not EMPire-building', *Generations Review*, Vol. 5, No. 1, pp. 7–8.

Craig, Y. (1996), 'Elder Mediation Project', *Elders*, Vol. 5, No. 2, pp. 16–24.

Craig, Y. and Woods, P. (1993), 'Elder Abuse', *Police Review*, 22 January, pp. 28–9.

Croft, S. and Beresford, P. (1992), 'The Politics of Participation', *Critical Social Policy*, Vol. 35, pp. 20–44.

Cumming, E. and Henry, W. (1961), *Growing Old*, Basic Books: New York.

Daatland, S. (1992), 'The Public–Private Mix', *European Journal of Gerontology*, Vol. 1, No. 3, pp. 38–51.

Danzig, R. and Lowy, M. (1975), 'Everyday Disputes and Mediation in the United States', *Law and Social Review*, Vol. 9. No. 4, pp. 675–94.

Davis, G. (1988), *Partisans and Mediators*, Clarendon: Oxford.

Davis, G. and Roberts, M. (1988), *Access to Agreement*, Open University Press: Milton Keynes.

Davitt, J. (1992), *The Patient Self-Determination Act*, Paper Presented to the 1992 NCCNHR Annual Meeting: Washington DC.

Decalmer, P. and Glendenning, F. (1993). *The Mistreatment of Elderly People*, Sage: London.

Derlega, V. , Metts, S. , Petronio, S. and Margolis, S. (1993), *Self Disclosure*, Sage: London.

Deutsch, M. (1973), *The Resolution of Conflict*, Yale University Press: New Haven, CT.

Dingwell, R. and Eekelaar, J. (1988), (eds), *Divorce, Mediation and the Legal Process*, Clarendon: Oxford.

Dispute Resolution Service (DRS), (1992), Information Leaflet: Olathe KA.

Dobash, R. and Dobash, R. (1980), *Violence against Wives*, Open Books, London.

Dolon, R. and Blakeley, B. (1989), 'Elder Abuse and Neglect', *Journal of Elder Abuse and Neglect*, Vol. 1, No. 3, pp. 31–49.

Donohue, W. and Kolt, R. (1992), *Managing Interpersonal Conflict*, Sage: London.

Donzelot, J. (1980), *The Policing of Families*, Hutchinson: London.

Downes, D. and Rock, P. (1970), *Deviant Interpretations*, Robertson: Oxford.

Downes, D. and Rock, P. (1988), *Understanding Deviance*, Clarendon: Oxford.

Doyal, L. and Gough, I. (1991), *A Theory of Human Need*, Macmillan: Basingstoke.

Duck, S. (1988), (ed), *Handbook of Personal Relationships*, John Wiley: New York.

Duck, S. (1991), *Friends, for Life,* Harvester: Sussex.

Duck, S. and Wood, J. (1995), (eds), *Confronting Relationship Challenges*, Sage: London.

Duke, J. (1976), *Conflict and Power and Social Life*, Brigham University Press: Utah.

Dukes, F. (1993), 'Building a Sustainable Democracy', *Interaction*, Vol. 5, No. 1, Spring, pp. 5, 7.

Eastman, M. (1984), *Old Age Abuse*, Age Concern: London.

Edwards. S. (1989), *Policing 'Domestic' Violence,* Sage: London.

Eisenberg, H. (1982), 'The Bargain and its Limits', *Harvard Law Review*, Vol. 95, No. 4, pp. 741–63.

Eisenberg, H. (1989), Private Ordering Through Negotiation', *Harvard Law Review*, February, pp. 637–81.

Elder Mediation Project (EMP), Yvonne Joan Craig, 27 Ridgmount Gardens, London WC1E 7AS.

Elias, R. (1985), *The Politics of Victimization*, Oxford University Press: New York.

Estes, C. (1981), *The Aging Enterprise*, Jossey Bass: San Francisco.

Estes, C. (1992), *The Aging Enterprise Revisited*, Paper presented to the Gerontological Association of America (GSA) Annual Meeting: Washington DC.

Evans, E. (1992), 'Liberation Theology, Empowerment Theory and Social Work Practice with the Oppressed', *International Social Work*, Vol. 35, No. 2, pp. 135–47.

Farley, S. (1991), 'Personal Commitments', in Jecker, N. *Aging and Ethics*, Humana Press: Cliftonville NJ, pp. 329–40.

Felstiner, W. , Abel, R. and Sarat, A. (1980/1), 'The Emergence and Transformation of Disputes', *Law and Social Review*, Vol. 15, Nos. 3–4, pp. 631–54.

Field, F. (1989), *Losing Out*, Blackwell: Oxford.

Filinson, R. and Ingham, S. (1989), (eds), *Elder Abuse*, Human Sciences Press: New York.

Fisher, R. , Kopelman, E. and Schneider, A. (1994), *Beyond Machiavelli*, Harvard University Press: New Haven CT.

Fisher, R. and Ury, W. (1990), *Getting to Yes*, Arrow: London.

Fitzpatrick, P. (1988), 'The Rise and Rise of Informalism', in Matthews, R. (ed), *Privatizing Criminal Justice*, Sage: London, pp. 178–98.

Flemming, A. (1992), Report, *Senior Consumer ALERT*, AARP: Washington DC.

Folberg, J. and Taylor, A. (1984), *Mediation*, Jossey Bass: San Francisco CA.

Folger, J. and Jones, T. (1994), (eds), *New Directions in Mediation*, Sage: London.

Formby, S. (1992), *Decision Making and the Impaired Resident*, Paper presented to the Atlanta Long Term Care Ombudsmen: Atlanta GA.

Formby, W. (1992) 'Should Elder Abuse be Decriminalised?', *Journal of Elder Abuse and Neglect*, Vol. 4, No. 4, pp. 121–30.

Foucault, M. (1981), *The History of Sexuality*, Penguin: Harmondsworth.

Freeden. M. (1991), *Rights*, Open University Press: Milton Keynes.

Freeman, M. (1984), *State, Law and the Family*, Tavistock: London.

Freire, P. (1970), *Pedagogy of the Oppressed*, Herder and Herder: New York.

Galanter, M. (1983), 'Reading the Landscape of Disputes', *University College of Los Angeles Law Review*, Vol. 31, No. 1, pp. 4–71.

Gaviland, H. (1992), 'Care in the Community', *Generations Review*, Vol. 2. No. 4, pp. 9–11.

Gelles, R. and Straus, M. (1988), *Intimate Violence*, Simon and Schuster: New York.

General Accounting Office (GAO), (1992a), *Gaps Between the Poor and Non-Poor Elderly*, GAO: Washington DC.

General Accounting Office (GAO), (1992b), *Elderly Americans*, GAO: Washington DC.

Gerontology Institute (GI), (1990), *Long Term Care Policy*, GI: Washington DC.

Giddens, A. (1990), *The Consequences of Modernity*, Polity Press: London.

Giles, H. , Coupland, N. and Weiman, J. (1990), *Communication, Health and the Elderly*, Manchester University Press: Manchester.

Gilroy, P. (1987), *There Ain't No Black in the Union Jack*, Hutchinson: London.

Girdner, L. (1990), 'Mediation Triage', *Mediation Quarterly*, Vol. 7. No. 4, pp. 365–72.

Glaser, B. and Strauss, A. (1967), *The Discovery of Grounded Theory*, Aldine de Gruyer: New York.

Goffman, E. (1961), *Asylums*, Anchor Books: New York.

Goffman, E. (1971), *Strategic Interactions*, Blackwell: Oxford.

Goldberg, S. , Green, E. and Sander, F. , (1985), *Dispute Resolution*, Little, Brown and Company: Boston MA.

Gottlich, V. (1992), Report, *NIDR Forum*, NIDR: Washington DC.

Greengross, S. (1986), *The Law and Vulnerable Elderly People, Age Concern:* London.

Griffiths, A. , Grimes, R. and Roberts, G. (1990), *The Law and Elderly People,* Routledge: London.

Griffiths, A. , Roberts, G. and Williams, J. (1992), *Shaping the Instrument,* British Association of Services for the Elderly (BASE): Newcastle under Lyme, Staffs.

Griffiths, A. and Grant, G. (1993), 'Shouting for a Samaritan', *BASELINE*, No. 52, June 1993, pp. 42–5.

Grimshaw, A. (1990), (ed), *Conflict Talk*, Cambridge University Press: Cambridge.

Gubrium, J. , Holstein, J. and Buckholdt, D. (1994), *Constructing the Life Course*, General Hall: New York.

Gudykunst, W. (1994), *Bridging Differences,* Sage: London.

Gulliver, P. (1979), *Disputes and Negotiations,* Academic Press: New York.

Gwyther, L., Gold, D. and Hinman-Smith, E. (undated), *Older People and their Families*, Duke University Medical Center: Durham NC.

Habermas, J. (1970), *Towards a Rational Society,* trans. Shapiro, J., Beacon Press: Boston MA.

Habermas, J. (1971), *Knowledge and the Human Interests,* trans. Shapiro, J., Beacon Press: Boston MA.

Habermas, J. (1987), *The Theory of Communicative Action,* trans. McCarthy, T., Beacon Press: Boston MA.

Habermas, J. (1990), *Moral Consciousness and Communicative Action*, trans. Leinhardt, C. , Harvard University Press: Cambridge MA.

Hampshire, S. (1989), *Innocence and Experience*, Penguin: Harmondsworth.

Hanawi, N. and Goodman, O. (1992), *Resolving Disputes in Nursing Homes*, NIDR: Washington DC.

Harding, S. (1987), (ed), *Feminism and Methodology*, Independent University Press: Bloomington IA.

Harkins, M. and Kelly, B. (1992), *The Impact of Adverse Nursing Home Care Survey Reports in Tort and Criminal Cases*, Presented to the NCCNHR Annual Meeting: Washington DC.

Harman, H. and Winn, L. (1991), *No Place Like Home*, National Association of Local Government Officers (NALGO): London.

Harrington, C. (1984), 'The Politics of Participation and Non-Participation in the Dispute Process', *Law and Policy*, Vol. 6, No. 2, pp. 203–30.

Harrington, C. (1985), *Shadow Justice*, Greenwood Press: Westport CT.

Harrington, C. and Merry, S. (1988), 'Ideological Production', *Law and Social Review*, Vol. 22, No. 4, pp. 709–35.

Harshbarger, S. (1989), 'A Personal Perspective on Protecting Older Americans', *Journal of Elder Abuse and Neglect*, Vol. 1, No. 3, pp. 5–15.

Haynes, J. (1981), *Divorce and Mediation*, Springer: New York.

Hedrick, T. , Bickman, L. and Hog, D. (1987), *Applied Research Design*, Open University Press: Milton Keynes.

Heisler, C. (1991), 'The Role of the Criminal Justice System in Elder Abuse Cases', *Journal of Elder Abuse and Neglect*, Vol. 3, No. 1, pp. 5–33.

Help the Aged, St. James' Walk, London, EC1.

Henry, S. (1984), 'Contradictions of Collective Justice', *Howard Journal*, Vol. 23, No. 3, pp. 158–69.

Henry, S. (1985), 'Capitalism, Society and Human Agency', *Journal of Law and Society*, Vol. 19, No. 2, pp. 303–27.

Hobman, D. (1993), (ed), *Uniting Generations,* Age Concern: London.

Hoffman, R. and Wood, E. (1991), 'Mediation: New Path to Problem Solving for Older Americans', *Senior Consumer Alert*, Winter 1991, AARP: Washington DC.

Hofrichter, R. (1988), *Neighborhood Justice in a Capitalist Society*, Greenwood Press: New York.

Hoggett, B. (1991), *Mentally Incapacitated Adults and Decision-Making: an Overview*, Law Commission No. 119, HMSO: London.

Hoggett, B. (1992), *Family Law Domestic Violence and Occupation of the Family Home*, Law Commission No. 207, HMSO: London.

Hoggett, B. (1993a), *Mentally Incapacitated Adults and Decision-Making*, Law Commission No. 128, HMSO: London.

Hoggett, B. (1993b), *Mentally Incapacitated Adults and Decision-Making*, Law Commission No. 129, HMSO: London.

Hoggett, B. (1993c), *Mentally Incapacitated and Other Vulnerable Adults,* Law Commission No. 130, HMSO: London.

Horl, J. (1992), 'Family Care of the Elderly in Austria', in Kosberg, J. (ed), *Family Care of the Elderly*, Sage: London, pp. 235–51.

Horley, S. (1990), 'Responding to Male Violence Against Women', *Probation Journal*, December, pp. 166–70.

Hudson, M. (1981), 'Analysis of the Concepts of Elder Mistreatment', *Journal of Elder Abuse and Neglect*, Vol. 1, No. 1, pp. 5–34.

Hudson, M. (1991), 'Elder Mistreatment', *Journal of Elder Abuse and Neglect*, Vol. 3, No. 2, pp. 1–19.

Hummert, M. , Weimann, J. and Nussbaum, S. (1994), *Interpersonal Communication in Older Adulthood*, Sage: London.

Hwalek, M. , Williamson, D. and Stahl, C. (1991), 'Community-Based M-Team Roles', *Journal of Elder Abuse and Neglect*, Vol. 3, No. 3, pp. 45–71.

Illsley, R. and Jamieson, A. (1990), 'Contextual and Structural Influences in Adaptation to Change', in Jamieson, A. and Illsley, R. (eds), *Contrasting European Policies for the Care of Older People*, Avebury: Aldershot, pp. 83–94.

Institute of Medicine (IoM), (1991) *Medicare*, IoM: Washington DC.

International Federation of Aging (IFA), (1992), *Declaration on Rights and Responsibilities of Older Persons*, IFA: Washington DC.

Jamieson, A. (1991), (ed), *Home Care for Older People in Europe*, Oxford University Press: Oxford.

Jamieson, A. and Illsley, R. (1990), (eds), *Contrasting European Policies for the Care of Older People*, Avebury: Aldershot.

Jannis, I. and Mann, L. (1977), *Decision Making*, Macmillan: London.

Jecker, N. (1991), *Aging and Ethics*, Humana Press: Clifton NJ.

Jefferys, M. (1989), (ed), *Growing Old in the Twentieth Century*, Routledge: London.

Jeffry, D. (1992), Report, *Community Care*, 26. 11. 92.

Jensen, A. (1991), 'Resentment and the Rights of the Elderly', in Jecker, N. *Aging and Ethics*, Humana Press: Cliftonville NJ, pp. 34–52.

Johns, S. , Hydle, I. and Aschjem, O. (1991), 'The act of abuse', *Journal of Elder Abuse and Neglect*, Vol. 3, No. 1, pp. 53–64.

Johns, S. , Juklestad O. and Hydle, I. (1992), *Developing Elder Protective Services in Norway*, Paper Presented to the Adult Protective Services Conference: San Antonio TX.

Johns, S. and Juklestad, O. (1994a) *Research and Action on Elder Abuse in Norway*, Paper Presented to the 2nd International Symposium on Elder Abuse: Stoke-on-Trent.

Johns, S. and Juklestad, O. (1994b) Personal Correspondence.

Johnson, R. (1989), 'Elder Mistreatment', *Journal of Elder Abuse and Neglect*, Vol. 1, No. 4, pp. 15–35.

Kanfer, F. and Goldstein, A. (1980), *Helping people change*, Penguin: Harmondsworth.

Kansas Mediation Services for Older Adults (KMSOA), (1985), Information Leaflet, KMSOA: Olathe KA.

KMSOA, (1985), *Mediation Services for Older Adults*, KMSOA: Olathe KA.

Kapp, M. (1990), 'Evaluating Decision Making Capacity in the Elderly', *Journal of Elder Abuse and Neglect*, Vol. 2, Nos. 3–4, pp. 15–29.

Kapp, M. (1991), 'Health Care Decision Making by the Elderly', *The Gerontologist*, Vol. 31, No. 5, pp. 619–23.

Kapp, M. (1992a), *Alternatives to Guardianship for the Elderly*, Wright State School of Medicine: Dayton OH .

Kapp, M. (1992b), 'Nursing Home Restraints and Legal Liability', *Journal of Legal Medicine*, No. 13, pp. 1–32.

Kingston, P. and Penhale, B. (1995), (eds), *Family Violence and the Caring Professions*, Macmillan: Basingstoke.

Kitwood, T. and Breden, K. (1992), 'Towards a Theory of Dementia Care, *Ageing and Society*, Vol. 12, No. 3, pp. 269–87.

Klein, R. and Milardo, R. (1993), 'Third Party Influence on the Management of Personal Relationships', Duck, S. (ed), *Social Context and Relationships*, Sage: London.

Knight, B. (1992), *Older Adults in Psychotherapy*, Sage: London.

Korbin, J. , Anetzberger, G. , Thomasson, R. and Austin, C. , (1991), 'Abused Elders Who Seek Legal Recourse Against Their Adult Offspring', *Journal of Elder Abuse and Neglect,* Vol. 3, No. 3, pp. 1–18.

Kosberg, J. (1983), (ed), *Abuse and Mistreatment of the Elderly,* John Wright: London.

Kosberg, J. (1992), (ed), *Family Care of the Elderly,* London: Sage.

Kreisberg, L. (1982), *Social Conflicts,* Prentice Hall: Englewood Cliffs NJ.

Kressell, K. and Pruitt, D. (1989), *Mediation Research.* Jossey Bass: San Francisco CA.

Kuhn, M. (1977), *Maggie Kuhn on Aging,* Westminster: Philadelphia MD.

Lee, R. (1993), *Doing Research in Sensitive Topics,* Sage: London.

Lerner, R. and Busch Ross Nagel, N. (1981), *Individuals as Producers of Their Own Development,* Academic Press: New York.

Lincoln, Y. and Guba, E. (1985), *Naturalistic Inquiry,* Sage: London.

Lisi, L. and Burns, A. (1992), 'Mediation in Guardianship Cases', *Clearinghouse Review,* No. 24, pp. 644–5.

Lloyd, P. (1991), 'The Empowerment of Elderly People', *Journal of Ageing and Society,* Vol. 5, No. 2, pp. 125–35.

Logstrup, K. (1971), *The Ethical Demand,* Fortress Press: Philadelphia MD.

Lukes, S. (1974), *Power,* Macmillan: London.

McCafferty, P. (1994), *Living Independently,* HMSO: London.

McCalman, J. (1991), *The Forgotten People,* King's Fund Centre: London.

McCreadie, C. (1991), *Elder Abuse,* Age Concern Institute of Gerontology: London.

McDowell, D. (1989), 'Aging America', *Journal of Elder Abuse and Neglect,* Vol. 1, No. 2, pp. 1–7.

McLaughlin, M. , Cody, M. and Read, S. (1992), *Explaining Oneself to Others,* Lawrence Erlbaum Associates: Hillsdale, NJ.

McThenia, A. and Shaffer, T. (1984–5), 'For Reconciliation', *Yale Law Journal,* Vol. 94, pp. 1660–8.

Mackie, K. (1991), (ed), *A Handbook of Dispute Resolution,* Routledge: London.

Maguire, P. (1987), *Doing Participatory Research,* University of Massachusetts: Amherst MA.

Marshall, T. (1985), *Alternatives to Criminal Courts,* Gower: Aldershot.

Marshall, T. (1988), 'Out of Court', in Matthews, R. (ed), *Informal Justice,* Sage: London, pp. 25–50.

Marshall, T. (1990), 'Perestroika and Mediation', *Mediation,* Vol. 6, No. 3, pp. 2–3.

Martin, L. and Tesser, A. (1992), (eds), *The Construction of Social Judgements,* Lawrence Erlbaum Associates: Hillside NJ.

Maslow, A. (1970), *Motivation and Personality,* Harper and Row: New York.

Maslow, A. (1976), *Religions, Values and Peak Experiences,* Penguin: New York.

Matthews, R. (1988), *Informal Justice,* Sage: London.

Matthews, R. (1989), (ed), *Privatizing Criminal Justice*, Sage: London.
Mediation UK, 82a Gloucester Road, Bishopston, Bristol, BS7 8BN, Avon.
Mediation UK, (1996), *Training Manual in Community Mediation Skills*, Mediation UK: Bristol.
Menkel-Meadow, C. (1984), 'Towards Another View', *University College of Los Angeles Law Review*, Vol. 31, No. 4, pp. 754–842.
Midwinter, E. (1992), (ed), *Citizenship*, Carnegie Inquiry Into the Third Age: London.
Minkler, M. and Estes, C. (1991), (eds), *Critical Perspectives on Aging*, Baywood Publishing Company: New York.
Moberg, D. (1990), 'Spiritual Maturity and Wholeness in Later Years', *Journal of Religion and Aging*, Vol. 7, Nos. 1–2, pp. 5–24.
Mohrman, A. and Lawler, E. (1984), 'The Diffusion of Quality of Life as a Paradigm Shift', in Bennis, W. , Benne, K. and Chin, R. (eds), *The Planning of Change*, Holt, Reinhart and Winston: New York, pp. 149–61.
Moody, H. (1992), *Ethics in an Aging Society*. John Hopkins University Press: Baltimore, MD.
Moore, C. (1986), *The Mediation Process*. Jossey Bass: San Francisco CA.
Myers, J. (1995), 'The Psychological Basis for Empowerment', in Thursz, D. , Nusberg, C. and Prather, J. (eds), *Empowering Older People*, Cassell: London.
Nathanson, P. (1983), 'An Overview of Legal Issues, Services and Resources', in Kosberg, J. (ed), *Abuse and Mistreatment of the Elderly*, John Wright: London.
National Aging Resource Center on Elder Abuse (NARCEA), Suite 500, 810 First Street NE, Washington DC 20002-4205.
National Citizens' Coalition for Nursing Home Reform (NCCNHR), 1424 16th Street NW, Washington DC 20036-2211.
National Eldercare Institute on Elder Abuse and State Long Term Care Ombudsmen Services (NEIEASLTCOS) (1992a), *Report on Elder Abuse*, NEIEASLTCOS: Washington DC.
NEIEASLTCOS, (1992b), *Report on Elder Rights*, NEIEASLTCOS: Washington DC.
NEIEASLTCOS, (1992c), *Report on Medicaid*, NEIEASLTCOS: Washington DC.
National Family Mediation (NFM), 9 Tavistock Place, London, WC1.
National Family Mediation (NFM), (1992), *Annual Report*, NFM: London.
National Institute of Dispute Resolution (NIDR), Suite 500, 1726 M Street NW, Washington DC 20036-4502.
National Institute of Social Work (NISW), 5 Tavistock Place, London, WC1.
Neill, J. (1989), *Assessing Elderly People for Residential Care*, NISW: London.
Neill, J. and Williams, S. (1992), *Leaving Hospital*, HMSO: London.
Norman, A. (1985), *Triple Jeopardy*, Centre for Policy on Ageing: London.
Norman, A. (1987), *Rights and Risks*, Centre for Policy on Ageing: London.

Nussbaum, J. Thompson, T. and Robinson, J. (1989), *Communication and Aging*, Harper and Row: New York.

Ogg, J. and Bennett, G. (1992), 'Elder Abuse in Britain', *British Medical Journal*, Vol. 6860, No. 305, pp. 988–9.

Ogus, A. , Walker, J. and Jones-Lee, M. (1989), *Summary of the Report of the Conciliation Project Unit*, University of Newcastle upon Tyne: Newcastle upon Tyne.

Oliver, M. (1990), *The Politics of Disablement*, Macmillan: Basingstoke.

Parkinson, L. (1986), *Conciliation in Separation and Divorce*, Croom Helm: London.

Parsons, R. and Cox, E. (1989), 'Family Mediation in Elder Caregiving Decisions', *Social Work*, Vol. 34, No. 2, pp. 122–6.

Pearson, J. and Thouness, N. (1984), 'A Preliminary Report of Client Reactions in Three Court Mediation Programs', *Mediation Quarterly*, No. 3, pp. 21–40.

Pepinsky, H. (1991), *The Geometry of Victims and Democracy*, Indiana University Press: Indianapolis IA.

Phillips, E. and Pugh, D. (1987), *How to Get a PhD*, Open University Press: Milton Keynes.

Phillips, L. and Rempusheski, V. (1986), 'Making Decisions About Elder Abuse', *Journal of Contemporary Social Work*, No. 67, pp. 131–40.

Phillipson, C. and Bigg, S. (1992), *Understanding Elder Abuse*, Longman: London.

Phillipson, C. and Walker, A. (1986), (eds), *Ageing and Social Policy*, Gower: Aldershot.

Pillemer, K. and Wolf, R. (1986), (eds), *Elder Abuse: Conflict in the Family*. Auburn House: Dover, MA.

Piven, F. and Cloward, R. (1982), *The New Class War*, Pantheon: New York.

Plotkin, M. (1988), *A Time for Dignity*, AARP: Washington, DC.

Policy Studies Unit (PSI), (1992), *Elderly People*, PSI: London.

Pritchard, J. (1992), *The Abuse of Elderly People*, Jessica Kingsley: London.

Putnam, J. (1970), *Old Age Politics in California*, Stanford University Press: Stanford CA.

Quinn, M. and Tomita, S. (1986), *Elder Abuse and Neglect*, Springer: New York.

Rawls, J. (1971), *A Theory of Justice*, Harvard University Press: Cambridge, MA.

Reason, P. (1988), (ed), *Human Inquiry in Action*, Sage: London.

Reason, P. and Rowan, J. (1981), (eds), *Human Inquiry*, John Wiley: Chichester.

Relatives Association, 5 Tavistock Place, London, WC1H 9SN.

Rex, J. and Mason, D. (1986), *Theories of Race and Ethnic Relations*, Cambridge University Press: Cambridge.

Robb, B. (1967), *Sans Everything*, Nelson: London.

206

Roberts, H. (1981), (ed), *Doing Feminist Research*, Routledge and Kegan Paul: London.

Roberts, M. (1988), *Mediation in Family Disputes*, Wildwood House: Aldershot.

Roberts, M. (1990), 'Systems of Selves', *Journal of Social Welfare Law*, pp. 6–19.

Roberts, S. (1983), 'Mediation in Family Disputes', *Modern Law Review*, Vol. 46, No. 5, pp. 537–57.

Roberts, S. (1986), ' Towards a Minimal Form of Intervention', *Mediation Quarterly*, No. 11, pp. 25–41.

Roberts, S. (1988), 'Three Models of Family Mediation', in Dingwell, R. and Eekelaar, J. (eds), *Divorce, Mediation and the Legal Process*, Clarendon: Oxford.

Robson, C. (1993), (ed), *Real World Research*, Blackwell: Oxford.

Rook, K. (1989), 'Strains in Older Adults', in Adams, R. and Blieszner, R. (eds), *Older Adult Friendship*, Sage: London, pp. 166–94.

Rook, K. (1990), 'Stressful Aspects of Older Adults', in Stephens, M. Crowther, S. , Hobfoll, D. and Tannenbaum, D. , *Stress and Coping in Later Life Families*, Hemisphere Publishing Co: London, pp. 177–92.

Royal Association for Disability and Rehabilitation (RADAR), 12 City Forum, 250 City Road, London EC1V 8AF.

Royal College of Nursing (RCN), *A Scandal Waiting to Happen*, RCN: London.

Ryft, C. and Essex, M. (1991), 'Psychological Well-Being in Adulthood and Old Age', *Abstracts in Social Gerontology*, No. 11, pp. 144–71.

Sanko, E. (1990), *Everyday Violence*, Pandora Press: London.

Sarton, M. (1973), *Journal of a Solitude*. Norton: New York.

SAVE Project, Laurence House, 1 Catford Road, London SE6 4RU.

Saveman, B-I, (1994), *Formal Carers in Health Care and the Social Services Witnessing Abuse of the Elderly in Their Homes*, Umea University: Sweden.

Schlesinger, B. and Schlesinger, R. (1988), (eds), *Abuse of the Elderly*, University of Toronto: Toronto.

Schonbach, P. (1990), *Account Episodes*, Cambridge University Press: Cambridge.

Schumacher, E. (1978), *Small is Beautiful*, Harper and Collins: London.

Seligman, M. (1975), *Helplessness*, W. H. Freeman: San Francisco CA.

Severance, J. (1989), 'Predictions of Elderly Participation in Long Term Care Decision Making', *The Gerontologist*, No. 29, p. 168.

Sherman, E. and Webb, T. (1994), 'The Self as Process in Later Life Reminiscence', *Ageing and Society*, No. 14, pp. 255–67.

Singer, L. (1990), *Settling Disputes*, Westview: Boulder, CO.

Smart, C. (1989), *Feminism and the Power of Law*, Routledge and Kegan Paul: London.

Smith, A. (1973), *Transracial Communication*, Prentice Hall: New York.

Smith, L. (1989), *Domestic Violence*, No. 107, Home Office Research and Planning Unit: London.

Social Services Inspectorate (SSI), (1992), *Confronting Elder Abuse*, SSI, Department of Health: London.

Spencer, C. (1993), 'Community Awareness and Response', *A Shared Concern (BC)*, Vol. 1, No. 4, p. 8.

Standing Conference of Ethnic Minority Senior Citizens (SCEMSC), 5–5a Westminster Bridge Road, London SE1 7XW.

Stein, K. (1991), 'A National Agenda for Elder Abuse and Neglect', *Journal of Elder Abuse and Neglect*, Vol. 3, No. 3, pp. 91–107.

Steinmetz, S. (1988), *Duty Bound*, Sage: London.

Stephens, M. , Crowther, J. , Hobfoll, S. and Tannenbaum, D. (1990), (eds), *Stress and Coping in Later Life Families*, Hemisphere Publishing Company: New York.

Stokes, G. (1987), *Aggression*, Winslow Press: London.

Swain, D. , Finkelstein, V. , French, S. and Oliver, M. , (1993), (eds), *Disabling Barriers*, Sage: London.

Taylor, J. (1972), *The Go-Between God*, Student Christian Movement Press: London.

Tinker, A. (1992), *Elderly People in Modern Society*, Longman: London.

Townsend, P. (1964), *The Last Refuge*, Routledge and Kegan Paul: London.

Townsend, P. (1987), *The Family Life of Old People*, Routledge and Kegan Paul: London.

Trubek, D. (1983), 'Turning Away from the Law', *Michigan Law Review*, No. 82, pp. 824–35.

Turk, A. (1975–6), 'Law as a Weapon in Social Conflict', *Social Policy*, No. 23, pp. 276–91.

Unger, R. (1975), *Knowledge and Politics*, Free Press: London.

Unger, R. (1987), *The Critical Legal Studies Movement*, Harvard University Press: Cambridge MA.

United States (US) House of Representatives, (1988), *Mediation and Older Americans*, United States Government Printing Office, (USGPO): Washington DC.

US House of Representatives, (1990), *Elder Abuse*, USGPO: Washington DC.

US Bureau of Census (USBC), (1990), *Poverty in the United States*, USGPO: Washington DC.

US Department of Labour, (1993), Report on California Unemployment, USGPO: Washington DC.

US Senate Special Committee on Aging, (1987–8), *Aging Americans*, USGPO: Washington DC.

Walker, A. (1996), (ed), *The New Generational Contract*, University College London: London.

Walklate, S. (1989), *Domestic Violence and the Criminal Justice Process*, Unwin Hyman: London.

Waller, K. and Bates, R. (1992), 'Health Locus of Control and Self-Efficacy', *American Journal of Health Promotion*, Vol. 6. No. 4, pp. 302–9.

Walters, J. (1992), 'Proximate Personhood', *Bioethics*, Vol. 6, No. 1, pp. 12–22.

Wehr, P. (1979), *Conflict Regulation*, Westview Press: Boulder, CO.

Weinstein, N. (1987), (ed), *Taking Care*, Cambridge University Press: Cambridge.

Wenger, G. (1992), *Help in Old Age*, Liverpool University Press: Liverpool.

Wertle, T. , Lekoff, S. , Cwikel, J. and Rosen, A. (1988), *The Gerontologist*, Vol. 28, June Supplement, pp. 32–7.

Willmott, P. (1988), 'Urban Kinship', *Social Studies Review*, Vol. 4, No. 2, pp. 44–6.

Willmott, P. (1989), *Community Initiatives*, Policy Studies Institute: London.

Wilson, G. (1993), 'When Being "Old" is Normal', *Generations Review*, Vol. 3, No. 2, pp. 2–3.

Wilson, G. (1994), 'Co-production and Self-care', *Social Policy and Administration*, Vol. 28, No. 3, pp. 236–50.

Wolf, R. (1990), 'Testimony on Behalf of the National Committee for the Prevention of Elder Abuse before the U. S. House Select Committee on Aging, Subcommittee on Human Services', *Journal of Elder Abuse and Neglect*, Vol. 2, Nos. 1–2, pp. 137–50.

Wolf, R. (1994), 'What's New in Elder Abuse Programming?', *The Gerontologist*, Vol. 34, No. 1, pp. 126–9.

Wolf, R. and Bergman, S. (1989), *Stress, Conflict and Abuse of the Elderly*, JDC Brookdale Institute of Gerontology: Jerusalem.

Wolf, R. and Pillemer, K. (1989), *Helping Elderly Victims*, Columbia University Columbia University Press: New York.

Wood, J. and Duck, S. (1995), *Understudied Relationships*, Sage: London.

Wood, E. and Kestner, P. (1989), *Mediation – The Coming of Age*, American Bar Association (ABA): Washington, DC.

Worrall, R. (1990), *Offending Women*, Routledge: London.

Wright, M. (1982), *Making Good*, Burnett Books, London.

Wright, M. (1991), *Justice for Victims and Offenders*, Open University Press: Milton Keynes.

Wright, M. (1996), (2nd ed.), *Justice for Victims and Offenders*, Waterside Press: Winchester.

Wright, M. and Galaway, B. (1989), (eds), *Mediation and Criminal Justice*, Sage: London.

Index

Amendments (1992) to the Nursing Home Reform Law/Omnibus Reconciliation Act 76, 83, 84, 92
American Association of Homes for the Aging 93
American Association of Retired Persons (AARP) 65, 77, 82, 86, 97, 130
  Coalition on Mediation and Older Americans 86
American Bar Association (ABA) vii, 7, 77, 86, 90, 138
American Economic Policy Institute 79
American Health Association 29
American Health Care Association (AHCA) 76, 77, 82, 83, 107
American Society on Aging 80
Americans with Disabilities Act 1990 (ADA) 86, 127, 130
anger 155
APS *see* adult protective services
areas of social deprivation 158
argumentation theory 155
Asian Americans 108, 109
Asian Family Mediation Service 30
assault 49
Association of Family and Conciliation Courts (AFCC) 48
Atlanta 10, 32, 57, 58, 131–7, 182
Atlanta Council on Elder Abuse 132
Atlanta, Justice Center *see* Justice Center of Atlanta
Austria 173, 190
autonomy 4, 17, 18, 20, 29, 59, 72, 78, 92, 93, 123, 127, 137, 147, 159, 185
avoidance 28

battered women 56
bed sores 34, 141
Berkshire Social Services Department 14
bioethics 15, 21
black people 64, 80
blaming 35, 36, 37
boundaries, personal 168
boundary
  disputes 179
  problems 152
breach of statutory duty 49
bridge-building 152
British Association of Services to the Elderly (BASE) 183
British Columbia 128

Coalition on the Prevention of Elder Abuse and Neglect 128
British Council of Organizations of Disabled People (BCOD) 186
budget cuts 102

California 10, 95, 99–130
  Advocates for Nursing Home Reform (CANHR) 100, 101, 111, 120, 127
  population 100
  socioeconomic profile 101
  State benefits 105
  unemployment rate 106
  University of 107
Californian Coalition on Elder Abuse 100, 110, 114, 128
Camden 15
Canada, national health insurance plan 105
CANHR *see* California Advocates for Nursing Home Reform
caregivers 6, 18, 87
caregiving options 79
carers 15, 17
  burden on 37
  responsibilities of 46–7
  stress of 36
CARIE *see* Coalition of Advocates for the Rights of the Infirm Elderly
Carter
  administration 131
  President 132
  Presidential Center 132
CEAN *see* Council on Elder Abuse and Neglect
Center for Dispute Resolution 86
Center for Social Gerontology (CSG) 86, 88
chaplain's imperative 91
Charity Commissioners 71
choice 4, 18, 20, 59
Christians 30
claiming 35, 36, 37
Clinton, Hillary Rodham 105
Coalition of Advocates for the Rights of the Infirm Elderly (CARIE) 94, 95
coalitions 65
coercive care 83
coercion 91
collective social action 149
Commission for Racial Equality 186
communication 29
  and relationship studies 153, 179

211

health care, costs 80
Health Care Financing Administration (HCFA) 82, 83, 94
health care insurance 81, 130
Health Care Reform Task Force 105
Health Insurance Association of America 129
helplessness, learned 148
Hispanics 80, 109, 142
home care 81
Home Office 178
home sales 14
homeless elderly people 135
homelessness 77, 80
hospital care 123–6
hostility 159
housebound persons 18, 133
human need theory 59
hygiene 34

identification 36
IFA see International Federation on Aging
immigrants 109, 157
impression
    formation 155
    management 153
imprisonment, false 49
incapacitated persons 47
incapacity 87
Incident Report 66
incompetence 34
incontinence 36
independence 17, 18, 29, 38, 59, 127, 147
infantilization 12
Institute of Gerontology 15, 176, 178
Institute on Law and Rights of Older Adults 87
Institute of Medicine (IoM) 93
institutionalism 38
institutionalized old people 18
interdisciplinary co-operation 140, 179
intergenerational conflicts 156
intergenerational equity 20
International Federation on Aging (IFA) 52
    Declaration on the Rights and Responsibilities of Older Persons 52, 53–4
interracial conflicts 109
intervention
    directive 25

minimal intervention 124; see also under Roberts, S.
    order 50
    strategic 154
intimacy 29
Ireland 183
isolation 139
Islamic stereotypes 187

JCA see Justice Center of Atlanta
Jewish Family Mediation Service 30
Joint Conference on Law and Aging 79
justice 21, 92, 127
    collective 43
    distributive 62
    participative 42, 55, 61
    relational 4, 19, 42, 55, 61, 159, 179, 187
    restorative 179
    social 4, 59–63, 77
Justice Center of Atlanta (JCA) 38, 131, 137
Justice Institute 128

Kansans for Improvement in Nursing Homes (KINH) 141, 142
Kansas 10, 32, 38, 40, 57, 58, 85, 91, 96, 131,137–43
    Elder Abuse, Prevention, Identification and Treatment Act 1985 140
    Legal Services (KLS) 137, 138, 142, 143
    Mediation Service for Older Adults (KMSOA) 138, 143
Kestner, Prue vii
KINH see Kansans for Improvement in Nursing Homes
KLS see Kansas Legal Services
KMSOA see Kansas Mediation Service for Older Adults

labelling 180, 192
Law Commission 46
    Consultation Paper No. 119, 46
    Consultation Paper No. 128, 46
    Consultation Paper No. 207, 47
    Consultation Papers, 51
law reform 46
lawyers 38, 40, 41, 42, 44, 76, 83, 85, 117, 139, 142
lay assessors 182–3
learned resistance 148

214

legal aid 85, 86
legalism 44
legislation
    American 60, 77, 92, 171
    Norwegian 166
Lewisham 15, 177
life-support measures 89
linguistic deficiencies 156
linguistic deficits 157
Living Trusts 97
Living Wills 89
local authorities 50
locus of control
    changes 193
    internal and external 193
    issues 18, 158
London Voluntary Service Council 151
long term care 130
long term care hospital 100
Long Term Care Ombudsmen (LTCO)
    viii–ix, 10, 77, 82, 83, 84, 85, 91, 92,
    97, 104, 132, 135, 136

Manglerud 169–72
Martin Luther King 131
    Center 132
Marxism 38
Massachusetts Health Research Institute
    66
mediation
    Cases 1–11 133–142
    in divorce legislation 5, 175
    in industrial conflicts 108
    low recorded rates 133
    morality 184–8
    on the spot 135
    services 6, 7
    training 107–8, 112, 120, 128, 131, 133,
    134, 137, 138, 141, 142, 152, 181
    training manual 132
    within criminal justice system 6
Mediation UK vii, 5, 6, 11, 54, 148, 149,
    150, 151, 152, 184, 185, 186, 187,
    189, 190
    Training Manual 184
mediators 6, 30, 35, 38, 40, 56, 60
    role of 163
    tasks 25
Medicaid 75, 79, 81, 82, 90, 96, 105
Medi-Cal system 100, 101, 105, 114, 115,
    119
medical bills 111

MEDICARD 82
Medicare 80, 81, 82, 90, 96, 100, 119
    Catastrophic Coverage Act 81
Mennonites 30
mental
    capacity, fluctuating 156
    frailties 69, 71
    incapacity 109
mentally frail elders and their carers 46
mentally ill homeless men 135
mentally impaired people 136
metacommunication 30, 164–6
Mexico 109
minimalism 23
miscommunication 164–6
Missouri 141
multicultural communities 150
multidisciplinary workers 126–30, 168
mutually abusive relationships 184

naming 34–5, 36, 37, 167
naming, blaming and claiming 102, 113,
    115, 117
National Aging Resource Center on Elder
    Abuse (NARCEA) 97
National Assistance Act 41, 51
National Citizens Coalition of Nursing
    Home Reform (NCCNHR) 83, 84,
    85, 89, 91, 92
National Council of Voluntary
    Organizations 151
National Elder Campaign 86
National Eldercare Campaign (NEC) 75
National Eldercare Institute on Elder
    Abuse and State Long Term Care
    Ombudsmen Services
    (NEIEASLTCOS) 75, 95, 96, 97
National Family Mediation (NFM) 5, 48
National Health Service and Community
    Care Act 50
National Institute of Dispute Resolution
    (NIDR) 76, 95, 107, 124, 129, 132
    nursing home mediation programmes
    132
    senior mediation project 111–3
National Legal Services Corporation 86
National Senior Citizen Law Center
    (NSCLC) 76
Navajo women 56, 57
NCCNHR see National Citizens Coalition
    of Nursing Home Reform
NDR see neighborhood dispute resolution

215